school of
KINGDOM MINISTRY

FIRST YEAR MANUAL

SECOND EDITION

ISBN-13: 978-0-9898321-1-3

Printed in the United States of America

Published by Coaching Saints Publications

Layout, cover design: www.webvisiongraphics.com

Endorsements

Rob Putman (Putty) has done a phenomenal job at developing a resource that individuals, small groups, and churches can use to equip their people for the purposes of doing kingdom ministry like never before. Having known Putty over the past couple of years, one of the things that I have admired about him is his passionate devotion to equipping the saints to do the ministry that Jesus and the apostles did. His approachability and accessibility with people will be realized in the reading of this book. My wife and I know him and his family well, and can vouch for the character and integrity of this man. He is not just a brain (although you will see that in this book), but he is also heart, and that comes through in his passion and his writing. This book is an awesome playbook on how to equip the saints for ministry according to Ephesians 5. I highly recommend church pastors and leaders to read this book and apply its principles to their church life.

Robby Dawkins
Author, Do What Jesus Did

Putty Putman has written an excellent Spirit-led guide to introducing students to kingdom lifestyle and walking in the supernatural power of the Holy Spirit. In a very deliberate, "line upon line, precept upon precept" approach, Putman leads readers from a consideration of worldview to a challenge of believing in the identity of who they have become in Jesus Christ. The "first being, then doing" path is very much the same teaching style as Jesus demonstrated with His disciples. Any leader who is seeking to raise up disciples of Jesus Christ will find this book to be a very helpful resource in their journey together.

Mike Hutchings, Director
Global School of Supernatural Ministry and
Christian Healing Certification Program
The Apostolic Network of Global Awakening

John 5:39 - *You search the Scriptures because you think that in them you have eternal life; and it is they that bear witness about me (Jesus).*

Dr. Putty (Rob) Putman is a man madly in love with Jesus. He searches the Scripture to discover a richer revelation of Jesus to the end that we, his students, may grow up into the fullness of Christ and continue his kingdom ministry on earth. The School of Kingdom Ministry Manual is overflowing with fresh faith-building insights plus plenty of practical instructions that will bring transformation to one's life. I heartily endorse this book and invite you to read and study with the Holy Spirit as your teacher. Expect to love Jesus more while being equipped for powerful kingdom ministry.

Dianne Leman/Co-Senior Pastor
The Vineyard Church, Urbana, IL

Putty Putman has put together some of the best resources on kingdom ministry I've seen. It is both informative and practical. Putty's not just a great researcher and thinker, he is a practitioner who has a heart to activate believers into their true identities in Christ and equip them to live out the mission of the kingdom. Putty's material embodies John Wimber's value that "everybody gets to play." If you are a pastor, leader, or equipper in your local church, these resources will help you build a kingdom culture. Whether you are a new believer or you've been doing ministry for years, the School of Kingdom Ministry is an invaluable resource that will mobilize you into a naturally supernatural lifestyle of kingdom activity.

Brian Blount
Co-author, From the Sanctuary to the Streets

Acknowledgements

The School of Kingdom Ministry has been a product of the journey I've been on the last five years of my life. As such, a number of people have been critical in making this book happen.

First and foremost, I'd like to thank my wife, Brittany, for supporting me on this journey of discovery these last five years and for walking the journey with me. Your support as God has begun to open my eyes and lead me to places where at the time it seemed like no one else was going has been essential. Thanks as well for supporting my hunger to read anything I could find in the early days; the financial sacrifice we made then fueled what is happening now. Your love and commitment to the ministry God has called me to regularly amazes me, and it couldn't happen without you being fully on board.

I definitely need to thank my parents, Bob and Pam Putman. Thank you for beginning a legacy of faith in our family. It is one I intend to pass on to my children. Thank you for demonstrating a value of the Word of God to me and modeling a faithful lifestyle to Jesus and what He is passionate about.

I'd like to say thank you to Happy and Dianne Leman. For years you have stood for the call of John 14:12—the same and greater works. Thanks for creating a church where I could explore these things and be celebrated. I'm beginning to see how truly rare that is. Secondly, thank you for seeing what you see in me and giving me the opportunities that you have. Without your leadership and your encouragement, my journey would have been very different.

I want to thank many of my ministry mentors along the way. What I've learned from each of you has been invaluable. Specifically Bob Shimmin, Alan Williams, and Arlene Brown have been instrumental in teaching and training me. Thank you for what you've passed on to me.

Thanks to Andrew Janssen for jumping on board with the vision in the early small group days. I can't believe how far we've come! Thanks as well to Daniel Putman, James Moreland, Stacey Snodgrass and everyone else that was a part of that group. The small group was so instrumental as an experimenting ground in my learning process. The School of Kingdom Ministry truly came out of what I learned there.

I want to express tremendous gratitude to Gayle Wildman for all the ways you've helped me through the years. You've proofread this so many times, and not only would this manuscript not exist without your help, the School of Kingdom Ministry wouldn't either. Your help has been a gift from God to me. Thank you.

I want to thank my editing team: Burnsey Eisenmenger and Joanna Machen. You guys make me sound better than I am! Every time you work through something I'm amazed by how much better it reads afterwards. Your strength there adds so much, and thank you for your help.

A special thanks goes to Jess Smuk for coordinating this project and helping out with it in a thousand big ways and then again in a thousand little ways. There is no way it could have happened without your help. Your contribution to the School of Kingdom Ministry team is immeasurable and your help has been absolutely critical to this publication. Thank you!

Finally, I want to say thanks to all the School of Kingdom Ministry students. Thank you for believing that more is possible, that we can live the way Jesus modeled, and that Christians were always meant to be dangerous.

Table of Contents

About School of Kingdom Ministry

This book contains the reading materials to accompany the teaching portion of the School of Kingdom Ministry. The School of Kingdom Ministry exists to provide training for everyday people in how to live a kingdom lifestyle. We're developing a network of churches that are raising up and mobilizing believers to do the works of Jesus wherever they live, learn, work, and play. Because we believe "everybody gets to play," we believe everybody should be trained, and our goal is to help make that possible.

The School of Kingdom Ministry began when Happy Leman spoke to the now-director of the School of Kingdom Ministry, Putty Putman, "Why don't we have a healing school? We should have a healing school." Putty began to condense the process and training he had been working through for a number of years into a training program that was named the School of Kingdom Ministry. The first class ran Fall 2011 to Spring 2012 and we graduated 50 students. By the next year, word had gotten out about the program and we tested a model of running the program in five churches concurrently spread across two states in the Midwest. Since that year, we've been working to build this into a program being hosted by a network of churches across the United States and around the world.

The School of Kingdom Ministry is a highly experiential course. The teaching component comprises less than half of the training program, and as such, it requires far beyond the teaching material contained here to have the full School of Kingdom Ministry experience. The teaching is a critical component, though, as the combination of teaching and practice shifts the student's worldview throughout the process of the course. These notes are meant to be an introduction to each topic that the students read before attending the lectures so they already have some thoughts stirring and can get the most out of the teaching portion of the school.

While this manual was originally designed as a reading supplement to the School of Kingdom Ministry, the readings and activation exercises contained here aren't cohesive on their own. The full experience of the school only occurs with the manual in conjunction with the other aspects of the School of Kingdom Ministry. In order to provide more space for students to take notes, we have included extra space at the bottom of each page for that purpose.

For more information about the School of Kingdom Ministry, including information about how to join our network and host a location, visit our website: http://schoolofkingdomministry.org.

Foreword

I am a product of the Vineyard and a spiritual son of John Wimber. For over 30 years, I've been interacting with kingdom of God principles and the supernatural ministry that flows from it. My wife, Dianne, and I are even the recipients of numerous miracles including five natural children who were not supposed to be born to us. Needless to say, I am one of the leading advocates throughout the entire Vineyard Movement regarding the issue of signs, wonders, and miracles. I believe they were part of the gospel in the days of Jesus and are just as important for our gospel today. Furthermore, I'm a longstanding proponent that "**everybody gets to play**." In other words, I believe signs and wonders should be commonplace among all Christians, both in and out of the church.

Having watched the body of Christ over that time period, I'm convinced we need more focused training aimed at developing our lay people into divine healing partners with the Holy Spirit. As I surveyed across the landscape of churches, I have seen very little effective, consistent training in this regard. For years, I've had a dream that we could develop a ministry that would really make a difference in equipping the saints.

A few years ago, I shared the dream with Putty Putman. He caught the understanding of what I was saying and set about to gather the resources. I assumed he would return to me with many ideas and need a considerable amount of help—especially since he had just graduated with a PhD in physics. However, as the months went on, I somewhat forgot what he was doing. You can imagine my surprise when the School of Kingdom Ministry emerged in the fall of 2011 with clear direction, focus, and written curriculum. I was overwhelmingly blessed at the quality of the material then and considered it a miracle in its own right.

Throughout 2011 and 2012, the material has greatly improved. Beginning in 2013, we were ready to export it to other churches with a similar vision and heart as ours. We believe the School of Kingdom Ministry will make a huge difference, not only in the lives in our church, but in the kingdom of God, wherever it is used. I give this school my highest endorsement and believe it is a ministry that is "built for such a time as this." Our prayer is that you enjoy it as much as we have.

Blessings,
Happy Leman
Co-Senior Pastor, Central Illinois Vineyard
Vineyard USA National Board Member

Code of Ethics

The following Code of Ethics provides a set of core values for those within the School of Kingdom Ministry and establishes a vision for each student, both individually and as a part of the group, to promote growth.

God

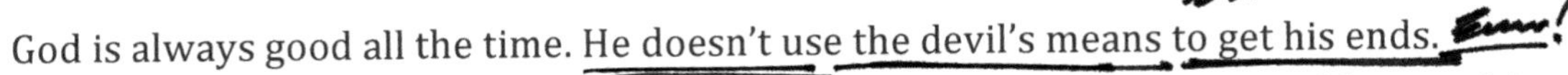

- God is always good all the time. He doesn't use the devil's means to get his ends.
- God has the ability to turn any situation any way he likes. There is no problem too big for God.
- My circumstances do not determine who God is. Jesus is the perfect image of God.
- My favor with God is unconditional because it is based on Jesus. I can never be un-forgiven or guilty in God's eyes.

Myself

- I am a child of the king, fully loved for who I am, not what I do.
- Jesus has defeated sin in me. I am no longer a sinner; I am a saint.
- Jesus tells me who I am, and my identity is in him. I won't look to anything else for my identity.

Family

- My spouse comes before all other human relationships.
- My children are my legacy, and I am to invest myself in them on their behalf.

Church

- I am fully committed to my local church as God's covenant people.
- I will honor the leadership of the church and support unity, not division, in spite of any differences.
- I will not participate or endorse gossip or slander in any form.

Others

- I love, respect, and honor all people, regardless of how they treat others or me.
- I will work to empower other people to get them to their destiny. I am not in competition with anyone else.

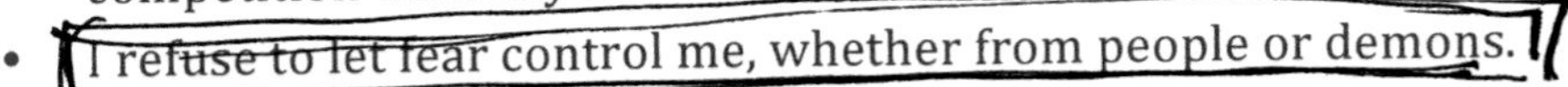

- I refuse to let fear control me, whether from people or demons.
- I choose to love others unguardedly.
- I will deal with confrontation and conflict as quickly as possible in person with an honoring and teachable posture.

Introduction

Welcome to the School of Kingdom Ministry! This manual is designed to accompany the first year of the School of Kingdom Ministry, and each student receives one as part of his or her experience. It is of course a useful tool for other discipleship programs or classes as well, and it serves as a good introduction to the School of Kingdom Ministry teaching content (although be aware—the majority of the School of Kingdom Ministry is the experiential component than cannot be captured in a book).

The general approach for the School of Kingdom Ministry combines education and practice. We believe true transformation always comes in the melting pot of learning and doing. We sum up the goal of the School of Kingdom Ministry in this way: understanding and accessing the kingdom. This describes both the goal and the process; we learn to do and we do to learn. Both aspects partner together to improve the other.

The focus for the first year of the School of Kingdom Ministry is a firm grounding in the student's identity in Christ. Our experience shows that the ministry of the Spirit is given fertile soil to grow in the firm grounding of identity in Christ. Once that has been established, the second year curriculum turns to focus on the issue of discovering your personal calling and beginning to take responsibility for walking that out:

	Understanding	Accessing
1st Year	Identity in Christ	Ministry of the Spirit
2nd Year	Identity in the Body of Christ	Calling

In order to help the manual be the most effective companion to the first year class, there are a few separate sections included in the manual. Understanding the purpose and the best way to use each section will help each student get the most out of the manual and the School of Kingdom Ministry experience:

- **Year One Readings**: These are the reading notes that accompany the teaching sessions of the School of Kingdom Ministry. They are designed to be read before the teaching sessions for that unit start. We have all students read the entire chapter before the teaching unit begins.

- **Theology Anchors**: These are interspersed throughout the readings and highlight the key ideas that many of the students experience as a paradigm shift. There is a complete list of them after the reading notes.

- **Developing Ministry Skills**: This section talks directly about developing different aspects of ministry skills and offers suggestions for how to grow in different areas of ministry. It is a useful tool for accompanying the activation portion of the School of Kingdom Ministry.

- **Ministry Practice Journal**: This is the final section of the manual and is a 28-week journal where the student can record the types of ministry he or she is engaging with during the course of the School of Kingdom Ministry. Reflecting on and reviewing this journal offers an opportunity to see where the student is functioning and where they are growing as their School of Kingdom Ministry experience progresses.

- **Margins**: Throughout much of this manual the margins at the bottom of the pages have been increased to give plenty of room at the bottom to take notes. This is encouraged and can be used in either the reading sessions or during class times in the teaching portions. This manual is designed to be more of a development manual than a book.

I hope you enjoy our experience! Thanks for being part of the School of Kingdom Ministry journey. I pray that God uses it powerfully in your life to bring glory to his name.

About the Author

The School of Kingdom Ministry was designed and this manual was written by Putty Putman. At the time of the development of this material, Putty was the Healing Ministries Pastor at the Vineyard Church in Urbana, IL, when Happy approached him about creating a school designed to empower people to live naturally supernatural lifestyles in the power of the Holy Spirit. This manual was largely written during the preparation and during the first year of classes held in Urbana, IL.

Putty (not actually his birth name, but a prophetic renaming that God gave him in early high school, saying he is "Putty in God's hands") has a PhD in theoretical quantum physics from the University of Illinois. During the process of completing that degree, he experienced some radical supernatural encounters in China on a short-term missions trip less than a month after he began praying for the sick. This began to direct the course of his life along the lines of pursuing the power and presence of God. After a number of years of devouring every resource he could find and pressing into new areas in his own personal practice, he was brought on staff at the church to oversee the healing and prophetic ministries. In the intervening time, his role has transitioned into oversight of the School of Kingdom Ministry internationally and involvement in the preaching team at the Vineyard Church.

Putty loves to see people discover all that Jesus really has made available for them and begin to live in light of that. He loves to teach and preach, to pray for anyone and to love people. For the most part, he's completely blown away and incredibly humbled by his role in the School of Kingdom Ministry and the way it's impacting lives all over the world. He is married to Brittany Putman, and at the time of this writing they have two children, Kayla and Benjamin.

Year One Readings

Worldviews and Culture

Everyone has a worldview. A worldview is a set of assumptions about the nature of reality. It involves our thinking patterns and the way we interpret our experiences. It acts as a lens that affects the way we see things, although we rarely are aware of it. These worldviews can differ greatly from one another. Here is an interesting example:

In a study done after World War II, thousands of people were interviewed and asked to respond to logical syllogisms—things like:[1]

- Cotton doesn't grow in countries that have cold weather.
- England is a country with cold weather.
- Will cotton grow in England?

Westerners would most likely answer that cotton would not grow in England. However, the majority of Easterners answered that they weren't qualified to answer the question because they had not been to England. This doesn't mean they were necessarily bad at logic. What it means is that they view the world as more complicated than logical arguments. They have a worldview that is different than ours, so when processing the same information, they arrive at a different conclusion.

This is a great example of a worldview. A worldview affects how we see; it determines how we take our perceptions and form coherent thought processes from them. It involves:

---

[1] This example and many of the ideas in this section are taken from chapter 18 of John Wimber and Kevin Springer's *Power Evangelism*.

Need to check this out!

- An explanation for the world—how and why things are and how and why they change.
- A standard of evaluation—what we measure as possible/impossible, credible/scandalous, etc.
- A standard way of life—it creates a community dynamic that acts as a common ground for those with the same worldview and a divide among those with different worldviews.
- A way to process experiences—the way we take new information and match it up with our prior experiences and so forth.

For our purposes, a worldview has two major effects:

1. It determines what seems reasonable and what seems ludicrous. It gives us a processing grid to determine what is and isn't realistic.
2. It describes the possibilities we'll consider when reasoning through a situation or series of events.

Basically, our worldview defines what *reality* is for us. It defines what we'll accept as real or what isn't. It gives a pathway that we use to process the input we receive to form an understanding of what has happened and why it happened. Like a set of train tracks that directs the possible routes for trains, our worldview is a set of tracks that our thoughts can follow.

Theology Anchor

Worldviews filter our perception and determine what we see.

Most of the time our worldview is almost completely unconscious. We have not learned to identify it because we assume that our perception of reality corresponds directly to reality, but that is one of the key points about worldviews: *everyone sees from an angle*. It's impossible not to. This is a reality of being human; we all have a worldview, and it affects us.

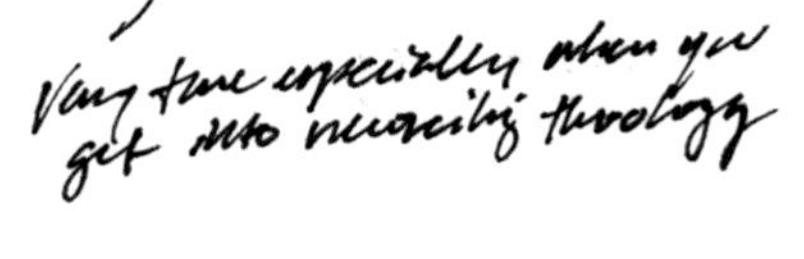

Our worldview will have multiple components. Part of our worldview will shape how we think of God. Sometimes this component is thought of as our worldview, but a true worldview contains more than our image of God. Another key part of our worldview is our *identity*. This shapes how we think of ourselves and who we believe we are. Another aspect is our *relational paradigm*. This is the view we take and the rules we follow when interacting with others. We also have a *cosmological picture*: what we view the world as made up of and how and why things happen. All of these together form our worldview. We will investigate each of these in turn during the first semester.

Now here's the catch: your worldview isn't determined by what you think, say, or try to believe. You have a worldview that exists completely independently of what you think it is. Your worldview is betrayed by how you act. When we pray for healing and don't expect God to heal, we are struggling with a deistic worldview, whether we say we believe God heals or not.

Because of the community aspect of a worldview, much of our worldview tends to be shaped by our culture. Cultures tend to have self-consistent worldviews.[2] Consider looking at a few aspects of the common American worldview:

- Futuristic: focused on the future more than the present or past.
- Individualistic: prioritizes the needs of the individual over the community.

Let's look at the social sense. If your social sense is individualistic, you will tend to prioritize the values of the individual over the values of the group. Imagine a hypothetical family situation in which the daughter falls in love with a man the father forbids her to marry even though there is no moral or social reason to do so. The daughter is at a crossroads: does she leave the man she loves or leave the family she

---

[2] Self-consistent means containing no logical contradictions. Worldviews are a coherent picture of the world.

loves? If you feel that the right thing to do is for the daughter to act on her feelings and marry the man anyway, your worldview is prioritizing the individual over the family.

Let's look at four other components of the American worldview:

- Secular: The belief that the universe is closed off from divine intervention.
- Self-reliant: Belief that we have the ability to provide anything we need for ourselves.
- Materialistic: Assumption that nothing exists beyond the material and its interactions.
- Rationalistic: Reason is the highest authority in life and that things which cannot be explained by reason in some fashion should not be trusted.

None of these line up with the worldview portrayed by Jesus' actions.

Spiritual Effects of Worldviews

Psychologists call the result of experiencing something that conflicts with your worldview *cognitive dissonance*: a discomfort that is a result of believing two conflicting ideas. A common example of cognitive dissonance happens when we experience a healing. Have you ever found yourself talking yourself out of believing what you just saw in front of your eyes only minutes later? This is because the event we've just experienced is trying to be processed within our worldview, and it doesn't fit anywhere. There doesn't seem to be any reasonable explanation, so we start to question the reality of what we just saw.

Jesus talks about this in what seems like a very strange text:

> *"No one after lighting a lamp puts it in a cellar or under a basket, but on a stand, so that those who enter may see the light. Your eye is the lamp of your body. When your eye is healthy, your whole body is full of light, but when it is bad, your body is*

full of darkness. Therefore be careful lest the light in you be darkness. If then your whole body is full of light, having no part dark, it will be wholly bright, as when a lamp with its rays gives you light." Luke 11:33-36

This is a very interesting passage. Jesus talks about our perception using the metaphor of our eye. Jesus doesn't say what you look at is the lamp of your body; he says it's your eye! He says that our perception determines how much light we shine. He warns us to be careful that our perception doesn't lead to darkness but to light.

This is an interesting shift. We would often like to think that what determines whether we shine is what we do. Jesus points more to who we are. We would like a list of things we know we can do to show him off, and instead Jesus just tells us to be a lamp! Yet this is exactly the shift that is important because our worldview always feeds into our identity; we cannot process the world without us having a place in it somewhere. We'll talk more about identity and this connection later; but for now, just notice that Jesus admonishes us to take care of our perception: our worldview.

> **Theology Anchor**
>
> Worldviews give us the grid of explanations we use to understand the world.

The reason this is so important is that our worldview determines what we can see. It is possible to have God right in front of your face and not see him because your worldview doesn't allow for it. This is referred to in Jesus' cryptic statements about people who have ears to hear and eyes to see.

And when his disciples asked him what this parable meant, he said, "To you it has been given to know the secrets of the kingdom of God, but for others they are in parables, so that 'seeing they may not see, and hearing they may not understand.'" Luke 8:9-10

The truth is that our ability to perceive God determines whether we'll see him everywhere, nowhere, or somewhere in between. This dynamic is captured in a fascinating passage where Jesus hears an audible voice from heaven:

> *"Now is my soul troubled. And what shall I say? 'Father, save me from this hour?' But for this purpose I have come to this hour. Father, glorify your name." Then a voice came from heaven: "I have glorified it, and I will glorify it again." The crowd that stood there and heard it said that it had thundered. Others said, "An angel has spoken to him." John 12:27-29*

The fact is that God spoke audibly to Jesus. Some of the crowd heard it and interpreted it as thunder (they must not have been able to hear specific words), and others interpreted it as the speaking of an angel.

Our Cultural Worldview

It is very useful to know the worldview into which we are sent "as lambs among wolves" (Matthew 10:6). Right now Western society is caught between two major worldviews (excluding the biblical worldview), scientific naturalism and postmodernism. A thorough study of these worldviews is quite interesting, and if you want to learn more than the meager introduction here, I recommend you read the book *Kingdom Triangle* by J.P. Moreland.

Scientific Naturalism

The worldview of scientific naturalism takes what can be learned by the scientific world and pushes that forward as true knowledge. Things that cannot be demonstrated scientifically are either lowered in status as a secondary truth or dismissed as unknowable. Furthermore, everything that exists is either physical or completely dependent on the physical world for its existence.

This worldview is dangerous because it dismisses matters of spirituality as something that cannot be known. God cannot be measured, so it cannot be known whether he is real or not. Right and wrong do not really mean anything to a scientific naturalist because our choices aren't physically measurable.

Postmodernism

Postmodernism is a reaction to the cold, purposeless picture painted by scientific naturalism, which actually just exacerbates the problem. The essential idea behind postmodernism is that because everyone sees through a worldview, there is no such thing as truth that exists independently of our interpretation. Since there is no absolute truth, reason is a meaningless concept. Postmodernism, then, in an effort to deal with the reality of a worldview that takes the idea to the extreme, and arrives in a world where nothing can be actually known, and there is no objective reality.

These two (as well as a few more) worldviews are summarized in the chart:[3]

	Reality	Man	Truth	Values
Naturalism: Atheism Agnosticism Existentialism	The material universe is all that exists. Reality is "one-dimensional." There is no such thing as a soul or a spirit. Everything can be explained on the basis of natural law.	Man is the chance product of a biological process of evolution. Man is entirely material. The human species will one day pass out of existence.	Truth is usually understood as scientific proof. Only that which can be observed with the five senses is accepted as real or true.	No objective values or morals exist. Morals are individual preferences or socially useful behaviors. Even social morals are subject to evolution and change.
Pantheism: Hinduism Taoism Buddhism New Age	Only the spiritual dimension exists. All else is illusion, *maya*. Spiritual reality, *Brahman*, is eternal, impersonal, and unknowable. It is possible to say that everything is a part of God, or that God is in everything and everyone.	Man is one with ultimate reality. Thus man is spiritual, eternal, and impersonal. Man's belief that he is an individual is illusion.	Truth is an experience of unity with "the oneness" of the universe. Truth is beyond all rational description. Rational thought as it is understood in the West cannot show us reality.	Because ultimate reality is impersonal, many pantheistic thinkers believe that there is no real distinction between good and evil. Instead, "unenlightened" behavior is that which fails to understand essential unity.
Theism: Christianity Islam Judaism	An infinite, personal God exists. He created a finite, material world. Reality is both material and spiritual. The universe as we know it had a beginning and will have an end.	Humankind is the unique creation of God. People were created "in the image of God," which means that we are personal, eternal, spiritual, and biological.	Truth about God is known through revelation. Truth about the material world is gained via revelation and the five senses in conjunction with rational thought.	Moral values are the objective expression of an absolute moral being.

[3] Table originally authored by Dennis McCallum. Taken from http://www.xenos.org/classes/papers/5wldview.htm. Accessed 8/24/11. Used by permission.

	Reality	Man	Truth	Values
Spiritism/ Polytheism	The world is populated by spirit beings who govern what goes on. Gods and demons are the real reason behind "natural" events. Material things are real, but they have spirits associated with them and, therefore, can be interpreted spiritually.	Man is a creation of the gods like the rest of the creatures on earth. Often, tribes or races have a special relationship with some gods who protect them and can punish them.	Truth about the natural world is discovered through the shaman figure who has visions telling him what the gods and demons are doing and how they feel.	Moral values take the form of taboos, which are things that irritate or anger various spirits. These taboos are different from the idea of "good and evil" because it is just as important to avoid irritating evil spirits as it is good ones.
Postmodernism	Reality must be interpreted through our language and cultural "paradigm." Therefore, reality is "socially constructed."	Humans are nodes in a cultural reality; they are a product of their social setting. The idea that people are autonomous and free is a myth.	Truths are mental constructs meaningful to individuals within a particular cultural paradigm. They do not apply to other paradigms. Truth is relative to one's culture.	Values are part of our social paradigms as well. Tolerance, freedom of expression, inclusion, and refusal to claim to have the answers are the only universal values.

There are a number of places that any of the non-theistic worldviews clash with the Christian worldview. I'm not interested in delineating all of them, but it is interesting to consider the ramifications of two most prevalent worldviews in our society (naturalism and postmodernism) and how they clash with the biblical worldview:

- There is no sense of good or bad. There is no way to live a meaningful or impactful life.
- Both of them relegate spiritual matters as something that can't really be known. This is actually a subtle change in what is defined as knowledge. There is a big jump between something being measureable and being knowable. Do all knowable things need to be measureable? The naturalist says yes, the postmodernist says nothing is knowable.
- Spiritual matters (including ethics) become a matter of opinion then, and for non-material matters, truth in general is lessened to something that depends on your point of view.
- Evil is completely factored out of these worldviews. (I wonder how that happened! Hint: Satan.) Both of these worldviews do not address the presence of evil in this world or how it is dealt with.

It is important for us to know and study the culture in which we live. As we grow in our ability to understand the worldview of those around us, we can more clearly articulate the gospel and point to Jesus.

Repentance

Jesus' ministry was characterized by a call to repentance:

> *Now after John was arrested, Jesus came into Galilee, proclaiming the gospel of God, and saying, "The time is fulfilled, and the kingdom of God is at hand; repent and believe in the gospel." Mark 1:14-15*

Repentance is a term that we've done a fair amount of religious violence to. We've turned it into a sin word. The word itself (*metanoia* in Greek) literally means something closer to "think differently" or "change your mind." Jesus calls us to completely change our thinking. It's not so much thinking a different way as it is thinking from a different starting point. This is the essence of repentance: a paradigm shift.

I believe it is a mistake to make sin the focus of repentance. The essence of repentance is not turning away from sin but rather turning towards God; otherwise, we don't know what we're turning towards. When you leave church to go home, you don't turn around and walk away from the church; you face your destination and you move towards it. It is the same with the Christian life. This is why Paul says,

> *Or do you presume on the riches of his kindness and forbearance and patience, not knowing that God's kindness is meant to lead you to repentance? Romans 2:4*

Turning towards God will always involve turning away from sin. This is why in Acts 15 when dealing with Gentile believers (remember these are genuine pagans that have been converted), the instructions the church settled upon were:

> *For it has seemed good to the Holy Spirit and to us to lay on you no greater burden than these requirements: that you abstain from what has been sacrificed to idols, and from blood, and from what has been strangled, and from sexual immorality. If you keep yourselves from these, you will do well. Acts 15:28-29*

These are remarkably short instructions that leave large gaps! What about instructions for how to treat other people? What about instructions on how to use money or anger or divorce, or any of dozens of other issues? All of that was left out because the early church knew that if they had truly turned towards God, the rest would follow; so they gave a few simple instructions to make sure the early converts would survive the process.

> **Theology Anchor**
>
> Repentance means changing our worldview; learning to think and see.

As mentioned before, the essence of repentance is a paradigm shift, or a change in worldview. It is to start thinking from a different place and therefore consider a different set of options in a circumstance. Jesus was constantly working to instill a different paradigm in his disciples than the one they came to him with. Here is a fantastic example:

> *Now they had forgotten to bring bread, and they had only one loaf with them in the boat. And he cautioned them, saying, "Watch out; beware of the leaven of the Pharisees and the leaven of Herod." And they began discussing with one another the fact that they had no bread. And Jesus, aware of this, said to them, "Why are you discussing the fact that you have no bread? Do you not yet perceive or understand? Are your hearts hardened? Having eyes do you not see, and having ears do you not hear? And do you not remember? When I broke the five loaves for the five thousand, how many baskets full of broken pieces did you take up?" They said to him, "Twelve." "And the seven for the four thousand, how many baskets full of broken pieces did you take up?" And they said to him, "Seven." And he said to them, "Do you not yet understand?" Mark 8:14-21*

The disciples misinterpret what Jesus is saying (as usual) and think that Jesus is complaining that they forgot to bring any food to eat. Jesus observes this and points out that they are thinking from the wrong perspective. He specifically brings their attention to the numbers of two multiplication miracles they'd seen. Jesus summarizes:

The wrong perspective will always see an accusation in an exhortation

Starting Loaves	People Fed	Leftovers
5	5,000	12 baskets
7	4,000	7 baskets

He's pointing out that when he started with less food, he not only fed more people, but there were more leftovers, too! The point is that the disciples were worried about the fact that they didn't bring something to eat, and Jesus points them back to the provision of God they'd already seen. He is pointing out that in the kingdom, you don't count your resources the same way you do on earth. You don't start by asking yourself how much you have because God comes in and changes the game completely. Because of this, you have to start from a different place.

Changing our Worldview

The good news is that changing our worldview is possible—otherwise Jesus wouldn't call us to it! Jesus has some interesting words in Matthew 13 when talking about why he spoke in parables:

> *This is why I speak to them in parables, because seeing they do not see, and hearing they do not hear, nor do they understand. Indeed, in their case the prophecy of Isaiah is fulfilled that says:*
>
> *You will indeed hear but never understand,*
> *and you will indeed see but never perceive.*
> *For this people's heart has grown dull,*
> *and with their ears they can barely hear,*
> *and their eyes they have closed,*
> *lest they should see with their eyes*
> *and hear with their ears*

and understand with their heart

and turn, and I would heal them. Matthew 13:13-15

Jesus draws a parallel between the condition of our heart and our perception. He says another interesting statement towards the beginning of the Sermon on the Mount:

> *Blessed are the pure in heart, for they shall see God.* Matthew 5:8

A large step towards our healing of the worldview has to do with our openness and humility. If we believe we already see things accurately and don't want to change, we will not. If we recognize our perception is flawed and open ourselves to God speaking and directing us, we position ourselves to receive the clarity God wants to bring. The truth is that this change has to come from God; we can participate with or resist it, but it has to come from God. Paul points to the same idea in Romans 12:

> *I appeal to you therefore, brothers, by the mercies of God, to present your bodies as a living sacrifice, holy and acceptable to God, which is your spiritual worship. Do not be conformed to this world, but be transformed by the renewal of your mind, that by testing you may discern what is the will of God, what is good and acceptable and perfect.* Romans 12:1-2

Paul exhorts us to offer every part of ourselves to God, which will result in the renewing of our mind (changing of our worldview), which will result in our ability to recognize God's will.

A second major tool we can take advantage of is the tool of culture. As we mentioned above, our culture tends to reinforce our worldview, which results in a common worldview across a set of people. If we learn to be intentional about this dynamic, we can sculpt a culture that helps reinforce a worldview we want to have. This is one of the keys to the success that Bethel in Redding has had in their church; they have been intentional about creating a culture that is conducive to producing a worldview that is much more in line with the worldview depicted by Jesus and the early church.

Culture is shaped by the way that we relate to God, each other, and ourselves. We can create a culture by determining a set of values we use as goals for how we interact. The Code of Ethics is the set of values that determine the culture we want to facilitate in this school. It gives us a set of values to be moving towards in life that help to shape a culture, which can then carry itself forward. As we move forward and study some of the other topics, we will see why some of the specific values are what they are.

Worldviews in Flux

As our worldview begins to change, we go through a process with being connected with the truth and the reality of the kingdom. Worldview goes through four stages:[4]

1. Unconsciously Unaware: We don't know that our worldview is an inaccurate understanding of the world. The power of God isn't even a question mark because we don't even think of it as a possibility. Modernism has created a worldview where most are unconsciously unaware of the supernatural.
2. Consciously Unaware: We begin to have awareness that our worldview isn't the whole story. There is a hunger to experience and know more of what is out there, and you see that you have been ruling the supernatural out of your understanding. This is the beginning of the shift of your worldview.
3. Consciously Aware: We begin to understand and embrace the worldview of the kingdom. You are in the learning stage here. You begin to see the world through a different lens and as a result, act differently. Kingdom resources and realities begin to be revealed to you, but it requires pressing in and intentionality.
4. Unconsciously Aware: Eventually the worldview of the kingdom becomes the natural processing grid you use, and it doesn't require effort or focus. As such,

[4] These four steps are taken from chapter 4 of Rick Evans and Tom Wadsworth's book *Willing*.

you live a naturally supernatural life where the kingdom is always on your mind.

I expect most of the students are somewhere in stages 2 or 3. One of our primary goals is for all of us (myself included) to continue to progress towards a stage-four kingdom worldview.

Kingdom Theology

The kingdom of God theology is the framework that the Vineyard uses for understanding the Bible. In essence, it actually articulates a worldview. As we discuss the theology of the kingdom of God, we'll discuss matters of worldview as well.

What Does Kingdom Mean?

A fair amount of discussion of kingdom theology actually revolves around what the word *kingdom* means. This is one of those unfortunate cases where there isn't a great parallel word from the Greek into English, which makes it hard for us to wrap our heads around. Biblically, *kingdom* is a much more active word than it is in English. In English when we say *kingdom* we usually think geographically; we think a place or a land that is under the rule of a king. *Kingdom* is a much more active word in the biblical meaning. Rather than pointing to the location of rule, it points to the activity of rule. It is the power, right, or ability to rule, or the ruling itself.

The phrase *kingdom of God* then means something more like the "ruling of God," the "intervention of God," or the "kingship of God." I actually like made-up words, so I think of it as the "king-ing of God." It is an intensely active phrase. I think of it this way: kingdom is a verb, not a noun.[5]

God exercising and exhibiting His kingship and authority through you.

---

[5] An astute reader of Scripture will identify that this phrase may go a little too far. Logically, the act of ruling implies that there is a location of rule, so in a sense "kingdom of God" can be a location as well as an act, and at times it is used like that in Scripture. However, the fact is that as English speakers we probably have a very inactive mindset towards the word "kingdom" and this phrase points us in the right direction.

Let's take a short aside and address worldviews again. Much of American Christianity lives in what is called *functional deism*. (This is a product of the enlightenment and the elevation of the natural at the expense of the spiritual.) They may believe that God is real and that he can do things in their everyday life but also believe that it is somehow exceptional for him to do that. This comes in different varieties:

- They don't expect God to do anything real in their lives. This comes up a lot with healing. They know God could heal, but probably only under exceptional circumstances such as for a really good person or someone who could help a lot of other people out.
- They have levels to things God will or won't do. Perhaps they may even believe and expect God to heal their body, but it would be strange to pray for a car to be fixed. Sure, God is in the people business, but he doesn't mess with mechanics. (A common variation to explain this is that because God cares about people he cares about your car, which is true, but that is again assigning a level of involvement to God's activity in the world).

The gospel of the kingdom will have none of that. It states that God is immensely involved in the world—every detail and every aspect. If we think that God interacting supernaturally is somehow special or abnormal, we are probably still wrestling with this mentality.

This phrase – the good news of God ushering and exercising His kingship and authority through you is that God is intimately engaged in everyday life through you.

The Jewish audience that Jesus spoke to had a framework for the kingdom of God, for God's direct interaction in the world; it was the end of time. The gospel that Jesus preached then was pretty intense! Jesus comes on the scene preaching a pretty bold statement: the end of the world is right around the corner. This brings us to the second critical aspect of the kingdom of God; it is fundamentally eschatological. It always has to do with the future—the end of time. The kingdom of God has to do with the apocalypse encroaching on the present.

→ revelation of the fullness of God.

The end of a covenant meant the death of a covenant which meant the end of that era – hence the end of time. — This is not a literal statement.

Interestingly, the aspect of the future breaking into the present comes into clarity when considering the history of revival. One of the common themes that carries across many different revivals is that shortly after the power of God is poured out powerfully, there is almost always a belief that the end of the world is right around the corner. When the kingdom of God is present, the end of the world *is* already there, so no wonder people start thinking Jesus is coming back very soon!

In conclusion, two keys of how we are to think about the kingdom:

- The kingdom refers to an action, not (just) a location.
- The action that happens is that the end of the world invades the present.

Two Kingdoms

> **Theology Anchor**
>
> This world exists on the battleground between two opposing kingdoms.

Surveying the entire New Testament, we see a cosmic picture unfold, which is a war between two forces. There is the force of good and the force of evil. The Bible uses a number of terms to refer to these forces:

Kingdom of God	Kingdom of Darkness
Kingdom of Heaven	The Present Evil Age
Kingdom of Light	
Age to Come	

These two kingdoms are depicted as being in a cosmic battle. Before Jesus comes, the world is under the dominion of the devil. Jesus comes and inaugurates the kingdom of God. These two forces are at war, and Jesus comes as the captain of the team of good.

> *The reason the Son of God appeared was to destroy the works of the devil.*
> *1 John 3:8*

This is the landscape on which we live our lives; everyday we are in a cosmic battle between good and evil, which both have their hands in the world and participate in the affairs of men. Jesus came bringing the kingdom of God, but after that the world exists as the battleground between two kingdoms at war. This is sometimes referred to as the tension of the kingdom. When Jesus returns, he will bring a final end to the kingdom of darkness as mankind is ushered into eternity. This idea is captured well in a diagram:

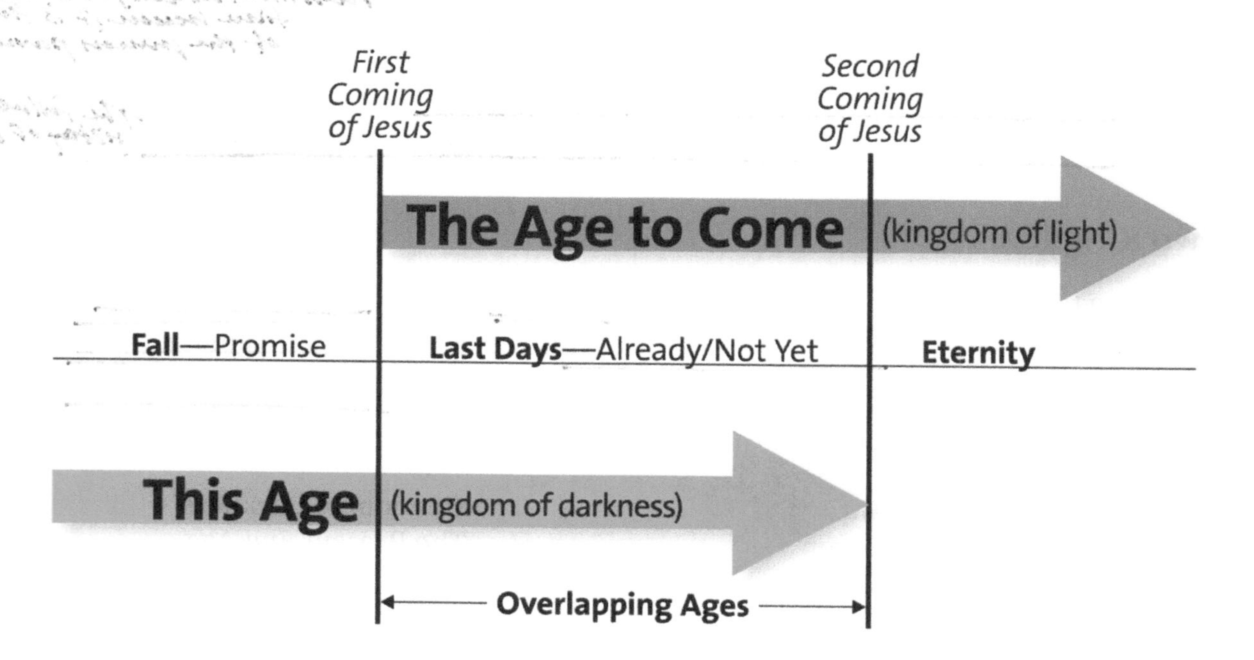

The battle between the two kingdoms is often referred to as the *Already/Not Yet* of the kingdom because the kingdom of God is already here, but it is not yet fully manifest. This language expresses the tension we live with in our world where God's will isn't always fully done. Sometimes the kingdom of God does break in, and people are healed, saved, and delivered; but sometimes, the kingdom of God doesn't manifest as well.

Historically, moves of God tend to start with a fresh revelation of some aspect of the *now* of the kingdom of God. The Spirit is moving and truth is revealed. This was certainly the case with the birthing of the Vineyard movement, when John Wimber was used to bring a powerful revelation of the message of the kingdom of God. What history shows us, however, is that as time goes on the *not-yet* increasingly tends to dominate the focus within the group created by that very same move of God until at times, tragically, the *now* is almost entirely excluded. Many of the denominations that today oppose the manifest moving of the Holy Spirit were birthed in powerful moves of God and then lost touch with their heritage. We would all do well to pray that the same does not happen in the future within our own movement.

To the end of retaining a healthy focus on the now while not excluding the reality of our experience as often being not yet, I'd like to propose a shift in language that personally I've found helpful. The term *not yet* is a term that causes us to focus on what God isn't doing, and gives focus to the devil. My suggestion is to change the language used when talking about the kingdom of God. Instead of using an already/not yet language, I suggest we implement a come/coming language. This has a multitude of benefits, the first being that it reinforces hope and keeps our focus on God. Regardless of whether or not the person is healed this time I pray, the kingdom of God is coming. The person will be healed at some point, on one side of eternity or the other. Furthermore, this actually seems to be the biblical language that is used as well:

> *"Truly, I say to you, there are some standing here who will not taste death until they see the Son of Man coming in his kingdom."* Matthew 16:28

> **Jesus said to him,** *"You have said so. But I tell you, from now on you will see the Son of Man seated at the right hand of Power and coming on the clouds of heaven."* *Matthew 26:64*

She said to him, "Yes, Lord; I believe that you are the Christ, the Son of God, who is coming into the world." John 11:27

Gospel of the Kingdom

Another question we ought to ask ourselves then is, what *is* the gospel of the kingdom? This is clearly the gospel that Jesus taught, and we see the same for Paul (Acts 28:31). A good beginning exercise is to consider how the picture we've painted in this chapter contrasts with the cultural worldview we discussed in the last chapter. To preach the kingdom of God then is to preach what the kingdom of God holds that is different from the society around us. This exercise is called *contextualizing* the gospel. This is what Paul did in the New Testament. If you read Paul's letters, at times it seems as if he is talking about an entirely different gospel than what Jesus talks about. Paul was preaching to a Greek-influenced gentile audience, whereas Jesus was speaking to a Jewish audience. The different worldviews required different methodologies and emphases on the gospel.

One of the implications of the kingdom message is that God is doing things in the world. This is something that oftentimes Christians need to hear! Christianity has been so demeaned that many, if not most, believers think that God can save their soul but not solve their problems!

Another implication is that God is uncomplicatedly good. The devil works very hard to convince us that God is the cause behind everything. This means that God sends sickness and death. The justification is that even though God sent this bad thing, he can use it to work good in my life, so really it's good. God doesn't need to use the devil's means to get his ends! The kingdom of darkness is real, and not everything that is God's will happens! Satan has as much a free will as you or I do, and he's behind all the bad

stuff. God's will is for good for us, all the time. God doesn't do bad-but-secretly-good things to us.

Likewise, the works of the devil all come from the same place. We can easily believe that somehow sin is more of a problem than sickness or death. No, they all have their root in the kingdom of darkness. It is very common for believers (or even non-believers) to believe that sin is more important than sickness. Both sin and sickness are symptoms of the kingdom of darkness, which is the real problem. This is a shift in thinking; the true problem of humanity is not chiefly sin, but the devil. The traditional protestant understanding is that humanity's problem is sin, and the devil is involved as the cause of that, but only secondarily. With this emphasis, sickness will always take a backseat to sin in terms of importance. If we understand the kingdom of darkness as our real problem, and that sin is the evidence of the kingdom of darkness at work within our in soul the same way that sickness is the evidence of the kingdom of darkness at work within our body, our understanding shifts. Although we still sin as believers, we do not tolerate sin since Jesus has made provision to redeem us from it; and we fight against it, regardless of whether it looks like we're making progress. It's the same with sickness.

Theology Anchor

The kingdom is what we're sent to bring. We bring the now to the not-yet.

Signs and wonders are part of the gospel. If the gospel is God taking action among mankind, then signs and wonders must accompany the gospel. They are indeed the very gospel we attest to. To say that God can rule over your life and not demonstrate it is incomplete. Signs and wonders then are not a merit badge to be worn or a sign of God's approval, and are not necessarily something God always does for a clear reason. Sometimes we can over rationalize God's motives for the miraculous. I don't believe that God really has an agenda many times when the

supernatural starts happening. God doesn't always heal people because he wants them saved; God heals people because he is good!

We get to live by a different set of rules as Christians. That is what it means to have a different worldview; the rule by which we live our lives isn't the same as others live by. We can choose joy and peace in every situation (see Romans 14:17). We always have a reason for hope, and we are connected to the source of eternal life. Our God is huge, and he can do whatever he wants, and he's just crazy about us! As we learn to demonstrate that, our lives follow a different set of rules than the others around us-we become living demonstrations of the gospel.

Sovereignty and Goodness

Kingdom theology provides a framework for addressing one of the most important questions that we as believers need to have settled deep in our hearts.

The question is one that philosophers and theologians have wrestled with for centuries and intersects our everyday experience. Put simply, it is this: if God is all-powerful and good, why do bad things happen?

How you answer this question makes all the difference in the world. Essentially to answer the question you have to end with one of two bottom lines: either you make God's goodness complicated or you make his sovereignty complicated.

The former is the more common solution: God's sovereignty is simple and his goodness is complicated. What does this mean? It means basically this: that what God wants to happen does happen. The events that occur in our life are the will of God. The reason that bad things happen is because we don't always have the biggest picture and that sometimes what we perceive as bad is really good. Verses like Romans 8:28 (And we

know that for those who love God all things work together for good, for those who are called according to his purpose) are used to substantiate this position.

The problem with this line of reasoning is that God becomes both the good and bad guy. While it is true that bad things happen in our lives and that God uses those bad things to work good in us, if God's will is always what happens, then God becomes responsible for a lot of bad things. What kind of a person gives someone cancer to develop their character? So while we know Scripturally that every good and perfect gift comes down from the Father (James 1:17), we lump a lot more than the good and perfect into the things that come from God.

Often in order to lessen the blow, the line of reasoning is expanded slightly to include the devil. Basically then, God wants the good stuff and the devil wants the bad stuff, but the devil still has to run his decisions by God before he blows our lives up. This isn't very comforting though; now instead of God causing evil, he's allowing it. Not really much of an improvement. Either way, a sense of dread and foreboding ought to begin to grow in our lives if we hold this view because we never know when something terrible will happen in our life that God allows so we can grow. God winds up seeming untrustworthy and unsafe.

Furthermore, this viewpoint undermines our faith as we pray. How can we know whether some negative circumstance is God's will for the person's life? If a disease is from God, we won't do well to pray for healing. The believer is left in a bit of a lurch—trying to pray the will of God, and hoping that it is for healing.

Finally the question that arises with this viewpoint is this: why does God use the devil's means to get his ends? Do the ends justify the means with God? That doesn't seem right. The Bible pretty explicitly says the ends don't justify the means for us:

If I speak in the tongues of men and of angels, but have not love, I am a noisy gong or a clanging cymbal. And if I have prophetic powers, and understand all mysteries and all knowledge, and if I have all faith, so as to remove mountains, but have not love, I am nothing. If I give away all I have, and if I deliver up my body to be burned, but have not love, I gain nothing. 1 Corinthians 13:1-3

So if the ends don't justify the means (love) for us, how can they justify them for God? Does God's toolbox really get bigger at the fall? Does he really have to use evil to form good?

The other viewpoint is actually the opposite of the kingdom viewpoint, which says that not everything that happens is God's will. If God's sovereignty means that his will always happens, then there really aren't two kingdoms; there is one kingdom. It's not a war if you win every battle. A real war means that there are two different forces that both have real power and the freedom to exercise that power. The kingdom worldview is a battle of the wills: God's will and Satan's will.

THIS IS GOOD

If this is the case, then God's sovereignty can't mean that God's will always happens. I know that this viewpoint might almost sound blasphemous if you've only heard the opposite, but I would encourage you to look at Jesus' own words about leadership:

But Jesus called them to him and said, "You know that the rulers of the Gentiles lord it over them, and their great ones exercise authority over them. It shall not be so among you. But whoever would be great among you must be your servant, and whoever would be first among you must be your slave, even as the Son of Man came not to be served but to serve, and to give his life as a ransom for many." Matthew 20:25-28

When Jesus talked with the disciples about leadership he specifically pointed out that he *didn't* lord over and exercise authority over others. He came from the bottom up, not the top down. He served rather than controlled; empowered rather than restricted. If this is the type of leadership that Jesus points to and models for us, how can we have a picture of the universe where God is forcing his will to always be done? If God's will is done all the time, then he's micromanaging the devil. The devil doesn't really have free will; God is checking him and cutting him off when he wants to do something outside his will. In other words God is lording over and exercising authority over the spiritual world—the very thing that Jesus points out as worldly and not the way of leadership in the kingdom!

So the picture we have here is that God's sovereignty is complicated, but his goodness remains simple. In this viewpoint what happens in our lives is not the barometer of God's will: goodness is. What is good is God's will, and what isn't good isn't God's will—it's as simple as that. Sometimes God's will happens and sometimes Satan's will happens. Either way, the bottom line that we use to determine whether something is God's will is straight from the mouth of Jesus:

> **Theology Anchor**
>
> God's goodness is simple and his sovereignty is complicated; not everything God wills happens and God is never the bad guy.

> *The thief comes only to steal and kill and destroy. I came that they may have life and have it abundantly.* John 10:10

If it's death, loss or destruction, then it belongs to the enemy; if it's abundant life, then it belongs to Jesus. These two wills are in competition in our world. God's goodness is never the question then—it's whether his good will actually happens that is the issue. As a result God is trustworthy. He's safe, and we can come to him knowing that he won't step on our toes to develop character or maturity in us.

The fact is that Jesus is meant to be the revelation of God. If we take the viewpoint that God's sovereignty means that his will always happens, then we take the circumstances and events of our lives as the determination of God's will. Our situation becomes our revelation of God. No, Jesus came as the revelation of the Father:

> *Long ago, at many times and in many ways, God spoke to our fathers by the prophets, but in these last days he has spoken to us by his Son, whom he appointed the heir of all things, through whom also he created the world. He is the radiance of the glory of God and the exact imprint of his nature. Hebrews 1:1-3*

Jesus is the exact imprint of God's nature; he is our picture of the will of God. How many times did Jesus let people remain sick or in pain? Never. Jesus healed every person that came to him for healing, and like wise we should recognize that it is God's will for healing for every person we pray for as well. This gives us confidence to pray with faith. The question of whether God wants to heal has been answered.

This viewpoint is difficult for many people to accept because they have been taught otherwise for so long. A common example I've heard many times is to take John 5:19 where Jesus informs us he can only do what he sees the Father doing and apply it to situations when we pray and the person isn't healed. We've been taught to shrug our shoulders and say, "I guess God isn't healing today."

The problem with this line of thinking is that Jesus never came to that conclusion with that same principle. Acts 10:38 says that Jesus healed all who were oppressed by the devil, so there was not a single time that Jesus asked the Father for healing and God said no. Rather Jesus asked how the Father was healing each individual person and cooperated with that. Even in situations where Jesus was asked to heal someone who was beyond his specific calling he still demonstrated the will of God was to heal (see Mark 7:24-30).

The question then that naturally arises is this: if God's sovereignty does not mean that his will is guaranteed to happen, what does it mean? It simply means that no situation is so bad that God cannot turn it around. God can win with any hand dealt him. This is what Romans 8:28 actually says in context: regardless of the badness of a situation, God can turn it for good. It is our never-give-up policy. The circumstances that we're in can never trump God. He did not put them there, but he can beat them every time.

Covenants

It's an interesting question to ask why Jesus had to come to be the revelation of the Father. God hasn't exactly been silent or removed from creation before Jesus came—why couldn't we look to any of that to see the imprint of his nature? There are a few verses in John 1 that hint at why that is:

> *For the law was given through Moses; grace and truth came through Jesus Christ. No one has ever seen God; [Jesus], who is at the Father's side, he has made him known. John 1:17-18*

The last verse starts with what we've been talking about - Jesus is the revelation of the Father. Without Jesus we aren't seeing God. Reflecting this on the verse before it, we see that in the context of the law, God wasn't made known. In the context of the grace and truth that Jesus brought, God is made known.

Well, that's kind of confusing. What does that mean? How is it that we can't fully know God through the law? Let's start with an interesting verse in the Psalms:

> *The heavens are the Lord's heavens,*
> *but the earth he has given to the children of man. Psalms 115:16*

This is a verse that gives a bit of commentary about what happened with the original assignment given to Adam and Eve:

> *And God blessed them. And God said to them, "Be fruitful and multiply and fill the earth and subdue it, and have dominion over the fish of the sea and over the birds of the heavens and over every living thing that moves on the earth." Genesis 1:28*

When God gives Adam and Eve dominion over the things on the earth, the Psalms say that God was giving us the earth. He wasn't loaning or delegating us the earth; he was giving it to us. That means when we didn't treat it well, it didn't default back to him. If I give you my car and you paint it some awful color and I take it back because I don't think you're treating it right, I haven't really given you my car; I just loaned it to you. If I give you my car, the decisions you make with it are no longer under my jurisdiction.

This is exactly what happened; God gave us the earth and we made some poor choices. We listened to Satan and with the fall in Genesis 3, Satan sowed his nature into our being. With that, he obtained access to the earth. By changing the nature of the stewards of authority on the earth, he begins to play the puppet master and control the earth. Authority that was ours became his through usurping our original nature. We see this mentioned in the dialogue between Satan and Jesus in the temptation Jesus experienced right before the beginning of his ministry:

> *[Satan] said to [Jesus], "To you I will give all this authority and their glory, for it has been delivered to me, and I give it to whom I will. If you, then, will worship me, it will all be yours." Luke 4:6-7*[6]

---

[6] You may recall that Satan is the Father of lies and as such give a second thought as to what he has to say as being true. That is a good thought, but remember that something being a lie doesn't mean that every part of it is false; I would suggest that all the temptations that Jesus faced were true options (otherwise they wouldn't actually be temptations) for him, but they would have been stooping to impure motives.

This point is worth reflecting on briefly. If God gave us authority on the earth and then Satan takes advantage of that authority by changing us from the inside to be like him, does God retain the authority he had delegated to Adam and Eve on the earth any more? The answer is actually no. That may seem shocking, but the reality is that's how God set it up. The authority God delegated to Adam and Eve was delegated to Satan from them at the fall. Notice that Jesus himself acknowledges the legitimate authority Satan has on the earth:

> *Now is the judgment of this world; now will the ruler of this world be cast out.* John 12:31

> *I will no longer talk much with you, for the ruler of this world is coming. He has no claim on me,* John 14:30

With this understanding many of the passages in the Old Testament begin to make a little more sense. For example, in Job chapters 1 and 2 we see a dialogue between God and Satan about Job. These verses have commonly been interpreted as God giving Satan permission to harass Job and destroy his family. The verses don't actually say that God gave Satan permission, but we read that into the text unless we understand that Satan already had permission to harass Job. He didn't need permission, and God didn't have it to give in the first place!

So after the fall, in a sense, God is running out of options: the people he's given the earth to have been infected with evil. How can his will be done on the earth? God can't

---

The reason this is a temptation is that what Satan says is actually true and Jesus knows it. It would be a shortcut of the cross and Jesus would be able to regain the authority and glory of the nations without the personal sacrifice of Jesus' life.

surrender his creation and humanity to the devil, but he doesn't have any entry point left on the earth. He's kind of in a bind here.[7]

This is where the idea of covenants comes in. Covenants are relational agreements in which two parties define the relationship and bind themselves to this kind of relationship. It is fundamentally an agreement about how the two parties are going to live their lives.[8] Covenants were agreements in which people would define what they are living towards, with the understanding that if they stopped living towards what had been agreed on in the covenant, their life would be forfeit.

So when God makes covenants with man on the earth, part of what is happening is he is actually getting a foot back in the door on this planet because he can demonstrate his will towards us. In this way when we agree with God, we empower his will to begin to work through us on this planet again.[9]

An interesting corollary of this line of thought is the following: this means that God is bound to the covenant just as much as we are. In other words, in a covenant in which God and man have agreed to a specific type of relationship, God is bound to honor that agreement just as much as we are. If the covenant dictates a certain type of response

[7] This of course only holds up through the death and resurrection of Jesus. Jesus as a man took back authority on the earth (Matthew 28:18), and as God he has all authority in heaven. As the unique God-man he actually holds authority in both spheres and under his ministry as the stewards of the earth, we are to reconcile these two realms to each other (2 Corinthians 5:18).

[8] You see this symbolism with the way that covenants were "cut." The two parties would sacrifice an animal and then cut it in half. They would then walk together through the distance between the two parts of the animal. This symbolized the walking together through to death. They would then slit their wrists/hands and shake, symbolizing their lives (life is in the blood) being bound together. For more information on how covenants were cut see http://www.rockofoffence.com/myst4.html.

[9] A moment's reflection on how the devil and how God are both working through humanity to effect their will on the earth reveals something we will return to when we discuss relationships: the devil works through control and dominance; he forces his will on ours and tries to subvert us. God on the other hand offers his will to us in such a way that requires our agreement. He celebrates and honors our freedom rather than subverting it.

from God to our actions, God is obligated to fulfill that type of action, whether he wants to or not.

In fact, this is exactly what happened. After God saves the people of Israel and leads them through the wilderness of Mount Sinai, he demonstrates his love and kindness to them every step of the journey. Every complaint and situation is dealt with mercy and grace. However, at the foot of Mount Sinai an interesting event occurs: as the people of God draw near, God establishes a covenant between them called the Law. The law essentially boils down to this: do good, get good; do bad, get bad:

> *And if you faithfully obey the voice of the LORD your God, being careful to do all his commandments that I command you today, the LORD your God will set you high above all the nations of the earth. And all these blessings shall come upon you and overtake you, if you obey the voice of the LORD your God... But if you will not obey the voice of the LORD your God or be careful to do all his commandments and his statutes that I command you today, then all these curses shall come upon you and overtake you... Deuteronomy 28:1-2,15*

From this point on when the Israelites fail to keep the entirety of the law, God is obligated to curse them. Sure enough, starting that very day every mistake the Israelites made resulted in death and destruction. In fact, as Moses comes down from the mountain after receiving the law, the people had been worshiping a golden calf and 3,000 people die as a result of their transgression.[10]

So here's the takeaway to realize: before Jesus came, God was actually bound to a covenant in which he had to curse his people based on their behavior whether he

[10] The parallel in the new covenant here is that on the day of the Holy Spirit being poured out, Peter preaches and 3,000 people are brought to new life.

wanted to or not. Even before then in the Abrahamic covenant God, in choosing to bless Abraham, has to curse those who dishonor Abraham:

> *And I will make of you a great nation, and I will bless you and make your name great, so that you will be a blessing. I will bless those who bless you, and him who dishonors you I will curse, and in you all the families of the earth shall be blessed. Genesis 12:2-3*

In differentiating Abraham from the rest of the world, God promises to bless those who bless Abraham and curse those who curse him.[11] Does God do this because he wants to curse other people? No! His very next sentence states the goal for this arrangement, so that every family on the earth will be blessed through Abraham. God sets this arrangement up so that he can bless every family on the earth; but even so, he's obligated to curse those who turn against Abraham.

The writer of Hebrews points to this line of thinking directly:

> *But as it is, Christ has obtained a ministry that is as much more excellent than the old as the covenant he mediates is better, since it is enacted on better promises. For if that first covenant had been faultless, there would have been no occasion to look for a second. Hebrews 8:6-7*

God found fault with the old covenant, so he wanted to enact a better one. What was wrong with the old covenant? Let's look at what comes next:

> *For he finds fault with them when he says:*

---

[11] This is an interesting kingdom principle that actually continues through to grace. If we honor those who the grace and anointing of God is on, we enter into the grace on their lives. If we dishonor them, we choose to shut ourselves off from the blessing God wants to bring us through them. We'll discuss this in more detail in our relationships unit.

"Behold, the days are coming," declares the Lord,
"when I will establish a new covenant with the house of Israel
and with the house of Judah,
not like the covenant that I made with their fathers
on the day when I took them by the hand to bring them out of the land of Egypt.
For they did not continue in my covenant,
and so I showed no concern for them, declares the Lord." Hebrews 8:8-9

The passage starts by saying he found fault with "them." What is "them" in this case? It's not the Israelites, but the promises of the old covenant! That's the context of the verses above. God found fault with the promises of the old covenant. He found fault with them because due to the Israelites' lack of continuing in the covenant, God had to show no concern for them. This is profound! God is saying that he didn't like the old covenant because it bound him to a set of behavior that he didn't find agreeable! What behavior does he want to abide by? The next passage writes of the new covenant, the one God wants to have:

> **Theology Anchor**
>
> God wants the new covenant. He's tired of the old one and he's not interested in going back.

For this is the covenant that I will make with the house of Israel
after those days, declares the Lord:
I will put my laws into their minds,
and write them on their hearts,
and I will be their God,
and they shall be my people.
And they shall not teach, each one his neighbor
and each one his brother, saying, 'Know the Lord,'
for they shall all know me,

from the least of them to the greatest.
For I will be merciful toward their iniquities,
and I will remember their sins no more." Hebrews 8:10-12

This is the covenant that God finds natural: everyone coming to know him and a covenant of mercy, not judgment.

This is the reason that Jesus has to become our anchor point of the Father. Before Jesus came, God was bound to covenantal behavior that he himself did not find ideal. He was, at times, forced to act in ways that did not align with his heart. Here is a description of an act of judgment described in the Old Testament:

For the Lord will rise up as on Mount Perazim;
as in the Valley of Gibeon he will be roused;
to do his deed—strange is his deed!
and to work his work—alien is his work! Isaiah 28:21

Acting on judgment puts God in a place that is strange and alien to him. He will do it if he has to, but he would really rather forgive and redeem. He did not have that option under the old covenant, and this is why God seems like a bad guy at times before Jesus shows up. Jesus is the first man who lived completely outside of the judgments and curses of unfulfilled covenants and could demonstrate the heart of the Father completely.

One final thought on the subject of covenants. You may be asking yourself why God put the law in place if it constrains him to behavior he doesn't want to have to do in the first place. That's a great question and I believe there are a few layers to the answer. The first is that the law serves as a mirror to the sinful state of unredeemed humanity:

Now we know that whatever the law says it speaks to those who are under the law, so that every mouth may be stopped, and the whole world may be held accountable to God. For by works of the law no human being will be justified in his sight, since through the law comes knowledge of sin. Romans 3:19-20

The law is a tool that humanity can use to come to awareness of sinfulness. The law brings knowledge of sin, and often knowledge of sin is the first step of the journey of turning towards Christ.[12] Beyond that I believe there is actually a deeper answer still though. Paul writes this in Galatians:

Why then the law? It was added because of transgressions, until the offspring should come to whom the promise had been made, and it was put in place through angels by an intermediary. Galatians 3:19

At first glance this text reads like Paul is saying that the law was put in place because there was so much sin and that the law helps to reel that in. While I do think the law does to some extent do that, I no longer think that is what he is saying here. Notice first the later half of the verse; the law was added because of transgressions until Jesus was here so the promise of Abraham could be fulfilled. The aspect to take note of is that the law was only put in place because the time wasn't ready for Jesus, and before Jesus came humanity was in it's unredeemed sinful state.

Paul repeats this same sentiment a few verses later:

But the Scripture imprisoned everything under sin, so that the promise by faith in Jesus Christ might be given to those who believe. Now before faith came, we were

---

12 What the law can never be is a tool to clean oneself up from sin; that is not the design of the law and the result of trying to do that will be legalism and bondage.

held captive under the law, imprisoned until the coming faith would be revealed. Galatians 3:22-23

Notice Paul's language: that the law imprisoned everything that was under sin (which in the next verse he says is us—we were under sin), until Jesus comes and the promise can be fulfilled. In other words I believe Paul is saying that the law was given because only redeemed humanity can live in faith and receive the fulfillment of the promise to Abraham. Because humanity had a sinful nature instead, the law was given in between.

So the law was given not necessarily because it was God's highest desire, but because of the sinful state of humanity. Why does the sinful state of humanity dictate the law? I would suggest it has to do with the source of the sinful state of humanity—the fall. Recall what the original sin was: the choice of the knowledge of good and evil instead of life. Every person born into that line is born living in the line of that choice. That means that when a fallen people who are the chosen people of God (the Israelites at the time of Moses) relate to God, they relate to God through that choice. The giving of the law was simply the physical manifestation of living according to the knowledge of good and evil. That is, after all, the essence of the law: the knowledge of what is right and what is wrong.

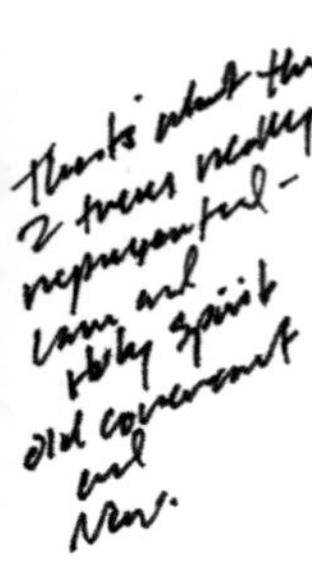

So why did God give the law? I would suggest He gave the law because Adam and Eve had already chosen the law. There was a time coming when the redeemer would come and God would be able to put aside the Old Covenant for the New, but until then humanity had chosen to live by the knowledge of good and evil and the law was simply the consequence of a fallen people in relationship with God.

Handling the Coming/Not-Yet

An important practical issue to address is how to handle yourself when the kingdom doesn't break in.[13] The reality of our experiences is that the kingdom doesn't always prevail on the earth in this age. If you haven't learned this lesson yet, you will! To be in the healing ministry is to have to face this question.

The issue is largely one of motivation. We know God's will is healing—if it wasn't, we couldn't think of the kingdom not having broken through. Rather the problem is more within ourselves: how can we maintain the intentionality and forward motion when we feel the emotional pain of the person we've been praying for not being healed or, even worse, dying?

Hebrews chapter two gives us a useful perspective on this question. Reflecting on some verses from the Psalms, the author explains that they apply to Jesus:

> *It has been testified somewhere,*
>
> *"What is man, that you are mindful of him,*
> *or the son of man, that you care for him?*
> *You made him for a little while lower than the angels;*
> *you have crowned him with glory and honor,*
> *putting everything in subjection under his feet."* Hebrews 2:6-8

Then continuing to reflect on this, there is a very interesting passage:

> *Now in putting everything in subjection to him, he left nothing outside his control. At present, we do not yet see everything in subjection to him.* Hebrews 2:8-9

[13] I actually almost used the word *failure*, but I don't think that is the right idea. God considers our obedience, not the final result that determines success or failure, and remember that love never fails.

This is the statement of the not-yet of the kingdom; we do not yet see everything in subjection to Jesus. How do we handle this?

> *But we see him who for a little while was made lower than the angels, namely Jesus, crowned with glory and honor because of the suffering of death, so that by the grace of God he might taste death for everyone. Hebrews 2:9*

Theology Anchor

When the kingdom doesn't come, keep your focus on Jesus, not your situation.

The not-yet is not the truth; *Jesus* is the truth. When our experience and Jesus don't line up, keep your eyes fixed on him; he is the author and perfector of faith (Hebrews 12:2). When we're faced with the coming of the kingdom, we keep Jesus as the revelation. As long as Jesus is bigger in our eyes than the circumstances, we have strength to continue forward in spite of discouragement.

The Kingdom in Us

The kingdom of God exists not only outside of us, but also within us as well. As we mature in Christianity, God rules not only over the events in our lives, but also in our relationships as well. Our identity and how we view ourselves is formed by the rule of God. The way we relate to others is shaped by God's intervention. This is why Paul not only says:

> *For the kingdom of God does not consist in talk but in power. 1 Corinthians 4:20*

but also

> *For the kingdom of God is not a matter of eating and drinking but of righteousness and peace and joy in the Holy Spirit. Romans 14:17*

The kingdom of God is power outside of us, but it is also power within us. The power of God at work within us is demonstrated by the quality of the life we have access to. Jesus often talks about the eternal life we have in him. This is another description of the kingdom—life that is connected to eternity. God's rule within our personhood results in an altering of who we are until the fruits of the Spirit radiate out of who we are. At the same time, our view of ourselves, who we are, and what we are called to do becomes sculpted by the work of God and conformed to God's view and calling.

Likewise, the rule of God can be expressed within the context of our relationships. Just as God can rule over who we are, He can also rule in our relationships; the manner in which we relate to others comes into alignment with the way God relates.

We will discuss the kingdom in us and in our relationships in much more detail in the units on identity and community later this semester. For now, let me point out one interesting observation. If you chart the standout important messages the Holy Spirit has been speaking over the last 30 years, you find something interesting:

	Principal message	How it relates to the kingdom of God
1980s	The kingdom of God	What the kingdom is
1990s	Sonship/identity	The kingdom in us
2000s	Culture of honor/community	The kingdom in our relationships

The Holy Spirit has been shaping our understanding of the various facets of the kingdom of God, and teaching us how they interconnect and work together.

What about the "Normal" Gospel?

This gospel of the kingdom is not what most people think the gospel is. The average Western description of the gospel is something that feels quite a bit different. The main summary points would be:

- Every human being has a sin problem.
- Jesus came and died to pay the penalty for our sin.
- If we turn to him, Jesus forgives our sin and we get to go to heaven.

This is a very different message than the message of the kingdom. Why is this? It is because in America, we focus more on what we are *saved from* than what we are *saved to*. The description above is true, but it is not the total gospel. The sin issue is also what stands between us and who God wants us to become.

> *Christ redeemed us from the curse of the law by becoming a curse for us—for it is written, "Cursed is everyone who is hanged on a tree"— so that in Christ Jesus the blessing of Abraham might come to the Gentiles, so that we might receive the promised Spirit through faith. Galatians 3:13-14*

The forgiveness of sin is not the point of the gospel; it is the means to the end of the gospel, which is the kingdom. The point of forgiveness of sin is that we can receive the Spirit. If we think that forgiveness of sin is the whole point, we'll have nowhere to go once we've been saved. No, the Holy Spirit is the point of the gospel, and the Holy Spirit always brings the kingdom. The kingdom of God is what we're saved to. So that means the truth about forgiveness of sin is part of the gospel. It is the means to the end of the gospel, which is the gospel of the kingdom.

This is encapsulated in a fascinating story in the book of Acts:

And it happened that while Apollos was at Corinth, Paul passed through the inland country and came to Ephesus. There he found some disciples. And he said to them, "Did you receive the Holy Spirit when you believed?" And they said, "No, we have not even heard that there is a Holy Spirit." And he said, "Into what then were you baptized?" They said, "Into John's baptism." And Paul said, "John baptized with the baptism of repentance, telling the people to believe in the one who was to come after him, that is, Jesus." On hearing this, they were baptized in the name of the Lord Jesus. And when Paul had laid his hands on them, the Holy Spirit came on them, and they began speaking in tongues and prophesying. Acts 19:1-6

Here is an interesting story that contrasts the difference between these two gospels. Paul runs into a set of disciples in Ephesus that apparently someone else had preached to. Paul asks if they had received the Holy Spirit, and when they said no, he asks into what they were baptized. They reply that they were baptized into John's baptism—that is according to what John preached. Let's look at what John's baptism was all about:

And Paul said, "John baptized with the baptism of repentance, telling the people to believe in the one who was to come after him, that is, Jesus." Acts 19:4

John appeared, baptizing in the wilderness and proclaiming a baptism of repentance for the forgiveness of sins. Mark 1:4

John's baptism is pretty much exactly what the western version of the gospel is: repent and turn from your sins and turn to the Messiah and you will be forgiven. Now, of course, John didn't know Jesus' name, but that's really the only difference. Here is the point: this is how people were saved *before* Jesus came. This is the *Old Testament* gospel. Jesus said it this way:

"The Law and the Prophets were until John; since then the good news of the kingdom of God is preached, and everyone forces his way into it." Luke 16:16

The point of the Old Testament is that humanity has a sin problem, and we need to turn to God to fix it. The point of the New Testament is the surprise of the kingdom! Since Jesus came, the message has changed: now the point is the kingdom! This is why Paul asks people he knows are believers if they had received the Holy Spirit; and when they hadn't, he takes care of it right away. If our gospel is focused on sin, we've not made it out of the Old Testament. We need to move to the next level and realize that forgiveness of sin is absolutely true, but Jesus came to bring the kingdom, not just to forgive our sin.

John said the kingdom is coming
Jesus said the kingdom is here

Sin and Grace

In order to move our understanding and experience into the reality of the kingdom gospel, we need to understand something important about the relationship between sin and grace. The primary message of the Old Testament focused on sin. Specifically:

- Everybody is sinful.
- Only God can take care of our sin.
- Sin contaminates.

The latter two are the primary message of the Law in the Old Testament. In the Old Testament God instituted a prophetic picture of sacrifice to point forward to the sacrifice that Jesus would make.

Indeed, under the law almost everything is purified with blood, and without the shedding of blood there is no forgiveness of sins. Hebrews 9:22

However, even so, this did not solve the problem. The shedding of blood allowed for a forgiveness of the sins that were committed, but it did not allow for the real solving of the problem. Forgiveness of sins is the symptom that is pointed to in the New Testament, which is sin at work within human nature. Sin within human nature resulted in sin behavior, which then required seeking forgiveness. The real problem, though, is not the behavior but the root of the behavior, which lies within humanity itself:

> *For since the law has but a shadow of the good things to come instead of the true form of these realities, it can never, by the same sacrifices that are continually offered every year, make perfect those who draw near. Otherwise, would they not have ceased to be offered, since the worshipers, having once been cleansed, would no longer have any consciousness of sins? But in these sacrifices there is a reminder of sins every year. For it is impossible for the blood of bulls and goats to take away sins. Hebrews 10:1-4*

Not only that, but sin is more powerful than the lack of sin. This is what is pointed to in all the rules about being clean in the Old Testament. In this framework whenever what was unclean touched what was clean, both objects became unclean. The message is to avoid sin so it doesn't contaminate you. Sin is more powerful than you are. Thus humanity is forced into a powerless situation where sin can rule over us. This state is called condemnation—a state of being victimized by sin.

Fortunately with the coming of Jesus, that all changed because with Jesus came a new concept: grace; although the reality of sin is true, the truth about grace is equally true and more powerful:

> *Mercy triumphs over judgment. James 2:13*

The stock definition of the term grace tends to be something along the lines of "unmerited favor." This is a poor definition. Why? Because grace comes from God, and why should we define something that belongs to God through us? Unmerited favor is a human-centric definition because it starts with us (unqualified), not a God-centric definition. What if grace was something with more substance? Something more like "unrestrainable favor" or "unlimitable favor"? Grace is favor so powerful that it doesn't matter if you're not qualified to receive it because grace is powerful enough to qualify you!

This paradigm shift is important because it moves us from a situation in which we are victimized by sin to one in which we are empowered by grace. Grace is so powerful that it not only meets your disqualification, but it qualifies you and empowers you to conquer what you were under before. Notice the language Paul uses in this passage:

> **Theology Anchor**
>
> Sin rules over humanity in the old covenant. Grace rules over sin in the new covenant.

For if, because of one man's trespass, death reigned through that one man, much more will those who receive the abundance of grace and the free gift of righteousness reign in life through the one man Jesus Christ. Romans 5:17

Death (and sin) reigned over us, but now we reign in life! The tables are turned with grace. Not only has God taken care of our sin behavior and our sin nature (this will be discussed more later), but he has also turned the tables on sin. We are no longer victims of sin. This is why in the New Testament we see that grace contaminates sin.

Let's consider the following examples:

- Leprosy: In the Old Testament we see that whoever has leprosy is unclean and whoever is touched by a leper becomes unclean. In the New Testament we see Jesus touching lepers and them being healed, and hence becoming clean.
- Diet: In the Old Testament there are dietary laws about what is clean and unclean. In the New Testament we see Jesus teaching that it is what is in your heart that determines whether you are clean or unclean. What you eat can no longer make you unclean. When we are under grace, we make unclean foods clean by eating them.
- Glory: In the Old Testament Moses goes up on the mountain and when he comes down his face is shining. He covers it up with his clothing so the people won't see him. In the New Testament Jesus goes up on the mountain and not only does his face glow, but his clothes are transformed as well.
- People: In the Old Testament, to become part of the people of God, one had to join the Jews; one had to conform to the standard ethnic group. In the New Testament, the people of God start spreading and perpetrating every ethnic group.

Do you get it? The point is that in grace what used to hold us back is now "infected" by grace and removed from disqualifying us. You are disqualified from being disqualified! Grace can't be stopped—it's too powerful!

This is an important message. Jesus has lifted us up above disqualification. We cannot be contaminated anymore; in fact, all we can do is spread grace around to others. When you get a hold of this idea, it changes your perspective. I'll pray for anyone in any situation because I know that the qualification and empowering on me can only spread to others. I have grace on my life and I know it, so I'm in the business of spreading that around to everyone I know and everyone I can get my hands on because God's favor is powerful and changes people's lives. Paul points to this dynamic as well:

Let no corrupting talk come out of your mouths, but only such as is good for building up, as fits the occasion, that it may give grace to those who hear.
Ephesians 4:29

Everything we say becomes useful for building up and tearing down. We must continuously be about building up.

The Holy Spirit

The Holy Spirit is a major part of the promise of the New Testament, just as the direct rule of God over and in his people is one of the major promises in the Old Testament. Paul links these together in an interesting verse in Romans:

> *For the kingdom of God is not a matter of eating and drinking but of righteousness and peace and joy in the Holy Spirit. Romans 14:17*

This verse identifies the source of the kingdom of God as the Holy Spirit. The Holy Spirit brings the kingdom of God to expression in our lives. The kingdom of God and the Holy Spirit are inseparable.

Roles of the Holy Spirit

The Holy Spirit has many roles in the life of a believer. To list all the verses out can be a bit dizzying. I think a useful study can be to see the prepositions used to describe his work. Generally, the Holy Spirit is described as being *in people*, and being *on people*:

> *until the Spirit is poured upon us from on high,*
> *and the wilderness becomes a fruitful field,*
> *and the fruitful field is deemed a forest. Isaiah 32:15*

> *And I will give you a new heart, and a new spirit I will put within you. And I will remove the heart of stone from your flesh and give you a heart of flesh. And I will put my Spirit within you, and cause you to walk in my statutes and be careful to obey my rules. Ezekiel 36:26-27*

And it shall come to pass afterward,
that I will pour out my Spirit on all flesh. Joel 2:28

And I will ask the Father, and he will give you another Helper, to be with you forever, even the Spirit of truth, whom the world cannot receive, because it neither sees him nor knows him. You know him, for he dwells with you and will be in you. John 14:16-17

I find this last Scripture interesting. Apparently there is a difference between the Holy Spirit being with us and being in us.[14] This is reinforced by the process we see the disciples go through after Jesus is raised from the dead and leading into Pentecost. Jesus is raised from the dead, and the first day he sees them again, we read:

Jesus said to them again, "Peace be with you. As the Father has sent me, even so I am sending you." And when he had said this, he breathed on them and said to them, "Receive the Holy Spirit. If you forgive the sins of any, they are forgiven them; if you withhold forgiveness from any, it is withheld." John 20:21-23

Jesus then hangs out with the disciples for 40 days teaching them and reminding them of things. Then on the day he is leaving, Jesus says,

And while staying with them he ordered them not to depart from Jerusalem, but to wait for the promise of the Father, which, he said, "you heard from me; for John baptized with water, but you will be baptized with the Holy Spirit not many days from now . . . But you will receive power when the Holy Spirit has come upon you,

[14] One could say that the Holy Spirit is already with them in the presence of Jesus; and if this was the only Scripture that implied there is a difference between the Holy Spirit being in and on, I could interpret it that way; but given the other discussion between the books of John and Acts, as well as the parallel in Jesus' life, it looks like Jesus may not have meant that.

and you will be my witnesses in Jerusalem and in all Judea and Samaria, and to the end of the earth."' Acts 1:4-5,8

Apparently even though the disciples had received the Holy Spirit, they were not yet baptized in the Holy Spirit. The Holy Spirit was *in them*, but Jesus says that the Holy Spirit has not yet come *on* them.

We actually see a similar progression in the life of Jesus as well. Luke writes this about Jesus' wilderness experience:

> *And Jesus, full of the Holy Spirit, returned from the Jordan and was led by the Spirit in the wilderness for forty days, being tempted by the devil. Luke 4:1-2*

> *And Jesus returned in the power of the Spirit to Galilee, and a report about him went out through all the surrounding country. Luke 4:14*

Jesus goes out full of the Spirit, and comes back in the power of the Spirit. It's exactly the same as the disciples, who receive the Spirit, and then have to wait for the Spirit to come upon them with power.

There is a whole lot of theological discussion that sits behind these ideas, as to the order of these events in a Christian's life, what it means to experience these things, when, and how often, etc. Honestly, I'm not interested in going there, but I do want to point out it is clear that the Holy Spirit is within us, and also comes upon us for works of power. These are two different things, and I want to consider each of them now.

By the way, if you consider the gospels, you'll notice that the synoptic gospels (Matthew, Mark and Luke) are primarily about the Spirit on believers, whereas the Johannine literature (the Gospel of John and 1st-3rd John) is primarily about the Spirit in believers. If you want to continue to study about this, I'd start there.

The Spirit In Us

The Holy Spirit's role in the believer is that of *transformation*. It is to change who we are on the inside from one person to another person.

> *Now the Lord is the Spirit, and where the Spirit of the Lord is, there is freedom. And we all, with unveiled face, beholding the glory of the Lord, are being transformed into the same image from one degree of glory to another. For this comes from the Lord who is the Spirit.* 2 Corinthians 3:17-18

Jesus, speaking about the Holy Spirit, says this:

> *And when he comes, he will convict the world concerning sin and righteousness and judgment: concerning sin, because they do not believe in me; concerning righteousness, because I go to the Father, and you will see me no longer; concerning judgment, because the ruler of this world is judged.* John 16:8-11

Now, notice something. Jesus says that the Holy Spirit convicts of three things: sin, righteousness, and judgment. Then he specifies subjects to those convictions: conviction of sin to unbelievers, and conviction of righteousness to his followers. Jesus doesn't say what we often quote this verse as saying, that the Holy Spirit convicts believers of sin; it says he convicts believers of righteousness![15] What righteousness? The righteousness of Jesus, because he's not with us anymore. Why do we need to be reminded of the righteousness of Jesus? Because that's the same righteousness we have!

> *For our sake he made him to be sin who knew no sin, so that in him we might become the righteousness of God.* 2 Corinthians 5:21

[15] To date I've not found a passage that says the Holy Spirit convicts believers of sin, which is often one of the first things we attribute to him. If you know of one, I'd like to hear it.

Now, many of us know we are righteous, but we can struggle to have the conviction that we're righteous. That's where the Holy Spirit comes in. He comes and reveals to us at such a deep level who we are in Christ that it literally changes us from the inside out.

> *No one born of God makes a practice of sinning, for God's seed abides in him, and he cannot keep on sinning because he has been born of God.* 1 John 3:9

The Holy Spirit operates on us and reveals God to us at the deepest levels of who we are, such that our desires come into alignment with his. In fact, every ounce of who we are starts to radiate God's very character:

> *But the fruit of the Spirit is love, joy, peace, patience, kindness, goodness, faithfulness, gentleness, self-control; against such things there is no law.* Galatians 5:22

As the Spirit works in our lives, what grows in us is the very personality of God himself.

Authority

Another aspect of the Holy Spirit in us is that with the Holy Spirit's presence comes spiritual authority. Scripture talks both about *authority* and *power* that Jesus bestows on his followers. Both are relevant and pertinent to our purposes.

Authority has to do with permission. It is about access or the right to do something. Power on the other hand has to do with the ability or means to do something. As believers, we need to understand both authority and power, learn to operate out of authority and out of power, and discern when to lean into which one.

First, let me observe that our authority is in proportion to our submission to God. The gospels make clear that authority isn't something that comes from ourselves, but rather something that comes from whomever is above us.

> *For I have not spoken on my own authority, but the Father who sent me has himself given me a commandment—what to say and what to speak.* John 12:49

> *Do you not believe that I am in the Father and the Father is in me? The words that I say to you I do not speak on my own authority, but the Father who dwells in me does his works. John 14:10*

> *"For I too am a man under authority, with soldiers under me. And I say to one, 'Go,' and he goes, and to another, 'Come,' and he comes, and to my servant, 'Do this,' and he does it." Matthew 8:9*

The point is that Jesus doesn't give us authority, but rather he puts us under his authority. As such, the authority to complete our mission doesn't come from us; it comes from Him:

> *And Jesus came and said to them, "All authority in heaven and on earth has been given to me. Go therefore and make disciples of all nations, baptizing them in the name of the Father and of the Son and of the Holy Spirit, teaching them to observe all that I have commanded you. And behold, I am with you always, to the end of the age." Matthew 28:18-20*

Authority then rests on Jesus and our obedience to do what he tells us to do. Our authority is in proportion to our submission to his mission. Indeed, as Jesus commissions the disciples, he points to the authority he has before sending them.

Let me take a brief aside. Before Jesus died and was resurrected, who had authority on the earth? The answer is Satan. This is something we need to take seriously, and an important thing to keep in mind while reading the Old Testament. Satan had legitimate access to the earth and could do what he wanted. We ought not to blame God for what Satan did during the Old Testament. One common example of this happens in Job 1, where Satan and God are dialoging about Job:

> *And the Lord said to Satan, "Behold, all that he has is in your hand. Only against him do not stretch out your hand." Job 1:12*

If we do not believe that Satan had legitimate authority, we read this verse as God giving Satan permission to harass Job. The reality though is that Satan had authority on the earth; he did not need God's permission to mess with Job—he already had it! With perspective we'll interpret this verse as God observing the authority that Satan already had. God wasn't giving Satan permission to destroy Job's life; he was observing that Satan already had that authority.

However, all that changes with Jesus. Jesus has taken back the authority that the devil had on the earth. He then commissions us under that authority; as proof, he gives us the presence of the Holy Spirit within us. Notice the language Jesus uses when the disciples receive the presence of the Holy Spirit within them:

> *Jesus said to them again, "Peace be with you. As the Father has sent me, even so I am sending you." And when he had said this, he breathed on them and said to them, "Receive the Holy Spirit. If you forgive the sins of any, they are forgiven them; if you withhold forgiveness from any, it is withheld." John 20:21-23*

Jesus connects the presence of the Holy Spirit within them with the authority to forgive sins. Paul talks about this when he talks about being sealed with the Holy Spirit:

In him you also, when you heard the word of truth, the gospel of your salvation, and believed in him, were sealed with the promised Holy Spirit, who is the guarantee of our inheritance until we acquire possession of it, to the praise of his glory. Ephesians 1:13-14

The presence of the Holy Spirit within us is the stamp on us that we belong to God, and as such we are under the authority that God has.

The Spirit on Us

The other part of the Spirit's work is the work of the Spirit on people (or things). The Holy Spirit coming on someone is linked to the manifest power of God. This comes up over and over in the gospels. We even see this in Jesus' conception. When Mary asks the angel Gabriel how she can be pregnant since she is a virgin, his reply is:

> **Theology Anchor**
>
> The Spirit is in us to transform us; he comes on us to release His power through us.

And the angel answered her, "The Holy Spirit will come upon you, and the power of the Most High will overshadow you; therefore the child to be born will be called holy—the Son of God. Luke 1:35

In fact, the power of the presence of the Spirit upon something is revealed all the way from the Creation account in Genesis 1.

In the beginning, God created the heavens and the earth. The earth was without form and void, and darkness was over the face of the deep. And the Spirit of God was hovering over the face of the waters. Genesis 1:1-2

The picture painted is that the Holy Spirit was upon the earth, acting as the catalyzing power of the spoken word of God to bring what was spoken into being. This is one of

the major keys to learn in power ministry: *the power comes with the manifest presence of God*. Wimber would put it this way: "The power is in the presence."

One aspect of moving in ministry works the same way-as we see the manifest presence of God on someone, we speak the word that the Holy Spirit uses as a catalyst to bring the kingdom of God.

Theology Anchor

The gifts of the Holy Spirit are given *situationally*. We can learn to flow in all the gifts because we have the giver living inside of us.

Paul lists nine gifts in a discussion about spiritual manifestations in 1 Corinthians 12. Paul's point here is not to provide an exhaustive list of spiritual activities, but rather that the source of all the manifestations is the same Holy Spirit in all the believers. Nevertheless, we can learn many things by studying what Paul says in this passage. We can sum this up in the following table.[16]

A careful reading of 1 Corinthians 12 shows that Paul is discussing spiritual manifestations, not spiritual gifts.[17] Some manifestations of the spirit come by gifts, and others through a different description, but Paul says,

> *Now there are varieties of gifts, but the same Spirit; and there are varieties of service, but the same Lord; and there are varieties of activities, but it is the same God who empowers them all in everyone. To each is given the manifestation of the Spirit for the common good. 1 Corinthians 12:4-7*[18]

---

[16] This table isn't my creation; it comes from another source, which I believe summarized a section of Alexander Venter's *Doing Healing*.

[17] For example, in 1 Cor. 12:1, the word *gifts* is not actually used in the Greek. Paul says, "Now, concerning the spiritual brothers, I don't want you to be uninformed."

[18] Interestingly, in the list of the manifestations of the Spirit, the only one listed as a "gift" is healings!

Manifestation	Classification	Explanation
Revelation (Mind of God)	Word of knowledge	Knowledge of a fact or truth that comes from the spiritual realm. Often something the person could not know in the natural. (Mark 2:8)
	Word of wisdom	Similar to a word of knowledge, except rather than information gleaned from the spiritual realm it is direction or a solution instead. (John 8:1-11)
	Discernment of spirits	The ability to perceive dynamics in the spirit realm directly and discern the source as human, angelic, demonic or divine. The ability to test and distinguish between spirits. (1 John 4:1)
Inspiration (Mouth of God)	Prophecy	Words spoken under inspiration that reveal God's mind and heart for a community or person. Used to strengthen, encourage and comfort the body. ~~May be related to~~ predicting future events. (1 Cor. 14)
	Different kinds of tongues	Also spoken inspired words, but in a language the person does not naturally speak or know—use both for personal worship and prayer, and when interpreted, ministry to others. (1 Cor. 14)
	Interpretation of tongues	Inspired interpretation of a spoken tongue, which reveals the meaning of what was said. (Daniel 5:22-28)
Demonstration (Hand of God)	Faith	A supernatural deposit of God's faith into an individual that often results in dramatic demonstration of God's power. (Acts 3:4-6, James 5:15)
	Gifts of healings	The ability given through faith and grace given to heal different kinds of sicknesses through spoken words and the laying on of hands. (1 Cor. 14)
	Working of miracles	The ability to work miracles, often creative in nature as a demonstration of God's power and his ability to meet human needs and rule over nature. (Acts 3:6-8)

Revelation Manifestations

Revelation manifestations reveal the mind of God to us. They are the information, understanding, and discernment from God being revealed to us. I think of revelation gifts as being our spiritual senses. The key to being released in revelation gifts is to recognize what you're looking for. Many people feel that God doesn't speak to them because they're looking in the wrong place. God lives on the inside of us now, so if we are listening to hear God, we need to be listening within ourselves, not for a voice from the outside. Once a person learns to begin to pay attention to what is happening within them—their thoughts, feelings, intuitions and so forth, he or she can often begin to recognize God speaking to them relatively quickly. From there it is simply a process of trial and error as he or she learns to recognize God's voice more and more confidently.

Word of Knowledge

Words of knowledge can be a very useful tool in ministry. It is a way of God highlighting what he is doing so we can work with him. Words of knowledge are relatively easy to get activated in and can give a great boost of faith for healing.

Theology Anchor

God speaks to us from the inside, not from the outside.

Different people tend to get words of knowledge differently. Some common avenues for words of knowledge are:

- **Seeing:** a mental picture of something (often a body part).
- **Feeling:** either emotionally or physically an issue someone else is dealing with.
- **Reading:** words written on a person or elsewhere.
- **Knowing:** an inner feeling or sense about a specific issue.
- **Speaking:** words just tumble out of our mouth having bypassed our mind.
- Hearing: words that pass through our mind.

Often people will operate in one or two of these with some frequency, and others only rarely. I've found that during different parts in my life, God has used different avenues at different times. I tend to get most of my words by knowing, although it is becoming less uncommon for me to operate through seeing, feeling, and speaking. To date I don't know that I've ever had a reading word of knowledge.

After you begin to move in words of knowledge, you'll want to learn to lean into whatever avenues you regularly receive revelation from. There is a growth process in each of these. I know that for knowing words, as I've practiced I've learned to be more sensitive to specifically what I "know" and have been able to get more specific words of knowledge. Likewise with picture words, you can grow in interpretive ability.

Word of Wisdom

Words of wisdom are quite similar to words of knowledge, except rather than information that is communicated, a word of wisdom is an insight, understanding or solution. A word of wisdom often unlocks a process or a direction for a person to pursue what the Lord wants them to undertake.

Words of wisdom take an additional faith component above words of knowledge because they are directional. If a word of knowledge is off, there usually is no harm done, but a word of wisdom gone wrong can cause the person to misuse time, energy, and resources. For that reason, people can tend to back off from words of wisdom. We need to learn to hear God accurately and trust what we hear, though, because there are many valuable insights that God wants to give us that we'll miss if we're too afraid to grow in words of wisdom.

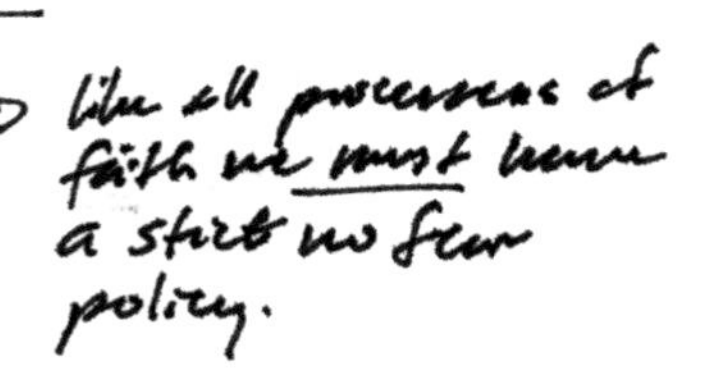

Discernment of Spirits

Discerning of spirits operates to two different ends. The first is to distinguish whether the source of an action or manifestation is demonic, human, or angelic in origin. It is kind of a red/green light that we can use to determine whether we should shut things down or continue. The second type of discerning of spirits involves recognizing the Holy Spirit's presence and/or work upon someone. It is learning to see the Holy Spirit hovering over someone just as we see in Genesis 1.

It is quite useful to learn to discern the presence of the demonic. It will help us decide whether to pursue deliverance or whether the person is being touched by God. Often it is difficult to tell the difference between these two because as the Holy Spirit encounters a person powerfully, often he drudges up a lot of hurt to bring healing. That process can sometimes look very similar to demonic manifestation. We often have a reaction in our spirit to the presence of the demonic. The following are common sensations:

- Feeling of nausea or queasiness.
- Inner uneasiness or restlessness.
- Difficulty retaining control of anger, lust, greed, or other sins that usually aren't a problem.
- Feeling inwardly violated.
- Confused thought processes and inability to perceive as you usually do.
- Permeating negativity.

As you learn to discern the presence of the demonic, use that information to correctly handle the situation. We'll talk much more about this later when we talk about deliverance.

Discerning the presence of the Holy Spirit is a much more enjoyable experience. As we learn to see the presence of God on people and follow that, we'll begin to have more powerful ministry experiences. Common ways of seeing the presence of God on people are:

- A person seems to be highlighted; they seem more real than real in some way.
- Feeling drawn to a person when you look at them.
- You find yourself looking repeatedly at a person for no particular reason.
- There are a whole host of physical signals of the Holy Spirit moving on someone. (See the following table)

Recipient	Minister
• crying • eyelids fluttering • trembling/spasms • glow • heat/cold in specific areas • sensations of power/electricity • trembling or shaking • stiffness or contortions • heaviness, loss of balance • peace, wooziness • drunkenness • trances • exhilaration, joy, laughter	• tenderness and compassion • heat, cold, or tingling in hands • sensations of power • sensations in our skin • disembodied detachment • aggressive engagement • overwhelming compassion • rising confidence in God • heaviness or sluggishness

Inspiration Manifestations

Inspiration manifestations refer to inspired speech; that is, God speaking through us.

Prophecy

Prophecy is more than speaking a revelation. If that were the case, words of knowledge and words of wisdom would be prophecy as well. Prophecy is speaking what God says about a situation or person. It is revealing God's heart. Revelation will always be a part of prophecy, but prophecy is much more than revelation.

Prophecy generally falls into two categories: inspirational and revelatory.[19] Inspirational prophecy is a form of prophecy that every believer can and should desire to move in:

> *Pursue love, and earnestly desire the spiritual gifts, especially that you may prophesy. For one who speaks in a tongue speaks not to men but to God; for no one understands him, but he utters mysteries in the Spirit. On the other hand, the one who prophesies speaks to people for their upbuilding and encouragement and consolation. 1 Corinthians 14:1-3*

The root of inspirational prophecy is speaking by the Holy Spirit for the purpose of building up, encouraging, and consoling the people of God. It is a kind of encouragement by the Spirit. Every believer can and should use this type of prophecy. This is a very common tool while ministering to others.

Inspirational prophecy tends to come by leaning into the revelation that God gives us. As the Lord speaks something to us, we ask the Lord what he meant and what that means in the context of what he is working in people's lives. We develop a picture of who that person is in the Spirit and the momentum that God is bringing to them right now. As that picture emerges, we release that to him or her.

---

[19] I take these categories from Graham Cooke's excellent book *Prophecy and Responsibility*.

Revelatory prophecy is a more weighty form of prophecy that requires a higher level of maturity and a proven track record in prophecy. Revelatory prophecy is much more intentional and requires more thought and prayer for how to handle it because it is highly directional. It shouldn't be given spontaneously because it provides an agenda for progress and needs the approval of the leadership before delivery to the whole church. Revelatory prophecy includes:

- Correction
- Direction
- Warning

Hence the need to weigh these types of words

We will talk much more in depth about prophecy when we come to our unit on prophecy in the second semester.

Speaking in Tongues

Paul informs us of the nature of the gift of tongues in 1 Corinthians:

> *If I speak in the tongues of men and of angels, but have not love, I am a noisy gong or a clanging cymbal. 1 Corinthians 13:1*

In Acts 2 on the day of Pentecost we saw the disciples burst forth speaking in tongues under the guidance of the Holy Spirit. They spoke in foreign languages, and the Jews of the Diaspora heard their native language being spoken. Paul adds a further insight here that speaking in tongues can also be speaking the language of angels.

Speaking in tongues is interesting in that is has a number of different uses. Those outlined scripturally are:

- Speaking to people in another language you don't know as seen in Acts 2. Interestingly the gift of tongues is the reversal of the splitting of language we

Unity without the Holy Spirit will accomplish demonic intention. Unity under the direction of Holy Spirit will accomplish Heavenly intention.

see in Genesis 11 at the Tower of Babel. At the Tower of Babel, God split the language because a unified group of evil people was too powerful. Yet, God wants us as believers to have unity, and the gift of tongues empowers that unity even though we still speak different languages.

- Speaking in a tongue publically which is then interpreted publically. This is referred to in 1 Corinthians 14. Pairing the gift of speaking in tongues with the gift of interpretation of tongues is a form of inspired worship that Paul says is useful to build up the church.
- Speaking in tongues privately. Paul informs us that speaking in tongues is a practice we can do to strengthen ourselves:

> *The one who speaks in a tongue builds up himself, but the one who prophesies builds up the church. 1 Corinthians 14:4*

- Speaking in tongues then is sort of a "weightlifting in the Spirit" that we can practice. As such it is an invaluable spiritual discipline! Smith Wigglesworth used to say that he never had to go on vacation because he would speak in tongues everyday and be refreshed.

Interpretation of Tongues

Interpretation of tongues is the partner gift to speaking in tongues used in a public setting. It is the supernatural disclosure of the meaning of a message that was spoken (or sometimes sung) in tongues in a public gathering. One interesting note on the interpretation of tongues: Paul makes it clear that one speaking in tongues is speaking to God:

> *For one who speaks in a tongue speaks not to men but to God; for no one understands him, but he utters mysteries in the Spirit. 1 Corinthians 14:2*

However, often in practice an interpreted tongue is delivered as a prophecy, as a message *from* God rather than *to* God. The interpretation of a tongue ought to be closer to worship than prophecy.

Demonstration Manifestations

Demonstration manifestations are acts of God. They are God in action and can be some of the clearest signs that point to the kingdom of God.

Faith

Faith is a term that seems to have many definitions and explanations. At the very least, it is complex because it is a gift (1 Cor. 12:9), and yet at the same time, it is also a fruit of the Spirit:

> *But the fruit of the Spirit is love, joy, peace, patience, kindness, goodness, faithfulness [literally faith, see the KJV], gentleness, self-control; against such things there is no law. Galatians 5:22-23*

The word *faith* translated in the Greek literally means "trust." I think we, as Westerners, tend to confuse the nature of faith because with our scientific/deistic worldview, we tend to have a hard time believing that God will do something we call supernatural. Because of that, we think that actually thinking that God could do something supernatural would be having faith. I think this is projecting our own worldview on to the Bible too much. Remember, the Hebrew and Greek worldviews that we see portrayed in the Bible were very different than our own. The Hebrews, for example didn't struggle with the same tendency to believe in a naturalistic world like we do. They would not have faced the same difficulty that we face, and yet Jesus faced a lack of faith in his followers.

On the other end of the spectrum, sometimes we reduce faith to an emotion. I've heard a gift of faith being described as a feeling of confidence that God will act. I'm not crazy about that description because I think it confuses the issue. A gift of faith can *result* in a confidence that God will act, but is that what it is? Doesn't it take more faith to pray when you don't feel like God will act than when you do?

Perhaps the clearest picture of the nature of faith comes out of the book of Hebrews:

> *Now faith is the assurance of things hoped for, the conviction of things not seen. Hebrews 11:1*

Note the word *conviction*. This is an issue we tend to have difficulty with. Faith is not belief. Belief is something that we think at a mental level; something we think or know is true. Faith is a conviction and operates out of a different place. Faith is to the heart what belief is to the head. This is why we cannot conjure up faith. We cannot talk ourselves into having faith because it isn't something that comes from our head.

> *And Jesus answered them, "Have faith in God. Truly, I say to you, whoever says to this mountain, 'Be taken up and thrown into the sea,'* ***and does not doubt in his heart****, but believes that what he says will come to pass, it will be done for him. Mark 11:22-23 emphasis mine*

Other translations may translate the word assurance as "substance" or "confidence." The word in the Greek means "a setting under or the foundation of" as well as "the substance of."[20] Faith then is both the foundation the intervention of God is built upon, as well as the avenue through which it moves.

---

[20] Blue Letter Bible, accessed 7/5/11.
http://www.blueletterbible.org/lang/lexicon/lexicon.cfm?Strongs=G5287&t=KJV

It is important to have both of these in mind. The miraculous is both built upon and comes through faith. Without a foundation of faith, there is no base for the miraculous to be put upon. Without the action of faith there is no path through which the miraculous can flow.

As we exercise whatever level of faith we have, faith grows in us. We have a foundation that gets built. This is why faith is called a fruit. The trust we exercise in God becomes something we don't have to reach for-it becomes something that is always there and grows in us.

Likewise the action of faith provides an opportunity for the miraculous to happen. Often the miraculous doesn't begin until the trust has been exercised:

> *But Peter said, "I have no silver and gold, but what I do have I give to you. In the name of Jesus Christ of Nazareth, rise up and walk!" And he took him by the right hand and raised him up, and immediately his feet and ankles were made strong.*
> *Acts 3:6-7*

Notice that the beggar's feet and ankles were not made strong until *after* Peter helped him up.

> *Then he ordered the crowds to sit down on the grass, and taking the five loaves and the two fish, he looked up to heaven and said a blessing. Then he broke the loaves and gave them to the disciples, and the disciples gave them to the crowds.*
> *Matthew 14:19*

Jesus did not multiply the loaves at this point; he gave them to the disciples. Only as the disciples started giving out the loaves were they multiplied.

This principle of acting and creating space for the miraculous is a key for healing. This is a big part of why Wimber would say that faith is spelled R-I-S-K. We activate our trust in God and who God is, and as we do that, we call into existence the things we hope for. This is the nature of who God is as well:

> *[Speaking about Abraham] as it is written, "I have made you the father of many nations"—in the presence of the God in whom he believed, who gives life to the dead and calls into existence the things that do not exist. Romans 4:17*

Notice as well the one failure in healing we have recorded in the Scriptures:

> *And when they came to the crowd, a man came up to him and, kneeling before him, said, "Lord, have mercy on my son, for he is an epileptic and he suffers terribly. For often he falls into the fire, and often into the water. And I brought him to your disciples, and they could not heal him." And Jesus answered, "O faithless and twisted generation, how long am I to be with you? How long am I to bear with you? Bring him here to me." And Jesus rebuked the demon, and it came out of him, and the boy was healed instantly. Then the disciples came to Jesus privately and said, "Why could we not cast it out?" He said to them, "Because of your little faith. For truly, I say to you, if you have faith like a grain of mustard seed, you will say to this mountain, 'Move from here to there,' and it will move, and nothing will be impossible for you." Matthew 17:14-20*

I do find it interesting that Jesus attributes their failure to lack of faith. There is a careful balance we have to walk regarding the role of faith with healing. There are some elements of faith teachings that result in some less-than-favorable practices, and I do believe that we ought to avoid those. I don't ever believe we should blame people for not being healed because they don't have faith. To do that puts a burden on the sick person that Jesus never put on them.[21] Yet at the same time we ought not to dismiss the importance and the role of faith. If Jesus thinks it is important, so should we.

> *For in Christ Jesus neither circumcision nor uncircumcision counts for anything, but only faith working through love. Galatians 5:6*

Gifts of Healing

Gifts of healing is actually the only manifestation of the Spirit that is described with the word *gift* in this passage, and actually it is described in the plural—gifts, not gift. If someone asks you if you have the gift of healing, you should ask which one they are talking about.

More important is looking at what the word *gifts* actually means. The word is *charismata*, which of course is where we get the word "charismatic." The singular is the word *charisma*, which comes from *charis*, the Greek word for grace. This connection is important: gifts flow through grace. This is an intentional word that has been chosen here to make this connection. Not every word translated in English as "gift" in the New Testament is this word, but this specific word has a clear connotation of grace. We see it as well in other passages that make this connection even more evident:

---

[21] Actually Jesus puts that burden on his disciples in this scripture, not the boy or his father. Biblically, it seems to me that if we make the "you didn't have enough faith" argument against anyone, it should be against the person praying, not the person receiving prayer. That being said, we still ought to be careful because, with this line of thinking, we can begin to blame ourselves as ministers when healing is not the result. To do that is to take credit for the devil's work. This is where kingdom theology has such a strong point—it keeps the focus on the enemy for the enemy's work. When we begin to hold ourselves to blame for people not being healed, we've inadvertently given the enemy a tool to attack and condemn us, and we've begun to take credit for the destruction he has caused. For this reason it seems to me the best biblical and practical stance on this issue is to adopt the following mindset when it comes to faith and lack of healing: "This may be a case where the enemy is really entrenched, and if I had faith here I'd be able to uproot him. It's not my fault he's here; it's his. I'm going to blame him for his work and I'm going to ask God to continue to grow me in faith." Let's blame the devil for his work, yet continue to ask God to empower us to overthrow every work of the enemy.

As each has received a gift, use it to serve one another, as good stewards of God's varied grace. 1 Peter 4:10

Having gifts that differ according to the grace given to us, let us use them: if prophecy, in proportion to our faith. Romans 12:6

Gifts of healing then are healings that come through grace. They are healings that come purely from the goodness of God as something he loves to give to his children.

To operate in a gift of healing then is to operate out of the grace of God. It is to lean into God's goodness and appeal to God to change the situation.

Working of Miracles

The manifestation of working of miracles is also described with two words. Let's examine them both:

Working is the word *energema*, which means "operating" or "working." Think energizing. The word *miracles* is actually the word *dunamis*, which means "power" or "ability." This is interesting; Paul is actually saying the operating of power! The focus on a miracle then is not just power, but the fact that the power is operated—by us!

An interesting question to ask then is: what is the difference between a healing and a miracle? By the common English definition, a healing is a miracle because miracle is a rather inclusive term in English. I've heard two common answers to this question:

- A miracle is an instant healing.
- A healing is when you're repairing things that already exist; a miracle is when you have to create something new.

I'm not crazy about either of those definitions honestly. I'm not sure what the reasoning behind the first one is; and from what I understand, the second comes from the Catholic tradition.[22]

I think the problem is really the question. If we want to get inside Paul's head, we need to be asking what the difference between a *gift of healing* and a *working of power/miracle* is. These are the terms Paul used, so I think those are the terms we should use when we're exploring the differences.[23]

When asking this question, Paul's point comes a little more into focus; it is that in one manifestation the channel is God's grace, and in the other manifestation is the operating of power. In other words, one moves around us and the other moves through us. God's grace works a gift of healing, whereas the working of a miracle happens in a partnership between God and us.

We could be tempted to draw a distinction between the two in terms of strength, where gifts of healing requires less power, but Scripturally we see the word *heal* as combined with power in the following verses:

> *And all the crowd sought to touch him, for power came out from him and healed them all. Luke 6:19*

> *God anointed Jesus of Nazareth with the Holy Spirit and with power. He went about doing good and healing all who were oppressed by the devil, for God was with him. Acts 10:38*

---

[22] This is an important distinction for the Catholics because miracles count toward becoming a saint; healings don't.

[23] Paul seems to be careful about maintaining that distinction. He includes the same two-word descriptions for these two manifestations later in the chapter in 1 Cor. 12:29-30.

So I don't think Paul is going after a difference in "strength" here although he does prioritize the working of miracles above gifts of healing:

> *And God has appointed in the church first apostles, second prophets, third teachers, then miracles, then gifts of healing, helping, administrating, and various kinds of tongues. Are all apostles? Are all prophets? Are all teachers? Do all work miracles? Do all possess gifts of healing? Do all speak with tongues? Do all interpret? But earnestly desire the higher gifts. 1 Corinthians 12:28-31*

Gifts and Character

Every so often I hear someone say something along the lines of "Character is more important than gifting." I appreciate the heart behind a statement like this, but I think it is not only wrong, but also creates a false dichotomy.[24] The heart of the statement is that gifting without character is dangerous, and so we should seek character and not gifting. I agree that gifting without character is often dangerous, but the flip side is that character without gifting is ineffectual. Try asking a person who is dying of cancer with one month to live who is asking you to pray for him or her whether gifting or character is more important. There are times when each comes to the forefront.

Character is the heart of God in us, and gifting is the hand of God through us. A much better statement would be that "gifting without character is incomplete." Of course, the likewise is also true. Character will influence the packaging of the gift, which often impacts how well it is received, and hence the effectiveness. Character and gifting work together then, not against each other.

Remember that we cannot accurately represent God without the power of the Holy Spirit. God is powerful and needs powerful people to be accurately portrayed:

---

[24] That is putting two things at odds that aren't actually opposed to each other.

> *"But you will receive power when the Holy Spirit has come upon you, and you will be [Jesus'] witnesses in Jerusalem and in all Judea and Samaria, and to the end of the earth." Acts 1:8*

Notice that becoming a witness only happens after the disciples have received power through the Holy Spirit. Why is this? Because without power we can only witness to what Jesus has *said*, with power we can witness to who he *is*. Our world doesn't need another person telling them what Jesus has said; they already know what Jesus said! Most people know Jesus tells us to love our enemies, turn the other cheek, and do unto others as we would have them do unto us. What they need is to see someone walking in the power that Jesus promised and offering that same power to them. For that we need gifting and character working together. We must have them both, and we must be growing in both of them.

Situational and Constitutional Gifts

Spiritual manifestations or gifts have long been a subject of discussion in the church. Those who believe and attempt to practice the gifts tend to put the spiritual gifts into two categories:

- Situational: gifts are available for anyone, so anyone can move in any spiritual gift.
- Constitutional: specific gifts are given to people, so you probably have a few spiritual gifts, but not others.

The reality is that both of these are depicted in Scripture, but in different places. The discussion we just had regarding 1 Corinthians 12 is about situational gifts.[25] How do we know this? Look at the last verse in that chapter:

> *But earnestly desire the higher gifts. 1 Corinthians 12:31*

Why would Paul instruct the people to desire specific gifts if they didn't have any chance to operate in them? This would be setting people up for failure and frustration.

Yet, constitutional gifts do exist. We see these mentioned in another famous passage:[26]

> *And [Jesus] gave the apostles, the prophets, the evangelists, the shepherds and teachers, to equip the saints for the work of ministry, for building up the body of Christ. Ephesians 4:11-12*

Notice the distinction though. In 1 Corinthians 12 the gift is the manifestation of the Spirit. In Ephesians 4 the gift is the person's calling (Ephesians 4:1). So for the gift of prophecy the gift is the prophecy itself, but for a prophet, the gift is the prophet.

Really the difference here is the difference between calling and gifting. Calling has to do with who you are; it has to do with identity. Gifting has to do with what you can do; it has to do with the ability to do something.

In the Ephesians 4 text, Paul lists five constitutional giftings sometimes called the five-fold ministry or the five offices.[27]

---

[25] It is a little more complicated than just situational gifts. The first part of 1 Cor. 12 is about situational gifts. After Paul uses the body metaphor he starts talking more about people and less about the spiritual gifts and bounces back and forth between the two.
[26] Parts of this discussion are from Kris Vallotton's book *Basic Training for Prophetic Ministry*.

- Apostles focus on governing and leading. They lead out of a sense of needing to establish what has been described in heaven and releasing that on the earth (see Hebrews 8:5)
- Prophets focus on seeing. They perceive the supernatural and are a source of guidance for what God is saying and what direction to be moving.
- Evangelists focus on saving the lost. Their hearts beat to gather people into relationship with Jesus.
- Pastors focus on caring for the found. They want to make sure that everyone's material and relational needs are met. They prioritize connection and community.
- Teachers focus on informing. They want to ground the relationship people have with Jesus in truth and provide real depth and strength to others.

These five offices are equipping offices; they exist for the betterment of the body of Christ and serve to equip the saints.[28] The five-fold ministry and calling will be discussed in much more detail for students who take the second year of the school.

The Parable of the Minas

Let's close by looking at a parable that Jesus said:

> *[Jesus] said therefore, "A nobleman went into a far country to receive for himself a kingdom and then return. Calling ten of his servants, he gave them ten minas, and said to them, 'Engage in business until I come.' . . . When he returned, having*

---

[27] Some exegetes believe this is a poor translation of Paul and that pastor-teacher is really one office, which results in four offices, not five. The common language is to discuss the five-fold office, so I stuck with that for the notes.

[28] As an interesting aside, consider 1 Cor. 12:28 as a comparison. Three of these offices are duplicated, an office or miracle worker is introduced (perhaps evangelists) and everything else is lumped into a non-descript group.

received the kingdom, he ordered these servants to whom he had given the money to be called to him, that he might know what they had gained by doing business.

The first came before him, saying, 'Lord, your mina has made ten minas more.' And he said to him, 'Well done, good servant! Because you have been faithful in a very little, you shall have authority over ten cities.'

And the second came, saying, 'Lord, your mina has made five minas.' And he said to him, 'And you are to be over five cities.'

Then another came, saying, 'Lord, here is your mina, which I kept laid away in a handkerchief; for I was afraid of you, because you are a severe man. You take what you did not deposit, and reap what you did not sow.' He said to him, 'I will condemn you with your own words, you wicked servant! You knew that I was a severe man, taking what I did not deposit and reaping what I did not sow? Why then did you not put my money in the bank, and at my coming I might have collected it with interest?'

And he said to those who stood by, 'Take the mina from him, and give it to the one who has the ten minas.' And they said to him, 'Lord, he has ten minas!' 'I tell you that to everyone who has, more will be given, but from the one who has not, even what he has will be taken away.'" Luke 19:12-13, 15-26

In this parable, Jesus explains that people have been given different amounts in the kingdom: different gifts, different skills, different insights and so forth. The sum message of this parable, though, is that responsible stewardship of whatever we've been given is the path to getting more. As we are faithful with what we have, we are given more. You may feel like you've been gifted much more or much less than others around you, and maybe you have. Honestly, it doesn't matter. What matters is what you do with what you've been given. Prove yourself faithful with whatever God has given you so far, and he will give you more. To everyone that has, more will be given.

Identity: How We View Ourselves

The issue of identity is of paramount importance to us as believers. As we learn to relate to ourselves the way that God relates to us, it provides stability for us to build upon in our interactions with others. The way we see ourselves is a powerful factor in the way we live and what we become. Jesus taught on identity in an interesting passage:

> *For no good tree bears bad fruit, nor again does a bad tree bear good fruit, for each tree is known by its own fruit. For figs are not gathered from thornbushes, nor are grapes picked from a bramble bush. The good person out of the good treasure of his heart produces good, and the evil person out of his evil treasure produces evil, for out of the abundance of the heart his mouth speaks.*
> *Luke 6:43-45*

Jesus says that if we want to have good fruit, we ought to be a good tree! That seems simple enough. Notice then what Jesus closes with: your fruit is determined by your heart. Being a good tree and producing good fruit then is a product of the good treasure in your heart, and vice versa for evil.

This is what we're interested in going after here. Identity is a complex term that can mean many things, but in this chapter I am referring to a knowing and confidence in who we are so that we have good treasures to draw from.

Identity is such a powerful message because it really is the gospel. The gospel is a message that has power within itself:

For I am not ashamed of the gospel, for it is the power of God for salvation to everyone who believes, to the Jew first and also to the Greek. Romans 1:16

As such, the message of identity empowers us to do the things that God calls us to. To get the message of identity, we need to reconsider our whole understanding of what we are saved from and how we are saved.

What We're Saved From

We all know that we are saved from sin, but often we are a little unclear exactly what the problem is with sin. It turns out that answering this question correctly makes clear why identity is such a critical issue.

Let's start by looking at the original identity as described by God when he created humanity. Here is the stated purpose for humanity by God himself:

Then God said, "Let us make man in our image, after our likeness. And let them have dominion over the fish of the sea and over the birds of the heavens and over the livestock and over all the earth and over every creeping thing that creeps on the earth." Genesis 1:26

We see two things here: first man was made in the image and likeness of God. What does it mean to be made in the image of something? Think of a statue or painting of a person that you know of, say the Lincoln Memorial. The Lincoln Memorial is a statue that was made in the image of Abraham Lincoln. What this means is that when you see the statue, you see the person it was made in the image of. When you look at the statue, the likeness that comes to mind is Abraham Lincoln, not a large rock that was dug out of a mountain somewhere.

That's what it means to be made in something's image; it means to be recognized as a visible representation of what that thing is. So for us to be made in the image of God means that when the rest of the earth was to see us, they would recognize God. We were the picture of God to the world.

Secondly, we see that humanity was given dominion, or rulership, on the earth. This makes perfect sense: if we're made in the image of the king, we'll have to rule. We wouldn't be able to be what we were made to be otherwise.

So the original identity of humanity could be summed up like this:

- Be God's face on this planet. (Our original identity)
- Do God's job on this planet. (Our original destiny)

God puts Adam and Eve in the garden and they begin to fulfill the destiny God has given them through intimacy and fellowship with God. Of course as we know, the story gets more complicated: Satan creeps into the garden in the form of the serpent, tempts Eve, and sin enters creation. Let's look at that account:

> *Now the serpent was more crafty than any other beast of the field that the Lord God had made.*
>
> *He said to the woman, "Did God actually say, 'You shall not eat of any tree in the garden'?" And the woman said to the serpent, "We may eat of the fruit of the trees in the garden, but God said, 'You shall not eat of the fruit of the tree that is in the midst of the garden, neither shall you touch it, lest you die.'" Genesis 3:1-3*

Satan enters the garden and brings up the tree. Eve correctly recalls that she's not supposed to eat from it (and incorrectly adds that she's not supposed to touch it). Notice the serpent's response:

But the serpent said to the woman, "You will not surely die. For God knows that when you eat of it your eyes will be opened, and you will be like God, knowing good and evil." Genesis 3:4-5

The enemy's lie is simply this: that God is holding out on you. If you eat this tree you'll become like him. There are actually two lies there: the first is that God is holding out on you, and the second is that you're not like God. The first lie is built on the second. God can't be holding out on us if Eve is already like him, which she is—we just saw that in Genesis 1! The original deception of the enemy starts with a lie about our identity.

This has been his strategy ever since. He comes after our identity and through that offers options to satisfy needs that are based on deception. Eve believes the lie about her identity, and her mindset shifts. She begins to think from lack-from who she's not.

Why did Satan attack here? Well beyond the fact that from our identity flows our actions, the Bible hints at another facet as well. Isaiah 14:12-14 is considered by many scholars to be a prophetic commentary on what happened in heaven with the fall of Satan. Look at what it says:

"How you are fallen from heaven,
O Day Star, son of Dawn!
How you are cut down to the ground,
you who laid the nations low!
You said in your heart,
'I will ascend to heaven;
above the stars of God
I will set my throne on high;
I will sit on the mount of assembly
in the far reaches of the north;

I will ascend above the heights of the clouds;
I will make myself like the Most High.'" Isaiah 14:12-14

This is interesting; in Lucifer's thinking he attempted to put himself in God's position. Why? In an attempt to become like him. What Satan wanted and what caused him to rebel against God was the likeness of God. After his rebellion he was thrown to the earth and began to wreak havoc on creation.[29] When he sees that humanity has been made in God's image and likeness, the very thing he wanted, he goes directly after it. Acting out of envy creates a mentality of "If I can't have it, nobody can."

Here is what happened after Eve fell for the deception about her identity:

> *So when the woman saw that the tree was good for food, and that it was a delight to the eyes, and that the tree was to be desired to make one wise, she took of its fruit and ate, and she also gave some to her husband who was with her, and he ate. Genesis 3:6*

With a mindset that's been rooted in a lie about her identity, Eve begins to consider the tree. As she does, her passions are ignited. Why are they ignited? Because the tree looks like it has something to offer. Her beliefs are based on a lie, and out of that her desires go astray. She acts on that desire and takes and eats the fruit. Adam eats the fruit as well when she brings it to him.

---

[29] There is reason to think that Satan had actually been actively destroying God's creation even before much of the creation account listed in Genesis 1. In Genesis 1:2 the earth is described as without form and void. The word translated "without form" (*tohuw*) is also listed in Isaiah 45:18: "For thus says the Lord, who created the heavens (he is God!), who formed the earth and made it (he established it; he did not create it empty [*tohuw*], he formed it to be inhabited!): 'I am the Lord, and there is no other.'" The choice of words in the verse in Isaiah cross-referenced with the words in Genesis 1 seems to point us to the conclusion that there was a gap in time between Genesis 1:1 and Genesis 1:2 where Satan already began to subvert and destroy God's handiwork.

When Eve acted on the enemy's lie, it became true. She was like God until she ate the tree. In following the actions of the enemy, she brought into reality the lie she acted on. This is again how the enemy works with us. He wants to sell us self-fulfilling lies that become true when we act on them.

Eve's sin is profoundly symbolic. She does not simply do something with the fruit she wasn't supposed to she actually takes the fruit and eats it; she brings within her being the sinful act that she's committing. It enters her, becomes part of her. Sin isn't just something she's done; it becomes something she is:

> *Then the eyes of both were opened, and they knew that they were naked. And they sewed fig leaves together and made themselves loincloths. Genesis 3:7*

Adam and Eve come to the revelation that the problem is internal. They're broken, and if they are seen for whom they really are at this point, they will be ashamed. So they do what humanity has done ever since then: they reach for something outside of themselves to cover up an internal problem. They try to use an external thing to fulfill an internal need.

The real problem of humanity is not that we've committed sinful acts; it's that our very being has become sinful. Sin is a living and active force within us and has destroyed the original identity that God gave us. We act out of that problem of sin living within us, which results in sinful actions.

The sinful actions are the symptom of the real problem: a nature that has been marred by sin. This is an important shift because if my sinful actions are the real problem, then it's a problem that exists outside of me and the solution will be outside of me. If the real problem is who I am, then the gospel will address that real problem. This is why

identity really flows directly from the gospel. The real problem is our identity, so the real solution provided in the gospel must be our identity as well.

This also ties into why Jesus came and died for us. The truth is it was possible for there to be forgiveness outside of Jesus' death, but only his death would change our identity.[30] There was already a system set up with the law that involved sacrificing animals to obtain forgiveness of sins:

> *Indeed, under the law almost everything is purified with blood, and without the shedding of blood there is no forgiveness of sins. Hebrews 9:22*

Clearly, Jesus' blood is a more complete forgiveness of sins than the blood of animals,[31] yet at the same time, there was a mechanism for the forgiveness of sins in the Old Covenant. If you'll allow me to speak a little tongue in cheek, you might say that if Jesus came and died to *only* forgive our sins, then really whom he saved were the animals! It was possible to be forgiven either way.[32] The point of this whole system, though, was to aim our attention at the internal problem: our identity. Animal sacrifices can't change who we are, so the fact that we needed to continue to make them points towards the real problem—that sin lived within us:

---

[30] At first glance that statement can sound heretical because the main content of the gospel is often summed up at "Jesus died for our sins." I don't disagree with that in any fashion, what I'm trying to do is tease apart the different between *forgiveness of sins* and *removal of sin*. Many people have given very little thought to the difference between the two and hence assume that dying for our sins is equivalent to forgiving our sins. The forgiveness of our sins does happen in the New Covenant, but it also happened in the Old Covenant—just through animal sacrifices instead of the blood of Jesus. The removal of sin only exists in the New Covenant and hence needs to be a critical aspect of our focus as well.

[31] Hebrews says that his blood was a once-for-all-time offering for the forgiveness of sins, whereas the blood of animals would offer a forgiveness that needed to be renewed year by year.

[32] Again, don't hear what I'm not saying—what I'm not saying is that forgiveness didn't need to be part of the New Covenant. I'm saying that forgiveness was possible before the New Covenant.

For since the law has but a shadow of the good things to come instead of the true form of these realities, it can never, by the same sacrifices that are continually offered every year, make perfect those who draw near. Otherwise, would they not have ceased to be offered, since the worshipers, having once been cleansed, would no longer have any consciousness of sins? But in these sacrifices there is a reminder of sins every year. For it is impossible for the blood of bulls and goats to take away sins. Hebrews 10:1-4

The point of the law was to reveal the heart of man. This is why salvation can never be by works. The law (a standard of works) wasn't ever intended for salvation; it was meant to show man who he is. In Galatians 3:24 Paul says that the law was meant to guard us until (some translations say tutor us to) Christ. The law was meant to function as a mirror, not a washcloth. The mirror is good at showing you what's on your face, but you don't try to use the mirror to clean your face! This is how it is with the law, God's standards of holiness. It doesn't empower you to meet the standards; it just shows you that you can't.

In 2 Corinthians 3 Paul refers to the law as the ministry of condemnation and the ministry that brings death. This is because the law is meant to point to the weakness of the flesh, and the result of our mind being set on the flesh is death (Romans 8:6). This was necessary to show us that we aren't what we were meant to be. In another passage Paul puts it this way:

Now the law came in to increase the trespass . . . so that, as sin reigned in death . . . Romans 5:20-21

Before we're in Christ, sin actually reigns within us. We were meant to rule this planet with and through the image of God in us but are actually ruled by sin within ourselves. Sin victimizes us. We are powerless to fight sin within our being, and the law brings the

problem to clarity because it provides the standard to measure ourselves against. Without the law, we could argue that our current state is natural; that being offended by others is a natural thing; that a tendency to manipulate and control to get our needs met at the cost of another's freedom is acceptable; that treating others based on the way they treat us is justice; that we should look out for ourselves first and others second and so forth.

Fortunately, none of that is how Jesus acted towards us! Jesus demonstrated to us what humanity was meant to be like: free and powerful.

Paul illustrates the experience of being victimized by sin in a powerful passage in Romans 7:[33]

> *Did [the law], then, bring death to me? By no means! It was sin, producing death in me through what is good, in order that sin might be shown to be sin, and through the commandment might become sinful beyond measure. For we know that the law is spiritual, but I am of the flesh, sold under sin. For I do not understand my own actions. For I do not do what I want, but I do the very thing I hate. Now if I do what I do not want, I agree with the law, that it is good. So now it is no longer I who do it, but sin that dwells within me. For I know that nothing good dwells in me, that is, in my flesh. For I have the desire to do what is right, but not the ability to carry it out. For I do not do the good I want, but the evil I do not want is what I keep on doing. Now if I do what I do not want, it is no longer I who do it, but sin that dwells within me. Romans 7:13-20*

---

[33] Many people interpret Romans 7 as being Paul talking in the present tense about his present experience as a believer. Looking at the context it is clear this is not the case. Paul makes it very clear that as a believer he is no longer under the law, which is the very subject of the whole discussion of Romans 7. The tense used in this passage is somewhat confusing (using present tense to describe a past state of being), but we do the same thing when telling stories.

Two sentences in that section sum up the whole state of humanity before Jesus: "For I know that nothing good dwells in me, that is, in my flesh. For I have the desire to do what is right, but not the ability to carry it out."

How We're Saved

So if the real issue is a problem of identity, how does the gospel address and solve that problem? Paul actually addresses this very question multiple times in his letters; we just haven't seen it yet because we've always kept the problem outside of us.

> *Do you not know that all of us who have been baptized into Christ Jesus were baptized into his death? We were buried therefore with him by baptism into death, in order that, just as Christ was raised from the dead by the glory of the Father, we too might walk in newness of life.*
>
> *For if we have been united with him in a death like his, we shall certainly be united with him in a resurrection like his. We know that our old self was crucified with him in order that the body of sin might be brought to nothing, so that we would no longer be enslaved to sin. For one who has died has been set free from sin. Now if we have died with Christ, we believe that we will also live with him. Romans 6:3-8*

In this passage Paul describes how the death and resurrection of Jesus are applied to us. Notice nowhere in this passage does Paul use substitutionary language. He never says Jesus died for us. Most Christians are trying to live their life according to the principle that Jesus died for us so we should live for him. That sounds good, but living for God was actually the subject of the Old Testament. Jesus empowers us to go beyond the Old Testament into the New!

So what language does Paul use in this passage? He uses language of *union*. He says that we have died with him and been resurrected with him. He says that we are united with

Jesus on the cross ("in a death like his" means death on the cross), burial and resurrection.

Paul uses this language over and over in his letters. Here are a few more examples:

> *I have been crucified with Christ. It is no longer I who live, but Christ who lives in me. And the life I now live in the flesh I live by faith in the Son of God, who loved me and gave himself for me. Galatians 2:20*

> *Set your minds on things that are above, not on things that are on earth. For you have died, and your life is hidden with Christ in God. Colossians 3:2-3*

This is a paradigm shift on the gospel. It means that the way the identity problem is solved is that the old us is killed, and a new us is born. When Jesus died, he brought the old us with him to the cross; and when he was resurrected, we were born to new life. We are quite literally a different person than we were before we believed in Jesus. In fact, Paul says exactly that same thing:

> *Therefore, if anyone is in Christ, he is a new creation (or creature). The old has passed away; behold, the new has come. 2 Corinthians 5:17*

The gospel message is that we are made new! We are a new person, and that new person is in no way who we were before. The person that was marred by sin died with Jesus and was buried with him in a tomb 2,000 years ago. The person that we are now is restored back into the image of God:

> *For those whom he foreknew he also predestined to be conformed to the image of his Son, in order that he might be the firstborn among many brothers.*
> *Romans 8:29*

. . . and to put on the new self, created after the likeness of God in true righteousness and holiness. *Ephesians 4:24*

See the whole point of this thing is about the likeness of God restored! Jesus is after restoring what was lost in the garden:

For the Son of Man came to seek and to save what was lost. Luke 19:10 NIV

Theology Anchor

The gospel saves us from sin to righteousness. It is about the image of God being restored. Jesus died as us so we could live as him.

This is why Jesus drafts us into his commission. In doing that, Jesus pulls us back up to the original mission given in the garden: to be the face of God on this planet. This commission is described repeatedly throughout the Scriptures. You can see it here in the commission given to the disciples in the Gospel of John:

Jesus said to them again, "Peace be with you. As the Father has sent me, even so I am sending you." And when he had said this, he breathed on them and said to them, "Receive the Holy Spirit." John 20:21-22

If you think about it, this is an astounding statement: As the Father sent me, so I send you. How was Jesus sent by the Father? He wasn't just sent to this world to save it (although that was definitely a big part of it); he was sent as the revelation of who the Father is. He was able to say to Phillip in John 14, "If you've seen me, you've seen the Father." We saw in the Kingdom Theology discussion on covenants that Jesus was the clear representation of the Father. No one had seen God, but Jesus made him known.

This is the way that Jesus was sent by the Father, and this is the way he sends us. We ought to be able to say, "If you've seen me, you've seen Jesus." We are now the face of

Jesus to the world. That's why we're called the *body* of Christ. Jesus was God incarnate; he was God in a body. He then commissions us to that same call and says in effect, "Alright, you're the body. Here comes God!" and he breathes on us, and God in the form of the Holy Spirit comes to live inside of us. We become God incarnated as well—the face of Jesus to the world.

You could sum it up like this: Jesus died *as* us so we could live *as* him.

I hope you're getting this. Even as I write, I'm so excited! This is the gospel; the good news, and it's pretty much so good that you'll have to have faith to believe it!

A Tale of Two Trees

Let's look at this thing from another angle. I find that hitting this identity message is such a paradigm shift that you need to see it a bunch of different times and in different ways for it to really start to sink in.

We've already looked at what happened in the Garden of Eden and the fall of humanity. Remember that as Eve ate the fruit of the tree, she brought sin within humanity and changed the nature of humanity in that one single act. We could put it allegorically like this: as Eve pulled the fruit off the tree and ate it, she was pulling sin off the tree and into humanity.

Now check this verse out:

> *For our sake [God] made [Jesus] to be sin who knew no sin, so that in him we might become the righteousness of God. 2 Corinthians 5:21*

This verse could be summarized as saying that God made Jesus who we were so we could become who he was. We were sin; it lived inside of us and had changed our very nature. Jesus was made into our nature so we could be made into his.

So God makes Jesus to become sin. What happens on Calvary is simply this: God makes Jesus sin, and puts sin back on the tree! Eve pulled sin off the tree; God (in Jesus) put it back on. Amazing! We make this thing too complicated—it's simple. Sin is back on the tree. We're back in the garden where we were always meant to be.

The House of God and Gate of Heaven

Let's look at it again from a different angle. In Genesis 28 Jacob has a dream that becomes part of the Jewish history and culture:

> *And he came to a certain place and stayed there that night, because the sun had set. Taking one of the stones of the place, he put it under his head and lay down in that place to sleep. And he dreamed, and behold, there was a ladder set up on the earth, and the top of it reached to heaven. And behold, the angels of God were ascending and descending on it! And behold, the Lord stood above it and said, "I am the Lord, the God of Abraham your father and the God of Isaac. The land on which you lie I will give to you and to your offspring. Your offspring shall be like the dust of the earth, and you shall spread abroad to the west and to the east and to the north and to the south, and in you and your offspring shall all the families of the earth be blessed. Behold, I am with you and will keep you wherever you go, and will bring you back to this land. For I will not leave you until I have done what I have promised you." Then Jacob awoke from his sleep and said, "Surely the Lord is in this place, and I did not know it." And he was afraid and said, "How awesome is this place! This is none other than the house of God, and this is the gate of heaven." Genesis 28:11-17*

Jacob has a dream where he sees a connection between earth and heaven. There is a ladder that stretches between the two, and angels go back and forth doing the will of God. Jacob's conclusion is profound: this is the place that God lives (house of God), and the place where his will is done (gate of heaven—remember we pray on earth as it is in heaven. Heaven is where God's will is done perfectly).

This place becomes an anchor point in Jewish history. God at times tells people to go to that place (Jacob named it Bethel, meaning house of God) and do specific things or wait for specific instructions.

In the calling of Nathaniel to be one of the disciples, Jesus makes an interesting comment:

> *Jesus answered him, "Because I said to you, 'I saw you under the fig tree,' do you believe? You will see greater things than these." And he said to him, "Truly, truly, I say to you, you will see heaven opened, and the angels of God ascending and descending on the Son of Man." John 1:50-51*

In the last statement, Jesus is undoubtedly referring to the dream Jacob had. Nathaniel would, of course, know this story. What is Jesus saying here? He's shifting his understanding of Jacob's dream. In the Old Testament, the house of God and gate of heaven was a place; but Jesus is saying it is no longer a place—it is a person.

Everywhere Jesus goes, he demonstrates that reality. God's will is perfectly done everywhere he goes, and he truly is the house of God on the earth.

Then in Acts 2, an interesting event occurs: the Holy Spirit is poured out on the disciples as they wait and pray in the upper room. Here is the description of what happened:

> *When the day of Pentecost arrived, they were all together in one place. And suddenly there came from heaven a sound like a mighty rushing wind, and it filled the entire house where they were sitting. And divided tongues as of fire appeared to them and rested on each one of them. And they were all filled with the Holy Spirit and began to speak in other tongues as the Spirit gave them utterance. Acts 2:1-4*

Often we focus on the last verse, the filling of the Spirit and speaking in tongues, but don't consider what the sound of wind and tongues of fire was about? The author of Hebrews, quoting the Psalms provides us a clue:

> *Of the angels he says,*
>
> *"He makes his angels winds,*
> *and his ministers a flame of fire." Hebrews 1:7*

What was happening on the day of Pentecost? Angels began to ascend and descend on whom? The disciples! What was a place in the Old Testament and became a person in the life of Jesus now becomes a people in the church. You and I are now the house of God and the gate of heaven. We are the place where God lives and his will is released; we are the access point of the will of the Father.

> **Theology Anchor**
>
> Jesus is 100% of the truth about God and 100% of the truth about man.

Righteousness Revealed from Faith for Faith

We started this discussion by looking at Romans 1:16. Let's continue to the next verse to find out one of the benefits of identity:

> *For in it the righteousness of God is revealed from faith for faith, as it is written, "The righteous shall live by faith." Romans 1:17*

Paul says that the gospel is the power of God for salvation because in it the righteousness of God is revealed from faith for faith. This sums up entirely everything we've been talking about in the last few sections. Righteousness means basically "rightness." The word used in this passage and is translated as "righteousness" 92 times in the New Testament means most literally "the state of him who is as he ought to be."[34] This state of being what we ought to be is revealed to us from faith. It is by faith we are saved and re-created as a new creation.

Paul then takes it a step further; righteousness is not only revealed from faith, it's revealed for faith. What does that mean? It means simply this: that faith unlocks righteousness for you, and righteousness leads you to faith. When you see who you are in Jesus, that you've been made new and put back the way humanity was always meant to be, it empowers you to live by faith. Faith isn't something you try to create; it naturally flows out of you. The person who is what humanity was always meant to be lives by faith. It comes as naturally to them as breathing. So faith leads us to identity, and identity leads us to faith.

Sin and the Flesh

One of the major pitfalls we run into is that we have some major confusion about what happens to us and to sin when we become believers. The Scriptures that address this issue are complex and require careful analysis, so let's walk through it carefully.[35] I'd

---

[34] Blue Letter Bible, accessed 6/26/12.
http://www.blueletterbible.org/lang/lexicon/Lexicon.cfm?strongs=G1343

[35] Please note that there is no universal agreement among theologians about this issue. I'm presenting one side of this argument that I believe is best supported by the Scriptures. The other arguments to me generally seem to be rooted in less careful exegesis and more reasoning from experience. In addition to

challenge you to read through many of these Scriptures for yourself and see if you arrive at the same results.[36]

First, the standard view of this situation is as follows:

- Before we are saved we have a sinful depraved nature and are in slavery to sin.
- God through his grace calls us, and we respond and are saved.
- When we are saved, that sinful nature is dealt a deathblow, and the Holy Spirit takes up residence in us.
- Moving forward from salvation, we are caught in a battle between the work of the Holy Spirit within us and the sinful nature we still carry while on this earth.

The major problem with this argument is that while it presents a coherent picture that feels very consistent with our experiences, to wind up at this place you have to force Paul to double-talk. Paul seems to make a pretty clear point that looks different than this picture:

> *How can we who died to sin still live in it? Romans 6:2*

> *For sin will have no dominion over you, since you are not under law but under grace. Romans 6:14*

> *We know that our old self was crucified with him in order that the body of sin might be brought to nothing, so that we would no longer be enslaved to sin. For one who has died has been set free from sin. Romans 6:6-7*

---

that, every other position seems to leave the person in a rather victimized state rather than being fully empowered, which is a major theme of the gospel and of importance when trying to do supernatural ministry.

[36] It should be noted that the translation you pick makes a difference here. I'd recommend a more word-for-word translation such as NASB, KJV or ESV (my preference); the less word-for-word you get, the more you get the translators introducing their theology into the translation.

The above argument puts a person in a position to be free to struggle with sin, but not to be set free from sin. Paul has made a very different point; these verses contradict any idea except for full freedom from sin. Even more directly than this is Paul's first injunctive[37] in the book of Romans:

> *So you also must consider yourselves dead to sin and alive to God in Christ Jesus. Romans 6:11*

The first thing that Paul tells people to do in the entire book of Romans doesn't come up until the sixth chapter; when it does, he tells people to consider themselves dead to sin. That word *consider* means to compute, calculate, or take inventory of.[38] There is a note on the definition of this word in Greek that clarifies:

> *This word deals with reality. If I reckon (*logizomai*) that my bankbook has $25 in it, it has $25 in it. Otherwise I am deceiving myself. This word refers more to fact than supposition or opinion.*

Wow, that should remove any shred of doubt. Paul chooses a word that makes it very clear that we are to recognize the reality that we are completely dead to sin. How does the picture I described earlier take this into account? It doesn't. It rather acknowledges the presence of sin still within us and consigns us to continue battling it until we pass into the afterlife. Not only would we not be dead to sin now, we wouldn't be until we're dead to our body as well!

---

37 Injunctive means "command" or "order."

38 Blue Letter Bible, accessed 7/6/11. http://www.blueletterbible.org/lang/lexicon/lexicon.cfm?Strongs=G3049&t=KJV Also the following note.

Most of the scriptural support for this discussion comes from Romans 5-8. The way you interpret this part of Scripture will shape the way you view yourself and what you expect your Christian experience to be. Generally the discussion breaks down like this:

- Romans 5:12-20: Because Adam sinned everyone born after him was born with sin and under condemnation. Fortunately because one person infected everyone with sin, so also one person (Jesus) can free everyone from sin.
- Romans 6:1-14: Through belief in Jesus we are united in his death and dead to sin. Sin no longer has power over us.
- Romans 6:15-6:23: Now that we are no longer in bondage to sin, we owe our allegiance to God.
- Romans 7:1-6: Being united in the death of Jesus also frees people from obligation to the law.
- Romans 7:7-15: The point of the law was to make us aware of sin. The problem was that it didn't provide the power we needed to overcome sin, so the law imprisoned those under it to a standard that could not be met.
- Romans 8:1-4: Not only did Jesus die and free people both from sin and the law, but the Holy Spirit empowers us to reach the righteousness the law pointed towards.
- Romans 8:5-16: In light of this we should live according to the Spirit, not the flesh.

The root of the problem with the previous argument involves the way we interpret the word "flesh" as it is used in Scripture. If we take flesh to mean our sinful nature, we wind up with the view described above; but is that how we should interpret the word flesh?

I've noticed two things that seem to be missing from this text that would point us toward the picture described above:

1. Paul never actually says we *have* flesh. He never ascribes ownership or says that it is part of us. His language is always something like "set your mind on the flesh" or "walk according to the flesh" or "live according to the flesh."[39]
2. We don't really see a picture of the flesh and spirit fighting against each other. Paul uses some language to describe the different outcomes of walking according to one or the other, but he doesn't use language that implies a conflict between the spirit and the flesh in us. In fact it seems by his language to be a simple choice.[40]

Furthermore, the term *flesh* is used to mean a number of different things in the Scripture, some of them having nothing to do with sinful nature. Sometimes it is just our physicality:

> *And the Word became flesh and dwelt among us, and we have seen his glory, glory as of the only Son from the Father, full of grace and truth. John 1:14*

This is the conclusion that I come to then; flesh means literally what it means: flesh—the natural and the physical. In light of this, how do we put all this together then? Consider the different phrases Paul uses in his discussion of flesh and spirit:

- "walk according to"—Romans 8:4
- "live according to"—Romans 8:5, 12-13
- "set their minds on"—Romans 8:5-7
- "in"—Romans 8:8-9

---

[39] The first time I noticed this I reread all of Paul's letters to try to see if he implies having flesh anywhere. He never does.

[40] The closest Scripture that implies a conflict between these two is Galatians 5:17—"For the desires of the flesh are against the Spirit, and the desires of the Spirit are against the flesh, for these are opposed to each other, to keep you from doing the things you want to do." Notice that this implies a conflict between the *desires* of the flesh and the *desires* of the Spirit, not the flesh and the Spirit.

Similarly in the book of Galatians chapter 5, Paul runs through a similar argument in which he uses slightly different terms:

- "walk by"—Galatians 5:16,25
- "led by"—Galatians 5:18

Culminating in a very interesting verse:

> *If we live by the Spirit, let us also walk by the Spirit. Galatians 5:25*

Throughout these discussions, Paul makes a point that the end of walking according to (or different phrases) the flesh or the Spirit produces righteous or unrighteous behavior.

The interesting thing about all of these phrases is that they are present tense, active phrases. He is instructing people to make a choice and pay attention to their worldview and their perspective. He instructs us to think about, meditate on, and align our values and decisions with the reality of the Spirit, not the flesh.

So let's bring all of this full-circle. Paul writes to us and informs us that sin within us has been defeated. We are dead to sin. We are not partly or mostly dead to sin; we are fully and completely dead to it. There is no part of you that is still sinful. You may still sin, but you are no longer sinful. Before the gospel, the principal problem wasn't your behavior, it was you: sin had infected who you were. That has changed; sin is no longer who you are. That doesn't mean you never do it anymore, but it means you're not the problem anymore. Your sin nature is dead. It isn't alive anymore; it is dead. The flesh is not

> **Theology Anchor**
>
> Our sin nature is completely killed at the cross. We struggle now because we think like our old selves, not because we are old.

your sin nature.

This is an important point. If we believe instead that we still have a sin nature, we will never feel at complete peace with God because we will always believe that there is some part of us that God is unhappy with. No, Jesus' blood bought complete peace with God. There is nothing left between you and God. God isn't against any part of you. Until we believe that our nature has changed, we believe that the work of the fall is more powerful than the work of the cross.

Paul then instructs us to start changing the way we live our lives so that we are living according to the Spirit, not the flesh. This means changing what we value and the very way that we think from the ground up. You see this in the Gospels a lot. Doesn't Jesus always seem to be frustrated that the disciples weren't tracking with him? That's because Jesus was trying to teach and demonstrate to them what a kingdom mindset (one might say a kingdom worldview) looks like. It is a call to true repentance: to learn to think from a different starting point. Paul writes about this in an amazing verse:

> *Do not be conformed to this world [literally "age"], but be transformed by the renewal of your mind, that by testing you may discern what is the will of God, what is good and acceptable and perfect. Romans 12:2*

This is an amazing verse. Let me point out two interesting things about this verse. First, the word transformed here is actually a unique word; specifically the word that is translated "transfigured" in the accounts of Jesus on the mount of transfiguration. This is a powerful word. It is not just change; it is the unleashing of another level of glory—that is, otherworldly. This word is used only four times in the Scriptures. Twice is describing Jesus' transfiguration, and the other is this verse:

And we all, with unveiled face, beholding the glory of the Lord, are being transformed into the same image from one degree of glory to another. For this comes from the Lord who is the Spirit. 2 Corinthians 3:18

This word points to the releasing of the divine into the human vessel. This renewing of the mind idea then is a really big deal! This isn't just learning how to think differently so we can be positive—this is a massive thing! Likewise, the word *discern* turns out to be a tricky word. Some other translations translate it as "prove." Here is what it means in the Greek:[41]

1. to test, examine, prove, scrutinize (to see whether a thing is genuine or not), as metals
2. to recognize as genuine after examination, to approve, deem worthy

The closest word in English might be something like "authenticate." It involves recognizing the validity of or approving the genuineness of. Allow me to give you Putty's translation of Romans 12:2 then:

Do not be conformed to this age, but be transfigured by the renewal of your mind, that by testing you may authenticate what is the will of God, what is good and acceptable and perfect.

This is amazing to me! Paul is saying that renewing our mind lifts us up to a higher level of existence from which we can recognize the will of God in situations and then release that into those situations![42] This is what Paul is pointing towards when he says to "walk according" to the Spirit. Walking according to the Spirit involves drawing off

---

[41] Blue Letter Bible, accessed 7/13/11.
http://www.blueletterbible.org/lang/lexicon/lexicon.cfm?Strongs=G1381&t=KJV
[42] Recall our discussion of the gate of heaven in the previous section. This is another Scripture that points to that dynamic.

of the presence of the Spirit within to the point where our very thoughts run on completely different tracks than they used to. Let's digest how this works a bit more.

Internals and Externals

We all live our lives on the boundary between our *internals* and our *externals*. The internals are things that come from us: our self-perception, thoughts, feelings, personality, our will, the way we respond to others, and so forth. Scripture is clear that we are accountable for and thus have control over our internals.

The externals are things that come from outside of us: the circumstances we find ourselves in, the things people say to us, the events at our jobs, etc. We don't have control over the externals. Our relationships happen at the border of these two worlds—where our internals and our externals meet. This is the ground on which we practice our relationships.

Our internal world is meant to draw off of something. Before we're saved the only place our internals can draw off of is our externals. Our feelings are the result of a situation we have, or our thoughts are because of a conversation we had, and so forth. Because of this, our internal space learns to draw off of the external space we live in. The lessons we learn in life and our worldview are shaped by the belief that *the environment I'm in determines the quality of life I experience*.

> **Theology Anchor**
>
> We never have to draw life from the world around us; we can always draw it solely from Jesus.

When we become Christians, something significant happens to our internal space. God brings new life to our spirit and the Holy Spirit moves in. Our internal space now has access to rooms that were locked up before. Within that expanded internal space is a new power source that our internals can run off of. The problem, though, is that we've spent our life learning that we need to draw from our externals. As long as we continue to look to our externals to determine our internal space, we will always be under the control of the environment around us to some extent. If the enemy chooses, he has the ability to set a situation up and change the quality of life we experience; thus, we give him control of our internals through the externals he has the ability to influence.

Naïve Christianity expects the point of Christianity to be that God will now start controlling our externals and as a result, our internal environment will be guaranteed to be enjoyable. This, as any Christian for more than a month or two will tell you, isn't the reality of the situation.

The catch is that God moves to start working in the internal space, not the external space. The enemy works from the outside in; he controls the external space and uses that to manipulate our internal space. God works from the inside out; he wants to renovate the internal space and use that space to change the external space through us.

Scripture is clear that God sets forth a destiny for us:

> *And we know that for those who love God all things work together for good, for those who are called according to his purpose. For those whom he foreknew he also predestined to be conformed to the image of his Son, in order that he might be the firstborn among many brothers. Romans 8:28-29*

> *He predestined us for adoption as sons through Jesus Christ, according to the purpose of his will, to the praise of his glorious grace, with which he has blessed us in the Beloved. Ephesians 1:5-6*

The subject of predestination is a large and complex discussion on which there are many points of view. I don't want to enter into that discussion other than to observe a

point most often not discussed: what we are predestined to is a process of growth. God sets in front of us a destiny to become someone new. That person is conformed to the image of Jesus and adopted as a son of God.

We often don't recognize the invitation to learn to draw from the Holy Spirit instead of the situations around us because that invitation is always *relational* in nature. Everything in God is relational in nature. God brings us into situations where He can *be* something for us, and in that situation is an invitation to experience relationship with Him in a way we haven't yet. This means being exposed to a situation where the current way we're living life is drawing off the externals. God brings us to a situation where we clearly aren't experiencing the quality of life He has for us and lets us lose control. Every loss of control in our life is an invitation to upgrade our experience of God.

Any place where our peace is under constant onslaught then is an opportunity for God to establish peace in us. We feel out of control because as soon as we fix one external problem, another one arises that steals our peace. All of this is exposing where we've yet to learn to access our peace from God. If we find ourselves in situations where we are always feeling right on the brink of bankruptcy, there is implicit in that situation an invitation to know God as provider. If you are frustrated a lot, perhaps that is the very place God wants to establish gentleness in you.

Lying within each of these situations is an upgrade if we have the eyes to see it. If we have the faith to believe that God has predestined an identity for us to become and that all things work together for our good, we start to see how we become more than conquerors in every situation. In every situation we find ourselves, God is working to become more to us, to establish us in our identity, and to strengthen our ability to draw off our internal space. This is the power of being predestined to *be* something.

Let's consider one of the more famous passages about the victory of Christianity:

> *Who shall separate us from the love of Christ* [an internal reality]*? Shall tribulation, or distress, or persecution, or famine, or nakedness, or danger, or sword* [external reality]*? As it is written,*
>
> *"For your sake we are being killed all the day long;*
> *we are regarded as sheep to be slaughtered."*
>
> *No, in all these things we are more than conquerors through him who loved us* [drawing from the internal reality]. *Romans 8:35-37*

Paul is commending us to focus on the internal reality of God's love and let that be what we draw from and focus on.

Now this doesn't mean that we'll never have negative emotions or thoughts, but what it does mean is that those emotions or thoughts won't have leverage over us. We may feel frustrated, sad, or lonely, but we'll be okay feeling those emotions. We won't feel out of control as a result of those feelings, because we know even the negative is an opportunity to do life with God.

Paul writes of this in Philippians 4:11-13:

> *Not that I am speaking of being in need, for I have learned in whatever situation I am to be content. I know how to be brought low, and I know how to abound. In any and every circumstance, I have learned the secret of facing plenty and hunger, abundance and need. I can do all things through him who strengthens me.*

Paul says that he knows how to exist in the mountaintops and the valleys of life and to be content in both and that the secret is to do it through God. As we learn to live our life

through the lens of our relationship with God, we gain the ability to be content in every situation. We are more than conquerors because God will only bring us into places in life where our relationship with him can grow and mature.

Once we are in Christ we have a choice, either we can try to convince God to save us from our circumstances, or we can ask him to save us through our circumstances. In one we try to leverage our relationship with God to change what is happening around us, and in the other we leverage what is happening around us to change our relationship with God. Our own valley then prophesies to us the growth that God wants to bring us. If we can learn to operate with this mentality, the cards start falling to us and we can live a conquering lifestyle. Our quality of life is no longer able to be affected by what happens in the externals of our lives.

When we start learning to live from our relationship with God, the truth starts being established *in* us. Jesus was clear that the truth is found in a person, not a teaching:

> *Jesus said to him, "I am the way, and the truth, and the life. No one comes to the Father except through me. John 14:6*

Truth is not something God wants to teach us; it's something He wants to write onto the very fiber of who we are. To have the truth in you is much more than just to have a correct understanding; it is to be changed in who we are:

> *So Jesus said to the Jews who had believed in him, "If you abide in my word, you are truly my disciples, and you will know the truth, and the truth will set you free." John 8:31-32*

The freedom that God wants to give us far surpasses a lack of bondage. In the kingdom there is always a two-fold process of getting out of the red and getting into the black—getting out of negative and getting into positive. The freedom that the truth will set us into is much more than freedom from the bondages we have; it is freedom to be and become someone. As God establishes the truth in us, we are released to be something otherworldly and glorious. Paul says this in Romans:

> *For the creation waits with eager longing for the revealing of the sons of God. For the creation was subjected to futility, not willingly, but because of him who subjected it, in hope that the creation itself will be set free from its bondage to corruption and obtain the freedom of the glory of the children of God.*
> *Romans 8:19-21*

In the first sentence the word *revealing* is actually the same word as the word *revelation* in the original Greek. This is amazing to me. Paul is saying that as we grow into being sons of God, which he says a few verses earlier in Romans 8:14 *"For all who are led by the Spirit of God are sons of God,"* we actually become a prophecy to creation about the freedom it will be released into.

Behavior Flows from Identity

We already touched on the idea that Jesus teaches that what we do flows out of who we are:

> *"For no good tree bears bad fruit, nor again does a bad tree bear good fruit, for each tree is known by its own fruit. For figs are not gathered from thornbushes, nor are grapes picked from a bramble bush. The good person out of the good treasure of his heart produces good, and the evil person out of his evil treasure produces evil, for out of the abundance of the heart his mouth speaks.*
> *Luke 6:43-45*

Jesus teaches that "the treasure of our heart" determines what we produce in this life. As we grow into our identity, we will see corresponding changes in our behavior as

well. Just as God's plan for bringing quality of life to us works from the inside out, so does God's plan for making us holy.

> *Behold, the days are coming, declares the Lord, when I will make a new covenant with the house of Israel and the house of Judah...But this is the covenant that I will make with the house of Israel after those days, declares the Lord: I will put my law within them, and I will write it on their hearts. And I will be their God, and they shall be my people. Jeremiah 31:31,33*

> *And I will give them one heart, and a new spirit I will put within them. I will remove the heart of stone from their flesh and give them a heart of flesh, that they may walk in my statutes and keep my rules and obey them. And they shall be my people, and I will be their God. Ezekiel 11:19-20*

So when we face a sin issue, we need to resist doing the sin, but we also need to ask ourselves the following question: What aspect of my identity needs to grow for this to lose control over me? Sin is often tied to a lack in our own person and that is part of why it carries leverage over us and is so difficult to break free from. People who are "conformed to the image of his Son" don't see sin as an attractive thing; they see it as repulsive. Any time sin attracts us, it is pulling on a hole in our identity that God wants to fill.

Let's look at a visual of how this process can be depicted. We often tend to think of our behavior existing along a spectrum:

On one end of the spectrum, we have carnality—being given over to fleshly desires. Carnality is the result of following the flesh to its conclusion. These sins are always characterized by excess and are destructive:

> *Now the works of the flesh are evident: sexual immorality, impurity, sensuality, idolatry, sorcery, enmity, strife, jealousy, fits of anger, rivalries, dissensions, divisions, envy, drunkenness, orgies, and things like these. Galatians 5:19-21*

> *Beloved, I urge you as sojourners and exiles to abstain from the passions of the flesh, which wage war against your soul. 1 Peter 2:11*

On the other side of the spectrum is religion. By this I mean that we try to earn something with God. We believe that our behavior actually gets us more favor with God. This results in a rules-based spirituality that prioritizes doing the right thing at the cost of relationship with God. The Pharisees were the consistent example of religion in the scriptures:

> *Woe to you, scribes and Pharisees, hypocrites! For you are like whitewashed tombs, which outwardly appear beautiful, but within are full of dead people's bones and all uncleanness. So you also outwardly appear righteous to others, but within you are full of hypocrisy and lawlessness. Matthew 23:27-28*

Jesus refers to these using a metaphor of leaven:

> *And he cautioned them, saying, "Watch out; beware of the leaven of the Pharisees and the leaven of Herod." Mark 8:15*

Clearly the Pharisees are representative of religion, but Herod we know less about. The Forerunner Bible Commentary says this in an entry about the leaven of Herod: "Herod

was involved in a great deal of lying in his political wheeling and dealing, abusing the power of his office, adultery, and general all-around worldliness."[43]

The power of religion and carnality is that they are self-reinforcing behaviors. They start to permeate the way we think and become part of our worldview. Paul says this using the same metaphor of leaven that Jesus did:

> *Your boasting is not good. Do you not know that a little leaven leavens the whole lump? Cleanse out the old leaven that you may be a new lump, as you really are unleavened. For Christ, our Passover lamb, has been sacrificed. Let us therefore celebrate the festival, not with the old leaven, the leaven of malice and evil, but with the unleavened bread of sincerity and truth. 1 Corinthians 5:6-8*

Have you ever had a conversation with someone who is in agreement with either religion or carnality? It is frustrating because they don't see things clearly; they run all their reasoning through their tainted mindset. This is the result of the leaven of religion or carnality. Paul informs us that because of Jesus' sacrifice, we can become unleavened bread—uninfluenced by our former traps of "malice and evil."

Between the middle of these two extremes is "unleavened" bread—a balance of behavior that we strive for. Here is the trick, though: if we think of holiness as a behavioral issue, we'll always be swinging back and forth along the spectrum, overshooting the middle and trying to head back towards what we missed. If we start out as carnal, we finally get ahold of ourselves and swing over into being incredibly religious and having no mercy on others. When we realize the monster we've become, we try and loosen up and we become carnal again. Because we're always moving away from something that's not our goal, we never wind up where we'd like to be.

---

[43] http://www.bibletools.org/index.cfm/fuseaction/Topical.show/RTD/cgg/ID/2914/Leaven-of-Herod.htm. Accessed 1/5/2011.

God looks less at our behavior and more at our heart:

> *But the Lord said to Samuel, "Do not look on his appearance or on the height of his stature, because I have rejected him. For the Lord sees not as man sees: man looks on the outward appearance, but the Lord looks on the heart." 1 Samuel 16:7*

What God is interested in is the inside of us: who we are. What we should do then is draw something that includes both aspects: the outward appearance (or the behavior) and the heart (or the identity).

When we first become a Christian, we are totally unaware of our identity as royal sons of the living God. As a result, we have a wide range of behavior that is consistent with our current self-perception. As we grow upwards in the identity that God has set before us and orchestrated our lives to grow us into, we find that the behavior that is

consistent with how we see ourselves shrinks. We find things that used to be attractive or tolerable to be repulsive, and our behavior conforms to that of God's law.

This is what it means when Jeremiah says that God will write his law on our hearts—that holiness isn't something we have to try and get to, but rather something that radiates out of who we really are.

This is what Paul is talking about in Romans 8 and in other passages. Paul commends us to set our minds on the Spirit and walk according to the Spirit. The Spirit then convicts *us* of our righteousness:

> *And when he comes, he will convict the world concerning sin and righteousness and judgment: concerning sin, because they do not believe in me; concerning righteousness, because I go to the Father, and you will see me no longer.*
> *John 16:8-10*

Out of that identity our behavior flows. This is why Paul refers to putting off the old self (your old identity) and putting on your new self (your new identity):

> *But that is not the way you learned Christ! . . . to put off your old self, which belongs to your former manner of life and is corrupt through deceitful desires, and to be renewed in the spirit of your minds, and to put on the new self, created after the likeness of God in true righteousness and holiness. Ephesians 4:20,22-24*

Note that to put on the new self requires being renewed in the spirit of our minds—our perception and our worldview. These two fit together.

You can probably see now that a major message of the New Testament is that of identity, realizing who we are in Christ and learning to think and act like who we are. This is foundational in Christian ethics. This is why the overall structure in many of

Paul's letters always comes back to who we are in Christ. He almost always spends the first half of the letter reminding his audience who they are in Christ and what Christ has already accomplished, and in light of that, how they should behave.

New Revelations of Who We Are

The New Testament has some amazing things to say about who we are as Christians. Let's take some time to consider the identity that is set forth for us in Scripture. There have been two major themes of identity that have been spread through the church in the last 15 or 20 years. Jack Frost has a teaching on sonship, and Kris Vallotton has a teaching on royalty, both of which God has used powerfully in the lives of many people. I'll discuss some aspects of them here, but I would highly suggest reading their books on these subjects.[44]

Before diving into the details, I want to talk a little bit about an overview of each of these teachings. Both of these teachings deal with who the Scriptures say we are and coming to terms with the identity God bestows on us. There are many similarities between the two, and much overlap. They differ in that they address slightly different lacks.

Sonship addresses a lack of love. It deals with an inability to have an intimate connection with the Father and receive his love. It is a revelation that deals heavily with the unconditional favor we have with God in Christ and maintaining a state of constantly receiving the love of the Father.

---

[44] The books are *Spiritual Slavery to Spiritual Sonship* by Jack Frost and *The Supernatural Ways of Royalty* by Kris Vallotton. Jack Frost's book is a little better organized and methodical. Kris Vallotton's book is very good, but it jumps around a lot, which can be frustrating to some people. Kris Vallotton's book also has an accompanying workbook,which I recommend as well.

Royalty addresses a lack of significance. It considers the destiny that God has laid out in front of each one of us and empowers us to become all that Christ died for us to be. This revelation deals with being part of the family of the King of kings and the significance of our royal heritage as believers.

Both revelations are true and important. You will probably resonate more with one or the other because your history has shaped you, and you probably need one of these revelations more than the other. These aren't in any kind of competition, nor do they really build on each other; they're just different. My guess would be that there are probably other potential revelations on our identity as believers that we'll see emerge in the future that will be important as well.[45]

Sonship

As mentioned earlier, sonship is a revelation that deals with the love of the Father and what it means to be in the family of God. Scripture is clear that we as believers are sons of God and Jesus' brothers and sisters:

> *See what kind of love the Father has given to us, that we should be called children of God; and so we are. 1 John 3:1*

> *For all who are led by the Spirit of God are sons of God. For you did not receive the spirit of slavery to fall back into fear, but you have received the Spirit of adoption as sons, by whom we cry, "Abba! Father!" The Spirit himself bears witness with our spirit that we are children of God. Romans 8:14-16*

---

[45] Remember how we discussed the empowering nature of grace? This could, for example, become a teaching on identity if it were fleshed out as it applies to us.

For those whom he foreknew he also predestined to be conformed to the image of his Son, in order that he might be the firstborn among many brothers.
Romans 8:29

These verses are true, whether we believe them or not, and whether we act like them or not. The problem is that we often don't really believe them or act like them. That is because we have what Jack Frost calls an *orphan heart.*

An orphan heart is the result of a process that starts with the rejection we all face at some point in our lives that eventually results in a stronghold in our life that becomes engrained in our worldview/identity. Here is how it works:[46]

1. We begin to focus on the faults we see in parental authority.
2. We receive parental faults as disappointment, discouragement, grief, or rejection.
3. We lose basic trust in parental authority.
4. We move into a fear of receiving love, comfort, and admonition from others.
5. We develop a closed spirit.
6. We take on an independent, self-reliant attitude.
7. We start controlling our relationships.
8. Our relationships become superficial.
9. We develop an ungodly belief that says no one will be there to meet our needs.
10. We begin to live life like a spiritual orphan.
11. We begin chasing after counterfeit affections.
12. We begin to daily battle a stronghold of oppression.

The key idea that happens with an orphan heart is this: it learns that others won't meet the needs that we have, and so we have to meet them ourselves. This results in a self-

[46] This list is taken from chapter 2 in Jack Frost's book *Spiritual Slavery to Spiritual Sonship* where he discusses this process in much more depth there.

focused mindset where we rely on ourselves to meet all our needs. We begin to control others and manipulate them to meet our needs, which causes increasing relational fracturing that prevents us from having our needs *actually* met.

As long as we live with the heart of an orphan, we will always be acting out of fear. Fear is what governs an orphan, and it results in a mistrust of authority, and an inability to submit to others. The orphan heart always blocks us from legitimately having our needs met, which requires interdependence with others and openness in relationships. The orphan heart and the heart of sonship are contrasted in this table taken from Appendix A of Jack Frost's book on sonship:

Orphan Heart		Heart of Sonship
See God as master	Image of God	See God as loving Father
Independent/self-reliant	Dependency	Interdependent/acknowledges need
Live by the love of law	Theology	Life by the law of love
Insecure/lack peace	Security	Rest and peace
Strive for the praise, approval, and acceptance of man	Need for Approval	Totally accepted in God's love and justified by grace
A need for personal achievement as you seek to impress God and others, or no motivation to serve at all	Motive for Service	Service that is motivated by a deep sense of gratitude for being unconditionally loved and accepted by God
Duty and earning God's favor, or no motivation at all	Motive behind Christian Disciplines	Pleasure and delight
"Must" be holy to have God's favor, thus increasing a sense of shame and guilt	Motive for Purity	"Want to" be holy; do not want anything to hinder intimate relationship with God
Self-rejection from comparing yourself to others	Self Image	Positive and affirmed because you know you have such value to God
Seek comfort in counterfeit affections: additions, compulsions, escapism, busyness, hyper-religious activity	Source of Comfort	Seek times of quietness and solitude to rest in the Father's presence and love

Orphan Heart		Heart of Sonship
Competition, rivalry, and jealousy toward others' success and position	Peer Relationships	Humility and unity as you value others and are able to rejoice in their blessings and success
Accusation and exposure in order to make yourself look good by making others look bad	Handling Other's Faults	Love covers as you seek to restore others in a spirit of love and gentleness
See authority as a source of pain; distrustful toward them and lack a heart attitude of submission	View of Authority	Respectful, honoring; you see them as ministers of God for good in your life
Difficulty receiving admonition; you must be right so you easily get your feelings hurt and close your spirit to discipline	View of Admonition	See the receiving of admonition as a blessing and need in your life so that your faults and weaknesses are exposed and put to death
Guarded and conditional; based upon others' performance as you seek to get your own needs met	Expression of Love	Open, patient, and affectionate as you lay your life and agendas down to meet the needs of others
Conditional and distant	Sense of God's Presence	Close and intimate
Bondage	Condition	Liberty
Feel like a servant/slave	Position	Feel like a son/daughter
Spiritual ambition; the earnest desire for some spiritual achievement and distinction and the willingness to strive for it; a desire to be seen and counted among the mature.	Vision	To daily experience the Father's unconditional love and acceptance and then be sent as a representative of His love to family and others.
Fight for what you can get!	Future	Sonship releases your inheritance!

All of us have an orphan heart to some degree. How do we deal with the orphan heart? The answer is it must be displaced. We must receive the love of the Father and experience the fact that we are at home and safe with him, and the orphan heart will be pushed out of us:

> *There is no fear in love, but perfect love casts out fear. For fear has to do with punishment, and whoever fears has not been perfected in love. We love because he first loved us. 1 John 4:18-19*

Jack Frost suggests this pathway to move from having an orphan heart to a heart of sonship:[47]

1. Forgive your parents for misrepresenting God's love to you.
2. Ask your parents to forgive you for the way you hurt or disappointed them.
3. Focus your life on being a son or daughter.
4. Forgive spiritual and governmental authorities.
5. You may need to seek forgiveness from those in authority.
6. Daily renounce ungodly beliefs and hidden lies of orphan thinking.
7. Begin sowing into your inheritance.
8. Entering into your inheritance.

The path moving from an orphan heart to sonship requires shifting our values. Rather than using people to meet our needs, we learn to value them for the relationship we have with them. Rather than rebelling against authority, we learn to joyfully submit to them. Rather than having to defend ourselves, we learn to let God defend us in his timing and with his methods. It is a road of learning to trust God fully.

---

[47] Taken from the last four chapters of *Spiritual Slavery to Spiritual Sonship* by Jack Frost.

Royalty

Royalty is a revelation that is focused on our *value*. It is about learning to love ourselves the way that God loves us. As we learn to value ourselves, we reflect that same value back towards others. If we don't value ourselves, we don't value others as well. Remember Jesus' words on identity:

> *The good person out of the good treasure of his heart produces good, and the evil person out of his evil treasure produces evil, for out of the abundance of the heart his mouth speaks.* Luke 6:45

This same dynamic is pointed to in an interesting proverb:

> *Under three things the earth trembles;*
> *under four it cannot bear up:*
> *a slave when he becomes king,*
> *and a fool when he is filled with food;*
> *an unloved woman when she gets a husband,*
> *and a maidservant when she displaces her mistress. Proverbs 30:21-23*

It is dangerous to take someone who isn't prepared for greatness and put them in a position of power because he or she will wield that power as a person who sees himself or herself as a powerless person and will make poor and dangerous choices.

The problem is that people who aren't prepared for greatness tend to define themselves by what they *don't* have. As long as we are defining ourselves by what we don't have, we are dangerous because we will do whatever we can to get that need met. We will sacrifice relationships and our integrity to supply our lack. Lack can exist in all kinds of different types; it doesn't just have to be economic. There can be lack in financial needs, material needs, relational needs, growth and nurture needs,

significance needs, educational needs, the need to be valued, and so forth. Anywhere in our lives that we don't realize we have our needs met, we will try to meet those needs on our own and take up that job at the cost of others. (This probably sounds familiar; it's the same story with an orphan heart.)

The catch is that as believers, we are now incredibly important! We have been promoted vastly!

> *But you are a chosen race, a royal priesthood, a holy nation, a people for his own possession, that you may proclaim the excellencies of him who called you out of darkness into his marvelous light. Once you were not a people, but now you are God's people; once you had not received mercy, but now you have received mercy. 1 Peter 2:9-10*

In fact, Jesus actually gave us the responsibility of discipling the nations ourselves. He has essentially put us in charge of the course of human history! It's hard to get more significant than that!

> *And Jesus came and said to them, "All authority in heaven and on earth has been given to me. Go therefore and make disciples of (note that word is "of," not "from," which is how we tend to read it) all nations, baptizing them in the name of the Father and of the Son and of the Holy Spirit, teaching them to observe all that I have commanded you. And behold, I am with you always, to the end of the age." Matthew 28:18-20*

So we find ourselves in the position described in that proverb. We have been promoted to massive significance, and we need to learn to value ourselves in the way that we can steward our responsibility towards others in positive ways.

There are a number of traits that Kris Vallotton esteems we should have as royalty:[48]

Destiny

People of royalty know they are destined for greatness. A prince is raised with the understanding that someday he will be king. He knows there are things set before him to walk into that are important and will affect the lives of others. Likewise, God promises us a destiny and an inheritance in him:

> *I do not cease to give thanks for you, remembering you in my prayers, that the God of our Lord Jesus Christ, the Father of glory, may give you a spirit of wisdom and of revelation in the knowledge of him, having the eyes of your hearts enlightened, that you may know what is the hope to which he has called you, what are the riches of his glorious inheritance in the saints, and what is the immeasurable greatness of his power toward us who believe Ephesians 1:16-19*

> *For we are his workmanship, created in Christ Jesus for good works, which God prepared beforehand, that we should walk in them. Ephesians 2:10*

Each one of us has a destiny laid out before us. We have purpose and importance in the kingdom of God. No one is in competition with us. We don't need to demonstrate that we're worth as much as anyone else because God has prepared something unique for each one of us that fits us perfectly.

Self-Value

Let me take a minute here and address humility. Humility is one of the highest praised attributes in Scripture. God actually resists those who are proud but gives grace to the

---

[48] These are taken from Chapters 8-13 of *The Supernatural Ways of Royalty* by Kris Vallotton. Much of the summarization is my own language.

humble. The problem is that in an effort to be humble, we often confuse humility and value. The church tends to teach us to self-deprecate in order to instill humility. We are told we are worthless slime and that only because God is nice, he chooses to save us. We are modeled a kind of self-deflecting reception of the praise of others so we do not take some of God's glory for ourselves.

This is a really twisted and confused attempt at demonstrating and maintaining humility. The true essence of humility is not thinking there is nothing good within us. It is not demeaning ourselves so that God looks better. God is not in any competition with us. As the people of God, we are his creation. If God's people look good, God looks good! Think of it like this. Suppose that an artist spends years of his life creating a masterpiece. When he asks you what your opinion is, if you say "Oh, that looks like garbage" because you don't want the artist to feel as if you like his painting more than you like him, does that praise the artist? No, an artist is praised through the praise of his art. God is not worried about sharing his glory with his people.

Now, clearly we could swing to the other end of the spectrum in error and start trying to take God's glory for ourselves. That is clearly the wrong answer, but that doesn't excuse us from learning to handle praise and value accurately. The true essence of humility is realizing where our value comes from. It is recognizing the praise of others and being rooted in what God has given us. The praise from others is on loan, as it were. We should learn to accept from others (otherwise we demean them if we dismiss what they say because God gave us the gift), and on our own reflect what we've received from others back towards God. Humility is recognizing the source of our greatness is God and not ourselves.

Furthermore, we ought to be convinced that as human beings, we have immeasurable value. Jesus wouldn't waste his time dying for trash. We ought not to think or speak of ourselves as worthless then if God has deemed us worthy. We are not worthless, and it dishonors the price that Jesus paid for us if we treat ourselves as if we are.

Honor

Honor at its root is reflecting the value we have for ourselves to other people. If we truly value ourselves and understand that we are not in competition with anyone else, we will naturally value others as well. We'll discuss honor extensively in the next unit that focuses on how we interact with others.

Covenant Relationships

As we saw in the discussion above on sonship, we are made to be interdependent on others, and our needs met through relational intimacy. God always designed relationships that provide the intimacy we need to be guarded by covenant. Covenant means choosing to support the relationship regardless of the personal cost to ourselves. It means looking out for others' needs above our own and holding up our end of the relationship whether the other person does or not. It means committing ourselves to opening ourselves fully to others and maintaining relational transparency.

One of the most prevalent and un-discussed covenantal trespasses happens with the corporate church body. God has put us in a church body for a reason, and he expects us to covenant with the people we call our local church body. Often people take a self-centered approach to church, choosing to attend the church while it serves their needs, then moving on if they feel like it. There is no commitment to the body on the personal level and the leadership specifically. This is sort of the spiritual version of cohabitation. God designed intimacy for covenant, not an "I'll be here while it works for me" approach. Instead, we need to shift our focus to being in the relationship for what we can give to it, not what we can get from it.

Warriors

The royal line was the one that led their people into battle. As such, they were people of war; people who would stand up and fight for justice on behalf of others and exercise the power they had to the benefit of others. Likewise, we are called to be warriors in the kingdom of light, wielding the power we have for the benefit of others and delivering them hope and freedom.

> *From the days of John the Baptist until now the kingdom of heaven has suffered violence, and the violent take it by force.* Matthew 11:12

Bravery

As leaders, royalty summon courage on behalf of others. They are the models that cast off fear and perform heroic deeds. They refuse to let the environment (externals) control their actions, and instead do what they know is right.

A New Creation

I would label my personal revelation of our identity as believers as "A New Creation." This comes from Paul's famous statement:

> *Therefore, if anyone is in Christ, he is a new creation. The old has passed away; behold, the new has come. 2 Corinthians 5:17*

As we discussed in the first few sections of this part of the material, this revelation revolves around the idea that the gospel restores us to the original created plan and identity. It puts us back to what we were created to be: image bearers of God. It is about restoration and redemption to our original identity and destiny.

I won't belabor the point any further since I've already written about this viewpoint in depth earlier. This viewpoint sees the work of Calvary and the new birth as a continuation of the creation account given in Genesis 1. Indeed the same voice that spoke things into being in Genesis 1 and saw that it was good never said that it was *finished* until he hung on the cross (John 19:30) and in that moment created us in Christ anew.

Our Eschatological Identity

As we begin to grow in our identity, we begin to start to differentiate between what goes on around us and who we are. We stop taking our circumstances as the definition of who we are or who God is and begin to learn to see our circumstance as an opportunity to demonstrate who God is and who we are instead.

The truth is that many of us look to our circumstances to see who God is far more than we care to admit. Letting our circumstances define the nature of God is always betrayed by asking the question "Why this, God?" or "Why me, God?" Whenever we cross the bridge to the question "why," we've let the circumstances define who God is.

This process is actually a major theme of the book of Job. The question underlying the book of Job is found in some of its first verses:

> *And the Lord said to Satan, "Have you considered my servant Job, that there is none like him on the earth, a blameless and upright man, who fears God and turns away from evil?" Then Satan answered the Lord and said, "Does Job fear God for no reason? Have you not put a hedge around him and his house and all that he has, on every side? You have blessed the work of his hands, and his possessions have increased in the land. But stretch out your hand and touch all that he has, and he will curse you to your face." Job 1:8-11*

The dialogue between God and Satan basically amounts to Satan asserting that Job only thinks God is good because the circumstances of his life have been good, and that if his circumstances go poorly, he won't think God is good anymore.[49] The question the reader is asking throughout the whole book of Job then is whether Job has the ability to keep believing in God's goodness regardless of his life situation.

Likewise, as the Lord shapes our identity within us, we have a deeper and fuller understanding of the truth that has been spoken about us. That understanding starts to sink down into the deep places in us, and our confidence in that truth begins to grow. In that process, our perspective starts to shift, and we begin to understand that our circumstances are the stage on which we can demonstrate the reality of our relationship with God. Either you look to the circumstances to define to you who God is, or you look at your circumstances as an opportunity to illustrate who God is to you. The latter is faith in action.

The truth is that our identity has already been established. There isn't any question of who we'll become:

> *And we know that for those who love God all things work together for good, for those who are called according to his purpose. For those whom he foreknew he also predestined to be conformed to the image of his Son, in order that he might be the firstborn among many brothers. Romans 8:28-29*

> *. . . even as he chose us in him before the foundation of the world, that we should be holy and blameless before him. In love he predestined us for adoption as sons through Jesus Christ, according to the purpose of his will. Ephesians 1:4-5*

---

[49] Interestingly this book has probably been used as much as any book in the Bible to question the goodness of God, because due to a misunderstanding of sovereignty, people have interpreted God as causing the work of the enemy in Job's life.

Notice both of these passages talk about us being predestined to become sons. God has already set forth for you a destiny, and that destiny is to grow into an identity as a son of God. Because of that, we can trust that all things in our life will work towards that. Whether they are good or bad, we have an identity that is our destiny, which cannot be derailed.[50]

In a sense then, who we are is a picture much like the picture discussed when we talked about Kingdom Theology. There is an eschatological identity that God has already established in front of us, and that identity is breaking into the present and establishing our current identity. Our identity is both come and coming!

This is one of the great promises of the New Testament. Every promise for us is already ours in Christ, but not only that, they have growing momentum![51]

> *For the Son of God, Jesus Christ, whom we proclaimed among you, Silvanus and Timothy and I, was not Yes and No, but in him it is always Yes. For all the promises of God find their Yes in him. That is why it is through him that we utter our Amen to God for his glory. And it is God who establishes us with you in Christ, and has anointed us, and who has also put his seal on us and given us his Spirit in our hearts as a guarantee. 2 Corinthians 1:19-22*

---

[50] This is a very different interpretation of these verses than is usually given in the standard discussion about predestination, which asks whether we're predestined to be saved or not. I'm not going to address that question, but rather take these verses as what they talk about, which is a growth process, not a salvation event.

[51] I believe this is why Paul says that not only is love eternal, but so are faith and hope. Furthermore Isaiah promises that of the increase of his government there will be no end (including in heaven). The process of our growth is not something that stops when we cross the divide of mortality. Indeed, even heaven gets better!

The Gospel of Growth?

Allow me to take a brief digression here. As Americans, we have a very strong value for improvement and growth. We see progress as our barometer of how well we're doing. Because of this, I think we can overemphasize this growth process and elevate it above other truths.

It is true that the gospel promises growth for us in all circumstances. Indeed, when the devil presents his plans, God can even use that to get his ends. However, this doesn't mean that the devil's means are justified. It doesn't mean that because some good can come out of bad things that the bad things are then good.

This perspective comes up often in healing. This happens because God uses a painful situation such as a disease to work some good in a person's life. What can happen is you can ask a person if they would like to be healed, and they will tell you they don't want to be healed because of the good that has happened in their life due to their sickness. It is true that God has used their sickness to work good, but this perspective comes out of three majorly flawed ideas.

First, this perspective comes out of an understanding that the goodness of God is limited. God doesn't need to use bad things to work good in our lives. He can use the bad things the devil puts there, but he doesn't need to use bad things. God can work the exact same good in a person with them completely healed as he could with them sick. Indeed, when a sick person gets well, often God uses the revelation of how much He loves them to work even more good in their life.

Secondly, the reality is that this response more often comes out of pain than it does theology. Due to the fact that people believe God has given them sickness to bring good in their lives, they don't feel safe with God. They'll put up a wall and not want to be healed. They don't trust God, and so they don't want to turn to him for healing. It is easier to hold God at a distance than open themselves to the vulnerability it requires to turn to God for healing.

Finally, we need to remember that the gospel that Jesus preached was not the gospel of growth, but the gospel of the kingdom. The good news is not that we can grow, but that God is on the move, and he is demolishing the work the enemy has done. We mustn't let our American perspective confuse these. God establishing His Kingdom has more priority than our own growth.

This is why I don't feel guilty offering to pray for people in wheelchairs or for blind people. I know it can be painful for us to force people to face the reality that they are sick, and I know it can drudge up hurt feelings and so forth; but the truth is the gospel we have to preach is that God is big and God is good. I cannot let another person's pain invalidate my gospel.

Growing in Identity

Identity is a journey you have to travel for yourself. It is something that needs to be written on who you are—a revelation that goes to the very core. As such it is not something that I can give you simple instructions about, but rather something you must seek the Lord for. It is a process that you must choose to embark on, but I want to give you a few pointers and suggestions for the road here.

So what actually changes us as we grow in identity? As we discussed before, it is a process of renewing our mind so that we can see ourselves the way we actually are, but what empowers and enables that process? Again, the answer is grace. Paul points to this dynamic in a verse that many of us know by heart:

> *For by grace you have been saved through faith. Ephesians 2:8*

Remember that *salvation* is a holistic term in the Bible. It means roughly "to save, keep safe and sound, to rescue from danger or destruction, heal or make well."[52] It is an encompassing term that means to be put right in every aspect of our lives. In this light it becomes clear that what heals us, what secures our eternal destiny, what delivers us, and what makes us whole is grace. Grace does all those things. No wonder the Holy Spirit is called the Spirit of Grace (Hebrews 10:29).

So what brings us to wholeness, what renews our mind is grace. How is that grace accessed? Through faith. Faith provides the runway for grace to land in your life. Grace, like the kingdom, has already come. It is already present:

> *For from his fullness we have all received, grace upon grace. For the law was given through Moses; grace and truth came through Jesus Christ. John 1:16-17*

Grace is here. Jesus brought it. What needs to happen is that grace needs to affect transformation and wholeness in our lives. The way that happens is through faith. Faith provides the channel for grace to flow and change us. This is the process of renewing the mind. Our mind isn't renewed through learning; it's renewed by grace. That grace is accessed through faith.

This brings us to the difference between revelation and information. Revelation is more than supernatural information; it is supernatural information with grace on it. Have you ever noticed that? When revelation comes, it has on it the grace to empower the change you see. Without grace on it, that information only has the power to show you what you should be; not change you to get you there.

---

[52] Blue Letter Bible, accessed 6/26/12. http://www.blueletterbible.org/lang/lexicon/lexicon.cfm?Strongs=G4982&t=KJV

Revelation releases an impartation and leads to transformation. Knowledge releases information and leads to education. Revelation releases in the heart the capacity to live out what the mind is seeing.

Our journey in renewing the mind is a journey of revelation; this is why you have to embark on it yourself. I can give you all kinds of pictures and teachings that describe it, but all of that is just information. If you want to live out identity (which is the whole point), it has to become a conviction in your heart, and God has to release the revelation to you for that. So engage with him. Ask for the revelation of who you are in Him. He promises to give good gifts to those of us who ask (Matthew 7:11).

Training in Righteousness

Paul gives us some interesting insight as to how he participates in the process of renewing his mind in a fascinating passage:

> *For though we walk in the flesh, we are not waging war according to the flesh. For the weapons of our warfare are not of the flesh but have divine power to destroy strongholds. We destroy arguments and every lofty opinion raised against the knowledge of God, and take every thought captive to obey Christ, being ready to punish every disobedience, when your obedience is complete. 2 Corinthians 10:3-6*

Paul starts off by saying that though he lives in a physical body, he has spiritual weapons with divine power. These weapons destroy strongholds. Strongholds are encampments; places an enemy has fortified for himself that need to be flushed out. This perfectly describes the condition of the mind that is being renewed. There are places where thought patterns sown by the enemy have made encampments into our thinking that need to be broken down and flushed out.

How does Paul destroy these strongholds? He gives us three steps:

1. Destroy arguments and every lofty opinion raised against the knowledge of God. This doesn't mean to make sure we have correct theology; it means to align our knowledge with God's. The "knowledge of God" is not knowledge about God; it's the knowledge that God has. God knows some things about us (who we are in him), and he forgets some things about us (who we were and our sin). Step one is to align our thoughts and opinions with God's.[53]

2. Take every thought captive to obey Christ. This refers to guarding our thought life. There are many thoughts we have that aren't yet in line with who we are. Paul admonishes us to make sure that every thought ends in obedience to Christ. If we have a thought about ourselves that's not true, we recognize it as a lie (which we can do because of the first step); and because we know it is a lie, we rejoice in the truth that it isn't true.

3. Punish every disobedience to obedience. What we do with our thoughts; we do with our actions. Every time disobedience slips forth through our actions, we turn around and begin to reinforce the truth through our actions. We act on the truth and make the place we disobeyed a place of obedience.

Not every thought or action has its source in the renewed mind, but Paul admonishes us to make sure that every thought or action does end in the truth. We make sure that no lie of the enemy slips through the cracks unnoticed; in everything, we train ourselves in the ways of righteousness.

---

[53] The studied student may be familiar with the idea of positional truth. Positional truth essentially means that there are some realities that are true from God's point of view that aren't true in our experience and life here on the earth. The reality that God sees/experiences is called the positional truth, whereas the reality that the believer walks in is called the conditional truth. I reject this notion entirely. As far as I can tell it explains away the realities of the new covenant by saying they hold true from God's perspective rather than our own and exalts our experience above what the Word says about us. It is a toxic doctrine.

Spiritual Disciplines

One tool that is very useful in our path of growing in who we are is to practice the spiritual disciplines. Paul refers to reading Scripture as a means to train ourselves in the ways of righteousness (see previous section):

> *All Scripture is breathed out by God and profitable for teaching, for reproof, for correction, and for training in righteousness, that the man of God may be complete, equipped for every good work. 2 Timothy 3:16-17*

Spiritual disciplines are simply practices that we do in an effort to open ourselves up to the work of the Lord within us. Generally, spiritual disciplines fall into two categories: disciplines of abstinence and disciplines of engagement.[54]

Disciplines of Abstinence

- Solitude: Spending time alone without other people or any of the distractions of life.
- Silence: Time spent with no noise, just you and God.
- Fasting: Abstaining from food, entertainment, or anything else.
- Frugality: Using your money on others' needs instead of your own.
- Chastity/Abstinence: Abstaining from sexual relations.
- Secrecy: Choosing not to disclose motivations or information that you could.
- Sacrifice: Giving of yourself willingly to learn to live with less and give more to others.
- Waiting on the Lord: Withdrawing yourself to commune with the presence of the Lord.

---

[54] This list is summarized (and expanded) based upon a list at http://quaillake.blogspot.com/2006/09/spiritual-disciplines.html.

Disciplines of Engagement

- Study: Memorization and thoughtful meditation on Scripture.
- Worship: Both corporately and alone. Not necessarily requiring music or song.
- Celebration: Practicing gratitude and thanksgiving with yourself and other believers.
- Service: Giving of your time and energy to your church or to others.
- Prayer: Time spent in intentional conversation with God.
- Fellowship: Time spent intentionally engaging in relationship with other believers.
- Confession: Owning and revealing the sin you've committed to another believer.
- Submission: Proper recognition and respect for the authority God has established.
- Speaking in Tongues: Practicing a personal prayer language that strengthens your spirit.
- Ministry Prayer: Ministering to others (or receiving ministry prayer) with the presence of the Holy Spirit.

Generally disciplines of abstinence are designed to break down the worldview of the flesh, and disciplines of engagement build up the mind of the Spirit.

I'd suggest practicing a variety of these disciplines and discovering your own needs and rhythm with them. Different people tend to be drawn to different disciplines; and at different points in your life, different disciplines will connect with you more than others. Learning to practice connecting with God and drawing our life from him through the seasons of our spiritual walk is a joy and keeps us focused on moving forward in everything. For those who want to learn more about these disciplines, I'd recommend starting with *The Spirit of the Disciplines* by Dallas Willard, or *Sacred Rhythms* by Ruth Haley Barton.

Relationships: How We Treat Others

I want to start by observing an interesting dynamic that Jesus discusses. Let's consider first a rich, if somewhat cryptic, passage in Matthew:

> *Now when Jesus came into the district of Caesarea Philippi, he asked his disciples, "Who do people say that the Son of Man is?" And they said, "Some say John the Baptist, others say Elijah, and others Jeremiah or one of the prophets." He said to them, "But who do you say that I am?" Simon Peter replied, "You are the Christ, the Son of the living God." And Jesus answered him, "Blessed are you, Simon Bar-Jonah! For flesh and blood has not revealed this to you, but my Father who is in heaven. And I tell you, you are Peter, and on this rock I will build my church, and the gates of hell shall not prevail against it. I will give you the keys of the kingdom of heaven, and whatever you bind on earth shall be bound in heaven, and whatever you loose on earth shall be loosed in heaven." Matthew 16:13-19*

First, notice that this is actually one of only two times that Jesus refers to the church in all of the Gospels. (We will look at the second passage next.) Notice as well that this is a very rich passage in terms of "doing the stuff"—keys of the kingdom, binding and loosing on earth and heaven. The kind of stuff we want to be doing!

So let's dissect this interchange and see what we can learn. First, Jesus asks the disciples who others are saying he is. When they reply that others have been suggesting that he is one of the prophets previously listed in the Bible, Jesus ups the ante and asks who they say he is. Peter jumps in and volunteers that Jesus is the Messiah.

Jesus' response is very interesting. He replies something along the lines of "Wow, you didn't figure that out, God gave you that revelation!" Then directly in line with Peter having asserted who Jesus is to him, Jesus turns around and bestows on Peter a new identity and a new destiny. As God starts to give us a revelation of whom He is, that flows into a new identity for ourselves. Deposited in that identity are the nutrients that God wants to draw from to grow us into our destiny.

Jesus then continues to declare Peter's destiny, "on this rock I will build my church, and the gates of hell shall not prevail against it." From the language in the verse it's not clear whether "this" refers to the revelation that Peter had, or the rock that Peter is (Peter means "rock"). We see later in the New Testament:

> *According to the grace of God given to me, like a skilled master builder I laid a foundation, and someone else is building upon it. Let each one take care how he builds upon it. For no one can lay a foundation other than that which is laid, which is Jesus Christ. 1 Corinthians 3:10-11*

At least to Paul, the foundation of the church is Jesus Christ. The church is built on the revelation of who Jesus is. We are the community of people who are discovering who Jesus is; as a result, we are the group of people discovering who we really are. As we discover who we really are, all hell should be pillaged.

> *. . . so that through the church the manifold wisdom of God might now be made known to the rulers and authorities in the heavenly places. Ephesians 3:10*

Finally, Jesus adds one more interesting phrase: "I will give you the keys of the kingdom of heaven, and whatever you bind on earth shall be bound in heaven, and whatever you loose on earth shall be loosed in heaven." This is a very interesting, and almost cryptic phrase. Let me add a few observations.

First, the word *you* throughout this passage is actually a different word than Jesus is using when he bestows a new name on Peter in the previous verse. It is actually the same word that Jesus uses a few verses before when he asks whom the disciples say Jesus is. Jesus is not referring solely to Peter here; he is referring to all the disciples.

Second, the verb tenses in the last phrase are ambiguous in the Greek. Some translations will translate it as it has been above; some will translate it "whatever you bind on earth shall have been bound in heaven, and whatever you loose on earth shall have been loosed in heaven." It appears there is some directional ambiguity as to whether the action starts on earth and then heaven responds, or vice-a-versa.

Third, the word *whatever* here refers to a class or a type of thing. It could be translated "whatever kind of thing you bind on earth."

Putting all of that together, what does Jesus' cryptic phrase mean? Notice that this phrase is being used in the context of Peter having received a revelation from God. In essence, he has had the cover taken off and had perception into the spiritual realm (into heaven). I believe what Jesus is pointing to is a fundamental spiritual principle: that as we see into heaven, as we receive revelation, not only is the payoff that we are bestowed with new identity, but also that revelation gives us access—it gives us permission, keys if you will—to release that same kind of thing on the earth.

This is why identity is so inseparably linked to destiny and a fundamental principle in releasing the kingdom of God here on the earth.

Let's look at the other passage where Jesus talks about the church now.

> *"If your brother sins against you, go and tell him his fault, between you and him alone. If he listens to you, you have gained your brother. But if he does not listen, take one or two others along with you, that every charge may be established by*

the evidence of two or three witnesses. If he refuses to listen to them, tell it to the church. And if he refuses to listen even to the church, let him be to you as a Gentile and a tax collector. Truly, I say to you, whatever you bind on earth shall be bound in heaven, and whatever you loose on earth shall be loosed in heaven. Again I say to you, if two of you agree on earth about anything they ask, it will be done for them by my Father in heaven. For where two or three are gathered in my name, there am I among them." ***Matthew 18:15-20***

This second passage where Jesus discusses the church entails a discussion of handling relationship. Notice as well that in this passage Jesus uses the same cryptic phrase referring to binding and loosing here that He did in the other passage in Matthew 16. Jesus clearly thought of the purpose of the church as being the agent of releasing the kingdom of heaven onto the earth.

For the purposes of this discussion I'm not going to analyze the steps of reconciliation that Jesus prescribes, but I do want to look at the second half of the passage. Again, let me make a few observations about the original language that will help us figure out what Jesus means by this statement.

First: the same ambiguity with tense that occurs in the passage we looked at in the last chapter occurs again here. It is not clear whether the meaning would be better rendered as "whatever you bind on earth shall have been bound in heaven, and whatever you loose on earth shall have been loosed in heaven."

Second: other than that, the phrase is the same, with one exception; the word *whatever* here means something different. In this passage *whatever* refers to a quantity. A good analogy might be something along the lines of "in as much as" or "to the extent that."

Earlier we found that revelation of heaven gives us access to releasing the same type of thing on the earth. This passage brings the understanding full circle. Jesus is talking about restoring the relationships we have among each other as brothers and sisters in Christ, and He inserts a statement to the effect of "as much as you bind or loose here on earth, that will determine how much is bound or loosed in heaven." Within the context of relationship, the binding and loosing might be binding division, or releasing forgiveness. In this statement, Jesus is painting a picture that the relationships we maintain here on earth influence the magnitude of response we get from heaven.

Jesus reiterates then, saying that agreement between people is a key factor that the Father responds to and that a community that is dedicated to Jesus releases his presence. This is the reason we want to be intentional about doing relationship and community with others in Kingdom ways.

God takes the way we do our relationships much more seriously than we tend to. Here are a few verses that address the way we do relationships, which may seem drastic, but they point to the importance of this principle:

> *So if you are offering your gift at the altar and there remember that your brother has something against you, leave your gift there before the altar and go. First be reconciled to your brother, and then come and offer your gift.* Matthew 5:23-24

> *For if you forgive others their trespasses, your heavenly Father will also forgive you, but if you do not forgive others their trespasses, neither will your Father forgive your trespasses.* Matthew 6:14-15

> *Likewise, husbands, live with your wives in an understanding way, showing honor to the woman as the weaker vessel, since they are heirs with you of the grace of life, so that your prayers may not be hindered. 1 Peter 3:7*

The two passages we've examined in Matthew 16 and Matthew 18 that talk about binding and loosing on heaven and on earth are each halves of the relationship between earth and heaven. In summary:

1. What we see bound or loosed in heaven gives us permission to bind or loose the same type of thing on earth. *Revelation gives us access.*
2. The amount that we bind or loose within the context of our relationships here on earth influences the size of response we get from heaven. *Relationship determines extent.*

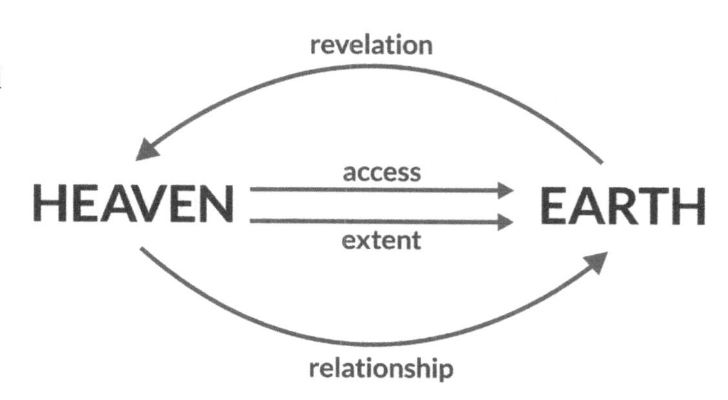

In the first step, the flow is from heaven towards earth. Heaven is the template, and earth is the canvas on which heaven paints. The second step relates to how much flows. Our actions on earth put constraints on how much flows from heaven to earth.

This means fundamentally that the ideas of identity and community go hand-in-hand. As we grow into our identity, we grow in step 1 and as we grow in community, we grow in step 2. Furthermore there is interaction between these two. As we grow in identity, we see how to do community better, which influences our identity even more, and so forth. There is an upward spiral of growth that has anointing swept up in the mix.

> **Theology Anchor**
>
> Our revelation gives us access to release the kingdom. Our relationships determine how much capacity we have to do so.

Unfortunately, what is true in the positive is true in the negative here as well. There can be an equally negative spiral that multiplies hurt and brokenness.

Jesus had some pretty strong things to say about that cycle:

> *At that time the disciples came to Jesus, saying, "Who is the greatest in the kingdom of heaven?" And calling to him a child, he put him in the midst of them and said, "Truly, I say to you, unless you turn and become like children, you will never enter the kingdom of heaven. Whoever humbles himself like this child is the greatest in the kingdom of heaven.*
>
> *"Whoever receives one such child in my name receives me, but whoever causes one of these little ones who believe in me to [stumble], it would be better for him to have a great millstone fastened around his neck and to be drowned in the depth of the sea.*
>
> *"Woe to the world for [stumbling blocks]! For it is necessary that [stumbling blocks] come, but woe to the one by whom the [stumbling block] comes! And if your hand or your foot causes you to [stumble], cut it off and throw it away. It is better for you to enter life crippled or lame than with two hands or two feet to be thrown into the eternal fire. And if your eye causes you to [stumble], tear it out and throw it away. It is better for you to enter life with one eye than with two eyes to be thrown into the hell of fire.* Matthew 18:1-9

In this passage I've changed the word usually translated "sin" to what the original word in Greek is—usually rendered as sin but more literally means "snare." Jesus uses this same word two chapters earlier:

> *From that time Jesus began to show his disciples that he must go to Jerusalem and suffer many things from the elders and chief priests and scribes, and be killed, and on the third day be raised. And Peter took him aside and began to rebuke him, saying, "Far be it from you, Lord! This shall never happen to you." But he turned*

and said to Peter, "Get behind me, Satan! You are a [stumbling block] to me. For you are not setting your mind on the things of God, but on the things of man." *Matthew 16:21-23*

Setting our mind on the things of man and influencing others to become that way causes us to become a stumbling block to others. We wind up shifting their mindset downwards towards our own, which Jesus considers a very bad thing according to the passage above.

However, if the negative cycle is that serious and powerful, how much more must the positive cycle be that way! Let's look at a few of the other places the words "bind" and "loose" are used in Scripture:

But if it is by the Spirit of God that I cast out demons, then the kingdom of God has come upon you. Or how can someone enter a strong man's house and plunder his goods, unless he first binds the strong man? Then indeed he may plunder his house. *Matthew 12:29-30*

And there was a woman who had had a disabling spirit for eighteen years. She was bent over and could not fully straighten herself. When Jesus saw her, he called her over and said to her, "Woman, you are freed from your disability." And he laid his hands on her, and immediately she was made straight, and she glorified God. But the ruler of the synagogue, indignant because Jesus had healed on the Sabbath, said to the people, "There are six days in which work ought to be done. Come on those days and be healed, and not on the Sabbath day." Then the Lord answered him, "You hypocrites! Does not each of you on the Sabbath untie his ox or his donkey from the manger and lead it away to water it? And ought not this woman, a daughter of Abraham whom Satan bound for eighteen years, be loosed from this bond on the Sabbath day?" *Luke 13:11-16*

> *And looking up to heaven, he sighed and said to him, "Ephphatha," that is, "Be opened." And his ears were opened, his tongue was [loosed], and he spoke plainly. And Jesus charged them to tell no one. But the more he charged them, the more zealously they proclaimed it. Mark 7:34-36*

> *this Jesus, delivered up according to the definite plan and foreknowledge of God, you crucified and killed by the hands of lawless men. God raised him up, loosing the pangs of death, because it was not possible for him to be held by it. Acts 2:23-24*

> *Whoever makes a practice of sinning is of the devil, for the devil has been sinning from the beginning. The reason the Son of God appeared was to [loose] the works of the devil. 1 John 3:8*

I don't know about you, but I want that kind of binding and loosing happening around me! It is precisely for this reason that we need to be intentional about the way we do relationship.

Relational Paradigms

The kingdom at work in our relationships involves embracing a different *relational paradigm*. It means starting to use a different set of rules and measures to govern the way we relate to other people. Most people never give much thought to their relational paradigm—the values they use to make decisions about how to relate to others.

As a result of this, most of us don't have a clearly defined relational paradigm, but that doesn't mean we don't have one. It just means we don't know what it is. Our relational paradigm is part of our worldview, just like our identity. Our identity is how we perceive ourselves within our worldview; our relational paradigm is how we perceive others.

Our goal, of course, should be not just to articulate our relational paradigm, but also to bring it in line with God's relational paradigm. God relates to people as well, and if we're smart, we'll try to learn to relate to people the same way that God does.

Let's look at a story from John that illustrates Jesus' relational paradigm:[55]

> *The scribes and the Pharisees brought a woman who had been caught in adultery, and placing her in the midst they said to him, "Teacher, this woman has been caught in the act of adultery. Now in the Law Moses commanded us to stone such women. So what do you say?" This they said to test him, that they might have some charge to bring against him. Jesus bent down and wrote with his finger on the ground. And as they continued to ask him, he stood up and said to them, "Let him who is without sin among you be the first to throw a stone at her." And once more he bent down and wrote on the ground. But when they heard it, they went away one by one, beginning with the older ones, and Jesus was left alone with the woman standing before him. Jesus stood up and said to her, "Woman, where are they? Has no one condemned you?" She said, "No one, Lord." And Jesus said, "Neither do I condemn you; go, and from now on sin no more." John 8:3-11*

Jesus is simply amazing here. What is the first thing that stands out here? Jesus is defending this woman from her accusers. Now, notice what happens after that, when the problem of what she's done is addressed: Jesus empowers her freedom and commends her to make good choices.

---

[55] As an interesting note, this story is not only specifically about one woman, but this story is equally a metaphor for Jesus' interaction with the world at large. The accusers are symbolic of the accuser, and the woman who was committing adultery is symbolic of Israel/humanity in general. Jesus writing on the ground vs. standing up is symbolic of Jesus position in heaven or on the earth.

There is a stark contrast that is painted here. The scribes and Pharisees are acting under a different relational paradigm here—one where what the woman has done is a problem for *them*, and so they have to punish her behavior. Jesus, on the other hand stands in stark contrast to that. He's not offended by her behavior. He doesn't try to control her behavior so she does what he wants. He doesn't threaten to punish her. He remains true to who he is, and he respects who she is.

This is so different from how many of us handle and process our interactions with other people. Jesus is clear about the fact that what the woman does cannot force his hand to the point where he will try to control what she does. In short, the externals of what she does can't control his internals.

Let me be very clear about this point because our society seems majorly confused about it. You are responsible for what you do. No one else is responsible for what you do. Someone else is responsible for what they do, and you are responsible for what you do. You are not responsible for what someone else does, nor are they responsible for what you do. If someone makes poor choices, those poor choices do not determine what your response is unless you let it. If you let their choices influence your response, then in essence that means you're allowing yourself to be controlled by other people. You let their poor choices determine your choices (which are usually equally poor).

In summation then, let me point out what seem to be the values Jesus is representing in this interaction. This is really important to catch here; this is the kingdom relational paradigm:

- I will love you regardless of your bad choices.
- I'm responsible for my behavior. I'm not responsible for your behavior.
- What you do can't control the way that I interact with you.
- I won't compromise your freedom or responsibility for your own behavior.

- I will not punish your bad choices, but I will empower you to make good choices with your freedom.

This is so different from how we tend to interact with each other! Usually we fail on all these points; as soon as we see people making bad choices, we appoint ourselves as being responsible for fixing their behavior, let them control our inner dynamics (we get angry, frustrated, or otherwise), then we compromise their freedom and try to control what they do so they don't make a stupid choice the next time. In this cycle, sin begets sin, and before we know it, we've partnered with control so much we're at least as much in the wrong as they are.

The trick here is to maintain our empowered status. I am empowered. What you do can't change that so I don't need to worry about what you do. We can fall prey to the mindset that what the other person does will infect me with their gunk, but remember our discussion about grace? We are un-infectable! I am actually so empowered that I can always choose to lift you up even when you've fallen on your face, and I can always choose to not lower myself to partnering with control or other tools of the enemy while I do it.

You can see how identity and relationship go hand in hand. If I know who I am, I'm not looking for you to tell me, and then I have a basis for how I interact with you. Who I am determines the quality in which I interact with you, and so what you do can never control what I do. You can never make me control you. You can never make me punish you.

This empowering of myself to always empower you is the mindset out of which Bethel has created their famous "Culture of Honor."

Responding and Reacting

A simple test we can apply to ourselves to tell whether we are walking in step with our identity as believers or in the mindset of the flesh is to examine whether we are responding or reacting. The difference between the two is very simple: when I respond, I choose what I do; when I react, you choose what I do.

Theology Anchor

We can always respond and remain in control of ourselves. The situation never has to control us.

This is certainly the way that God relates to us. No amount of our own sin forces God to lose control of himself with us. He is never offended or manipulated by us: he always responds out of who he is to the situation at hand.

There are so many pictures of this in the Scriptures where we can see how Jesus does relationship. One clear picture happens when Jesus reassures Peter of his calling after the resurrection.

> *When they had finished breakfast, Jesus said to Simon Peter, "Simon, son of John, do you love me more than these?" He said to him, "Yes, Lord; you know that I love you." He said to him, "Feed my lambs." He said to him a second time, "Simon, son of John, do you love me?" He said to him, "Yes, Lord; you know that I love you." He said to him, "Tend my sheep." He said to him the third time, "Simon, son of John, do you love me?" Peter was grieved because he said to him the third time, "Do you love me?" and he said to him, "Lord, you know everything; you know that I love you." Jesus said to him, "Feed my sheep. John 21:15-17*

Jesus is making sure that Peter has not lost his sense of calling. Jesus called Peter specifically to minister to his church (Matthew 16:18), but a lot has happened since then, most recently Peter betraying Jesus three times before he was crucified.

Imagine yourself in this situation. You've spent three years of your life pouring everything you have into a group of people, and Peter most of all since he'll be the leader. You've sacrificed, modeled, taught, prayed and just about everything else together. At the end of everything, the one who you've invested in the most turns his back on you and explicitly denies he knows you three times while you go through the most excruciating experience of your life. In fact, not only did Jesus know Peter would do this, he heard him do it.[56]

Would you be hurt? Would you be offended? Would you feel betrayed? I'm fairly certain I would. The next time I saw Peter, I'd have a difficult time trusting him and opening up to him. But that's not Jesus' response. What does Jesus do? His main concern is with Peter. He wants to make sure that Peter hasn't lost his sense of calling or who he is. He reassures Peter that he hasn't disqualified himself. Jesus doesn't even address Peter's mistake! There is no mention of the fact that Peter missed the mark on that one (of course, he already knew that). No, Jesus' full attention seems to be on restoring Peter. The situation has not provoked anything in him because there is no weakness or lack of identity. In no way can Peter's denial make Jesus lose a sense of who he is.

Another amazing example of this happens shortly before the crucifixion. The Jews have just asked Pilate to crucify Jesus. At this request, Pilate privately questions Jesus:

> *When Pilate heard this statement, he was even more afraid. He entered his headquarters again and said to Jesus, "Where are you from?" But Jesus gave him no answer. So Pilate said to him, "You will not speak to me? Do you not know that I have authority to release you and authority to crucify you?" Jesus answered*

[56] See Luke 22:61.

> *him, "You would have no authority over me at all unless it had been given you from above. Therefore he who delivered me over to you has the greater sin."*
> *John 19:8-11*

Pilate in an effort to figure out who Jesus is threatens him. In essence, Pilate is saying, "Jesus, I can kill you. You better answer my questions here!" That's pretty intense because that's exactly what's at stake. Pilate is trying to manipulate Jesus and force his hand. What does Jesus do? He refuses to be manipulated and simply observes that Pilate's own authority is being manipulated by Satan. Amazing.

Jesus isn't living for himself, so he can't be manipulated. Manipulation always threatens pain for you if you don't do what the other person wants. That will always work if you're living for yourself. But if you aren't living for yourself, your concern isn't for your own pain; it's for the well-being of others.

Like Jesus modeled, we need to learn to respond, not react. We always have the choice to control ourselves; there is no situation that *forces* us to become reactive. My feelings are my responsibility. You can't cause feelings in me—only provide opportunities for me to feel any specific way. My view of the situation is what determines what feelings will arise in any given situation.

Anytime that our feelings are out of proportion with the stimulus, we have become reactive. Why have we become reactive? Because we feel our needs are being threatened. This happens because we aren't established in our own identity.

Here is a simple example: what happens when someone cuts you off while you're driving? Many people will lose it. Why? Not because they got cut off. Unless they actually hit you, the situation is actually a relatively minor problem. The real issue is that the situation provokes a perceived lack of value. The message we receive is "That person thinks they're more important than I am so they'll inconvenience me to make their own life easier." The reason our feelings throw themselves out of control and we potentially blow up is because we're not secure in our own identity, so their assessment of our identity threatens us. If you're secure in your identity, you don't need someone else's affirmation; someone else's lack of affirmation doesn't threaten you.

We choose to become reactive when we let ourselves act when we're in that state. When we do that, we allow the devil to control our behavior and force us to act like he does through orchestrating the situation around us. Don't do that! No situation forces you to react. Take responsibility for yourself and center yourself in your identity before you act.

This practice has been key in my life. The instant I realize I've slipped into that reactive state, I try to remove myself from whatever situation I'm in and reconnect with God. When you connect with God, you center yourself in who you are and reposition yourself in a position of strength. Only after I've positioned myself in that place of strength do I re-engage with the situation and try to move forward.

Bringing Strength to Relationships

Once we learn this lesson we are freed from ourselves in relationships. Here is the fundamental problem most people have with relationships: *they come to relationship needing something*. They come to relationships to get instead of to give. This isn't how relationship is done in the kingdom:

> *Remember the words of the Lord Jesus, how he himself said, "It is more blessed to give than to receive." Acts 20:35*

The critical misconception is this: that we can't actually have our needs met by God. Many of us know in our heads that God *should* be able to meet all our needs, but we don't walk in the reality of that by faith so our experience is that God isn't meeting all our needs. We turn to our relationships to meet whatever needs we don't see God fulfilling in our lives.

This isn't the way it should be! We can walk by faith in the reality that God really does meet all our needs; in that case, when we come to relationships, we come from a place of strength instead of weakness. Relationship is now about you instead of me. It is now about what I can bring and give to you rather than what you can do for me. Because of this, we can come to relationship always from a place of strength. If my main motivator in relationship is to bless you because I'm already fulfilled, then your response to me can't be a threat. It doesn't matter whether you are responding or reacting; neither affects me. I'm covered either way.

This is the way that Jesus did relationship. Jesus never lost touch with who he was or his completeness in the Father because of the actions of those around him. He at times had the worst possible circumstances (being betrayed by one of your disciples to be killed in an extremely painful way comes to mind), but never let his circumstances control his inner state. He always chose to respond out of who he was instead.

Our Motivation in Relationships

If we choose to not control or scare people into doing what we'd like for them, what does that mean in terms of working with others through disagreement? How can I get what I want?

In short, the answer is you can't, or rather that you never could in the first place. What happens is a paradigm shift in our relationships. What happens when we operate from a paradigm of control or fear is that we trade in on the relationship for the behavior we want. I am willing to do wrong by our relationship in order to get the behavior from you that I want. I am willing to raise my voice at you or threaten to isolate myself from you in order to get you to do the dishes, mow the lawn, or whatever else I'm trying to convince you to do. In the process, I'm sinning against our relationship to bring about behavior.

The paradigm shift is that we now decide that no behavior is worth trading in on the relationship. Our relationship is more valuable to me than anything I'd like you to do or believe, and so your behavior becomes a secondary issue. Now we need to learn to address behavior without sacrificing the relationship in the process. This requires needing to use a new set of tools for doing relationship.

Theology Anchor

The only motivation the kingdom recognizes is love.

The motivation we use now is love rather than fear. Our appeal is not based on trying to scare someone into doing something, but rather a clear communication of our desire or need and expecting the person to respect the relationship. It is their choice whether they choose to do what we would like them to. Clearly some choices will affect the relationship we have in negative ways and others in positive ways, but the choice is up to them.

Now, of course, this can be pushed too far. I'm not saying we should deliver the person a relational ultimatum. What I'm saying is we make clear that some choices will hurt us. We choose to love them regardless of the choice they make, but make clear the choice they make may affect the quality of the relationship because it isn't possible to maintain intimacy with someone who doesn't care if they hurt the other person(s).

This is a much more dangerous form of relating. It leads to the type of relationship in which people can hurt you deeply, but it also develops the soil in which people may grow. It is the way God relates to us. God never tries to manipulate but always reveals his heart and invites us into what he has for us. Jesus stands at the door and knocks; he doesn't guilt us into letting him in. Likewise, we choose to make ourselves vulnerable to others in order to not compromise their freedom. Will it result in not getting what we'd like all the time? Probably. God doesn't get what he wants all the time either, but he doesn't change his approach to relationships. Likewise, we will do well if we settle in our minds that the ends never justify the means in relationships. It's not okay to use sinful means to get positive ends.

Conflict

This relational paradigm is tested when people disagree with you. It isn't hard to empower people who agree with you or not control people who are making good choices. It is when they're making dumb choices and running people (or you) over in the process, making your ability to stay true to your choice to honor others difficult.

People are people though, and so conflict is inevitable. There will always be disagreements, differences in values, and miscommunication, so we will always have opportunities to get better at building up one another.

The key to successfully navigating conflict in relationship is to properly handle the tension that arises as a result of the disagreement. This tension will naturally arise in any relationship within the process of conflict. It's actually a good thing; it means you value the relationship. You don't feel tension with people unless there is something you care about at stake.

The way we handle that tension makes all the difference. The important thing to distinguish between is the tension that arises within the relationship and the issue that is provoking the disagreement. The issue may affect the relationship, but it really is outside the relationship. Where people go wrong is they lose the relationship as the context for addressing the problem. When this happens, people wind up letting the issue come into the middle of their relationship and split them to opposite sides of it.

A better approach is to navigate the conflict within the context of the relationship. When a conflict arises, the conflict does not mean the relationship is fractured. As a result, we still honor and value the person, and we address the conflict as a unit together. We stand together both addressing the issue, not as two individuals on opposite sides of the issue.

In the kingdom, no issue is big enough to sacrifice our relationships. God defines his relationships with covenants; he's not splitting relationships over disagreements. His commitment is bigger than any issue we may not see eye-to-eye on. As a result, we can approach conflict safely. We don't tiptoe into conflict worried about losing the relationship because our commitment to each other as people goes deeper than whatever issue is at hand.

When handling conflict within the context of hierarchical relationships,[57] there are a few principles that are helpful to keep in mind. In order to successfully navigate conflict while honoring and empowering others, our goals are to:[58]

- Introduce consequences into a situation in order to teach and strengthen.
- Bring to the surface what people forget about themselves after they've failed.
- Send an invitation to strengthen a relational bond with someone.

---

[57] Parent to child, employer to employee, spiritual overseer to person overseen, etc.
[58] Taken from Chapter 7 of Danny Silk's book *Culture of Honor*.

- Apply pressure strategically in order to expose areas needing strength and grace.

There is a difference between consequences and punishment. The difference is that with consequences, people are empowered to clean up their own mess whereas with punishment, people are forced into compliance and hence disempowered. Every choice has consequences; there may be a breaking of trust in a relationship, or loss of privileges that the person is no longer considered worthy of.

When people face the consequences of their actions, a road back to intimacy is created. If someone intentionally makes a choice to hurt us, one consequence is that we may not feel safe around that person anymore. We make it clear to that person that as a result of what he or she has done, we don't feel safe with him or her anymore; and until he or she is ready to own the fact that his or her actions have hurt you and work through that, you're not going to be around him or her. This informs the person you still love him or her, empowers the person to clean up the mess, and extends an invitation to restored relationship when the person is ready to take responsibility for the consequences of his or her actions.

To learn how to manage relationships this way is a complete change for most of us. Take some time to reflect on how you interact with others. What is your current relational paradigm? How can you practice loving others and not controlling them?

Permission

In the process of growth in community, we continually come face-to-face with the fact that we have not yet arrived. God works through our circumstances and relationships to expose where He wants to bring us to maturity next. The way we view this process will either cause us to work with or against the maturing process.

There are two chief obstacles towards participating with the growth process. The first is pride. The extent to which we harbor pride within our heart is the extent to which we will feel hurt when God exposes something immature within us. As we let go of our pride, we drop any need to keep a pretense that we've got everything worked out. We can embrace the joy of living in reality: we are all on a journey and each person needs to grow in different places.

The second obstacle is that a skewed view of God can cause us to approach the process of growth from the wrong starting point. In the process of pointing us towards our next phase of growth, we can begin to feel that God is unsatisfied with our current place of maturity. We can believe that God is upset because of issues that we feel we should have already overcome by now.

The reality is that this kind of thinking projects an inaccurate picture onto God. God is love, and love is always patient and kind, full of goodness and mercy and bears, believes, hopes, and endures all things. When the work of God in our lives brings not-yet-redeemed sinful habits or other immaturities to the surface in our lives, this does not mean God is upset with us. It does not mean that God is on the verge of coming against us. It does not mean that God is removing favor from our lives; it means the Holy Spirit is allowing you to participate in the process of your growth.

As believers, we carry a wonderful amount of permission on our lives; when the Spirit of God starts to work in a specific area, permission to upgrade is implicit. The very nature of God's activity points to the next area of freedom. When God works to expose immaturity in our lives, we are always faced with a choice: we can come down on ourselves for having another area in our lives that needs attention, or we can view it as a prophetic word of the freedom that God wants to bring us into.

I want to choose to believe that any character flaw that God exposes is a prophecy of freedom to me. God never starts a work that he has not planned to bring to completion:

> *And I am sure of this, that he who began a good work in you will bring it to completion at the day of Jesus Christ. Philippians 1:6*

None of us have arrived, and we don't need to pretend that we have. God is at work in all of us; when God begins a process by exposing things in our lives, we can rejoice because we know the process of freedom has already begun. We can choose to agree with the upgrade and cooperate with our freedom, or we can choose to get upset and prolong the process.

When we learn to let go of our pride and really believe in the goodness of God, there is an incredible freedom. The process of growth is always in God's hands, whether we believe it is or not:

> *What then is Apollos? What is Paul? Servants through whom you believed, as the Lord assigned to each. I planted, Apollos watered, but God gave the growth. 1 Corinthians 3:5-6*

I don't even want to spend too much time watching my own process of growth. Why would I want to focus on that when I can focus on God instead? God is the one able to keep us from falling, not ourselves:

> *Now to him who is able to keep you from stumbling and to present you blameless before the presence of his glory with great joy. Jude 1:24*

So we can give him that burden and instead focus on who we are becoming in Him.

Celebrating Each Other's Gifts

It is imperative that as believers we learn to celebrate each other's gifts and to promote one another above ourselves. Jesus has a very interesting statement on the way that we view each other's giftings in Matthew:

> *"Whoever receives you receives me, and whoever receives me receives him who sent me. The one who receives a prophet because he is a prophet will receive a prophet's reward, and the one who receives a righteous person because he is a righteous person will receive a righteous person's reward. And whoever gives one of these little ones even a cup of cold water because he is a disciple, truly, I say to you, he will by no means lose his reward." Matthew 10:40-42*

Jesus draws a very interesting parallel here. He begins by asserting that the way we receive or accept or believe the Father is how we receive him. This passage follows one in which Jesus is discussing his purpose here on the earth. In effect, this statement is saying, "Look, this is who I am and the mission I'm on. I am the *gift* from God, and the way you receive that gift is the way you receive God."

Then Jesus turns that same concept around and points it at our interactions with each other. He says that to receive a prophet because he is a prophet means receiving a prophet's reward. In other words, if you bless and respect the gifting the person is walking in, you get to enter into the same rewards that person walks in. Likewise, the measure to which you receive someone (as a prophet or a righteous man) will determine the measure of reward that you get to enjoy, all the way down to a cup of cold water.

Paul actually refers to this same dynamic when talking about prophecy:

On the other hand, the one who prophesies speaks to people for their upbuilding and encouragement and consolation . . . the one who prophesies builds up the church. 1 Corinthians 14:3-4

Did you notice that? Paul says that prophecy is aimed at a *person*, but upbuilds the *church*. This is, in fact, Paul's main thrust of this whole section of scripture about tongues and prophecy: prophecy benefits everyone present, whereas tongues only benefits those that can understand. But how does prophecy upbuild the church if it's only aimed at individual people? Paul lets us know a few verses later when he reveals the reason tongues isn't upbuilding:

Otherwise, if you give thanks with your spirit, how can anyone in the position of an outsider say "Amen" to your thanksgiving when he does not know what you are saying? 1 Corinthians 14:16

Paul says the reason tongues aren't profitable is that people can't say "Amen." They can't come into agreement because they don't understand. With prophecy, because people understand, they can come into agreement. This corporate agreement unlocks corporate upbuilding. All are built up because all enter into the grace on the prophetic word whether it is directed at them or not.

Theology Anchor

The more we honor each other and each other's gifts, the more we gain access to their breakthrough.

Furthermore, Peter tells us:

As each has received a gift, use it to serve one another, as good stewards of God's varied grace: whoever speaks, as one who speaks oracles of God; whoever serves, as one who serves by the strength that God supplies—in order that in everything

God may be glorified through Jesus Christ. To him belong glory and dominion forever and ever. Amen. 1 Peter 4:10-11

Peter refers to using our gifts as stewarding God's varied grace. I love this picture! God's gifts on our lives are packets of grace that he enables us to walk in. Now remember our discussion of revelation and how revelation gives us access. If God puts grace on our lives in the form of gifts, then we can actually be revelations to each other of who God is, and in that process we gain access to that same gifting the other person has access to.

Let me give a specific example. Let's say we have someone with a pastoral gifting in the church. Their heart is to love and compassionately walk people through the pain they carry with them in life. In addition to that, let's add a prophetic person, someone whose passion is to hear the voice of God and experience what is happening in the spiritual realm. As these two interact, if they choose to recognize and bless each other's gifting, then it is possible for the pastoral person to begin to get a revelation of God as the God who speaks to his people, and the prophetic person will begin to get a revelation of God as a compassionate Father. As they begin to see who God is through each other, they gain access to that grace to give it away, and we have a pastoral person with a prophetic person's reward and a prophetic person with a pastoral person's reward.

This is brilliant and powerful because it means that as we learn to hold each other in right relationship and see God through each other, we get multiplicative impact. If we start with two people honoring and receiving each other, we get 2x2 = 4 total people-gift combinations. If we start with 10 we get 10x10 = 100!

Again, the issue of identity is paramount here. If we are not established in who we are and have not moved beyond the competitive nature of the orphan or poverty mentality, we'll always have a struggle fully celebrating the gifts God has put in others. We'll be

struggling against the void we feel internally; our celebration of others will be contingent on them not threatening our own performance.

Power Evangelism

Power evangelism played a critical role in the birthing of the Vineyard movement. In a real sense, it is part of our birthright.[59] John Wimber was working at Fuller Theological Seminary when through discussions with missionaries in other parts of the world, he discovered through their stories and insights that the supernatural was a powerful key to evangelism and church growth. Around the same time, Wimber was getting involved with the activity of signs and wonders in his church in Anaheim. In the early 1980s, John Wimber taught a course at Fuller that was called "MC510: Signs, Wonders and Church Growth," which featured teaching on the supernatural as well as clinic time to practice moving in the power of the Spirit. The main thrust of the teaching was that power evangelism—when the power of God accompanies a presentation of the gospel—is a biblical model of evangelism and a powerful tool for the church.

The course was both a little scandalous and a runaway success. In future iterations, people from all over the country came; however after a few rounds it was shut down at Fuller, and Wimber switched gears to become the founding father of the Vineyard movement. In my understanding, it was the opportunity to put this message to the test—that the power of God is a key tool for witnessing to the lost—that was one of the motivators for Wimber to start a church planting movement. Throughout the early days of the Vineyard, the main message didn't change: the power of God is a key tool to witness to the lost. It is deep in our Vineyard DNA. In my opinion, to lose power

---

[59] I recognize that not every church or student participating in the School of Kingdom Ministry calls the Vineyard their home church or movement. That's okay—while you're in the School of Kingdom Ministry you're participating in the fruit and destiny of the Vineyard as a movement, and you can consider it your birthright as well.

evangelism would be to lose an essential part of what God created the Vineyard for; it is something God has called us to as a tribe.

In the book of Romans, Paul writes this about the Israelite people who were the original people of God and had now largely turned against God:

> *For the gifts and the calling of God are irrevocable. Romans 11:2*

God has not removed the gift or the calling to power evangelism on the Vineyard and he never will; when he bestows a gift, he doesn't take it back. Whether we have been faithful to that call or not makes no difference. God has put it on the Vineyard as a movement permanently.[60] The only question is whether we will choose to step into it. I believe we would all do well to embrace that calling and run with it as far and as fast as we can.

The Process of Evangelism

It takes a process to make a Christian. While it is true in some sense that salvation is an event in that at one point a person turns their life over to Jesus and from then on their eternal salvation is secure, it is a process to lead up to that point and a process to move forward from that point. This process is captured in a diagnostic tool called the Engel scale:

---

[60] From what I understand the question of whether we have been faithful to that call is a subject of some disagreement in the movement. I'm not really interested in suggesting that we have or haven't, either as a movement or on a more individual level. What matters is whether we choose to embrace that call *now*. Whether we've been faithful or not, the option to choose to say yes *now* is always on the table.

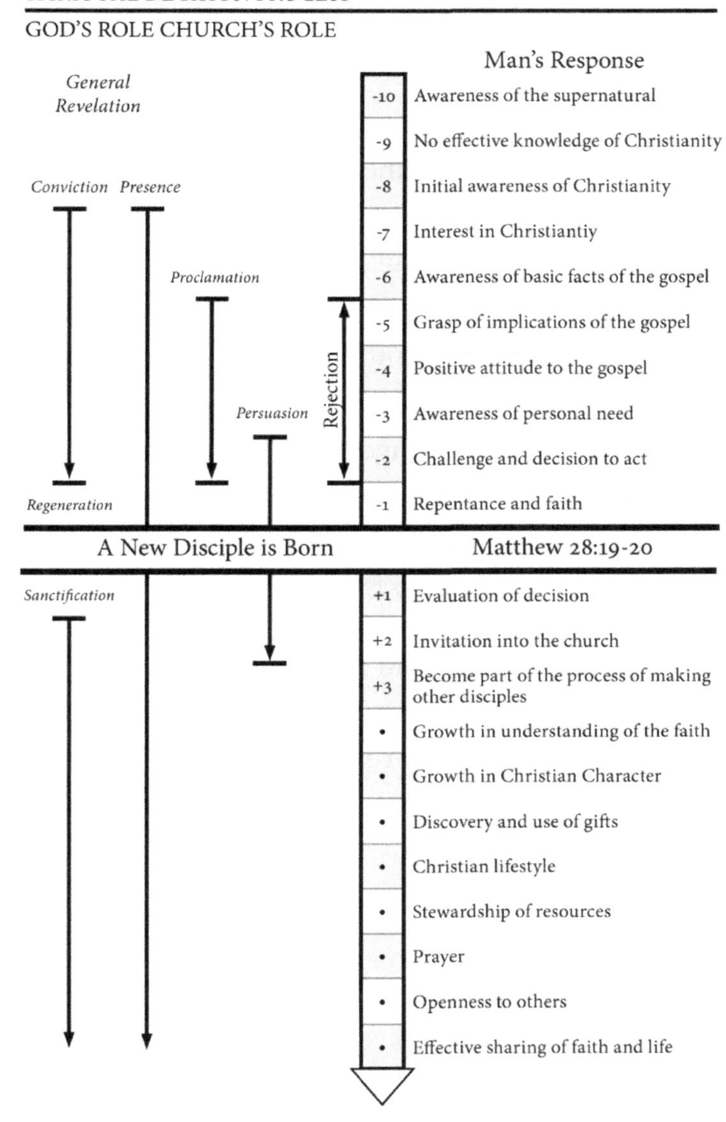

On the Engel scale shown above,[61] each person is described by a number that ranges from -8 to +5. Negative numbers aren't believers, and positive numbers are. The goal of evangelism then is to move people from wherever they are on the spectrum towards the positive direction.

While evangelizing, it is important to know where the person you are working with is at in that process. If we wind up treating a person like he or she is further along the process of becoming a Christian than he or she is, there is a significant chance we may push him or her away rather than help them. What Wimber found when he studied power evangelism is that power encounters tend to move a person forward on the Engel scale much more quickly than he or she otherwise would move. A person who is closed to the gospel message may change his or her mind when a Christian prays for healing for them or gives an accurate prophetic word about his or her life. This is the prime time to move into evangelism because the power encounter has opened him or her to the reality of the gospel in a way that rational arguments wouldn't be able to do.

This was the argument that Wimber put forth about power evangelism. Allow me to elaborate on it somewhat. Rather than creating a graph in one dimension, consider one in two dimensions, where two things are plotted: on the horizontal a person's openness to the gospel, and in the vertical a person's knowledge about the gospel. This is called the Gray Matrix:[62]

---

[61] Graphic from *Power Evangelism* by John Wimber and Kevin Springer, page 109 Copyright (2009), Gospel Light/Regal Books, Ventura, CA 93003. Used by permission. Adapted from *What's Gone Wrong with the Harvest?* by James F. Engel and Wilbert Norton (Zondervan, 1957).
[62] For more information about the Gray Matrix, see http://thegraymatrix.org/.

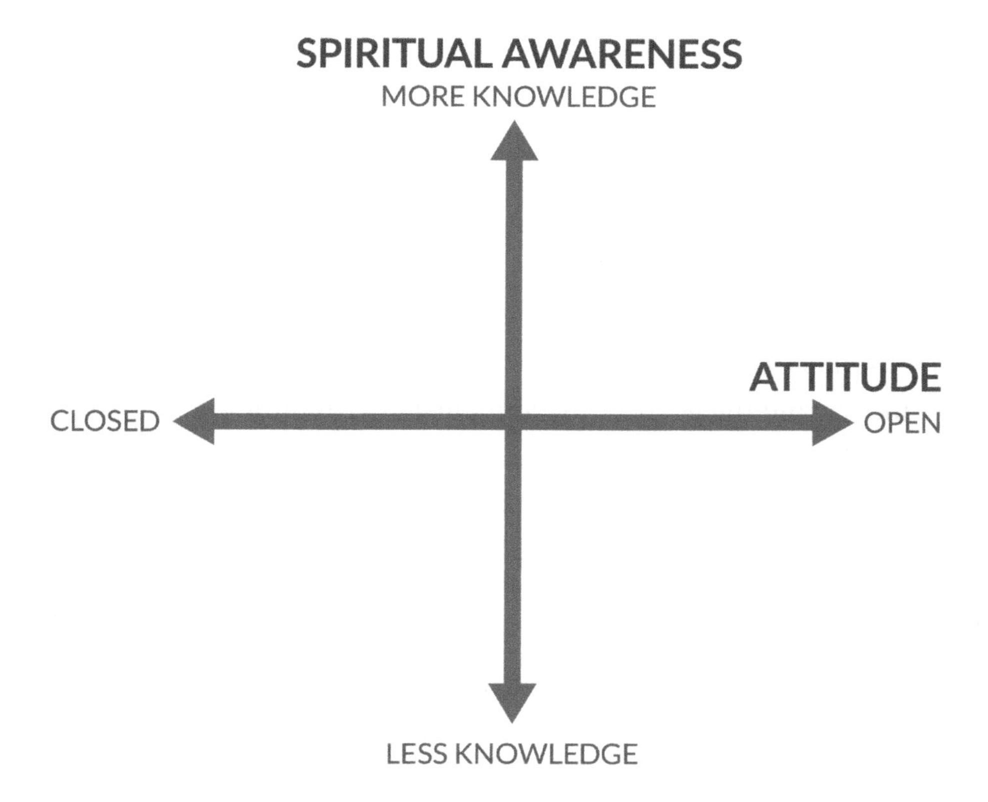

Any person then can be represented with a point on the plane. People will fall into one of four quadrants:

Lower Left: No Knowledge and Closed Attitude

This is the "don't know, don't care" section of the graph. People who are actively involved and committed to another faith (including atheism or agnosticism) tend to fall into this quadrant.

Lower Right: No Knowledge but Open Attitude

This is the seeker quadrant. Most evangelism is aimed at this quadrant. Once a person has interest in the gospel, the task of evangelism is largely educational in nature. As a person who is already interested is educated, all he needs is to be presented with an opportunity to accept salvation.

Upper Left: Knowledge but Closed Attitude

This is the post-churched quadrant. People who know the gospel but have since lost interest go here. This tends to be a difficult quadrant to reach because they feel that since they already understand the gospel they don't feel Christianity has more to offer. The truth, of course, is that if they really knew Jesus as a person and were relating to him as such, they wouldn't have lost interest because Jesus is amazing. People here tend to see Christianity as largely doctrinal or philosophical, not relational.

Upper Right: Knowledge and Open Attitude

This is the healthy quadrant where we want to be moving people towards: a person who understands and is invested in the gospel.

Now as I mentioned before, most evangelism is targeted at the lower-right quadrant. The two left quadrants are typically very difficult to reach evangelistically because it is difficult to *create* interest in someone. Education will move a person along vertically on this graph, but horizontal motion is trickier.

A person will move horizontally due to *experience*. This is the real strength of power evangelism. A power encounter provides horizontal motion. A person generally won't learn much about the gospel in a power encounter. They may learn some about God, but the true strength is that it forces the reality of the gospel. When people encounter God, they become interested.

It becomes clear that power evangelism is a unique tool because it is designed to reach people that most other evangelistic methods aren't targeted at. *We've got the tool that the church needs to reach the other group of people out there*! Does a power encounter

by itself do everything? No, because in addition to their experience, people need some education so they can be moving along horizontally and vertically; but a power encounter is a power tool for inducing rapid horizontal movement in the person as depicted on the Gray Matrix.

As people experience motion towards the right in the Gray Matrix, that opens them up towards experiencing motion upward as well. If we try to move people upwards above the level of their openness, our attempts are usually dismissed as irrelevant. At that point, we can either choose to make the person care about something because it is important to us (this is manipulation and is *bad*), or we can give up. Experiencing the gospel opens people to education about the gospel.

> **Theology Anchor**
> The message educates; power creates interest.

This is why the sharpest edge of power evangelism is not with complete strangers. Power evangelism with strangers is great and very good practice, but adding a relationship evangelism dynamic as well results in multiplied fruit. There are multiple opportunities to influence the person and move them along the process, both in experience and in education. Friends and family are prime targets for power evangelism.

Power Evangelism and Evangelism Contexts

One common misconception that I've seen is that power evangelism is primarily practiced in the context of street evangelism. I think that to view power evangelism as nothing more than street evangelism is really to miss the point entirely. Power evangelism is a *strategy* of evangelism; our evangelism strategy is to introduce the power of God into the discussion as evidence of the reality of God. There are many strategies of evangelism; seeker sensitivity is one, discussion of the afterlife is another.

Street evangelism on the other hand is a *context* of evangelism. It describes the format of evangelism and really is only one context for practicing power evangelism. It is a useful training ground because it is an opportunity that is accessible to anyone (not everyone has the opportunity to minister to large crowds for example, which is another context of evangelism), and it is a place where opportunities are readily available. This is why we practice evangelism in this context in class. The thinking is that if we work out our skills in an environment where practice is readily available, then they will be ready when we need them in the other contexts.

Our goal then, in training power evangelism is not to produce a crew of street evangelists. Some people will enjoy that context and do well, but others won't. All believers are called to evangelize, but each of us will feel most comfortable in a unique context. So part of your journey is to discover what context is the best fit for you and try to be most effective in that context.[63] There are a number of evangelism contexts in Scripture:[64]

---

[63] Of course there are opportunities that arise outside of our most comfortable context, and we can't use this line of reasoning as an excuse to avoid the ways to partner with God right in front of us either.
[64] This list originally comes from Andrew Wommack. http://www.awmi.net/devotion/jesus/dec_18

Context	Scriptural Examples
House to house	Acts 5:42—And every day, in the temple and from house to house, they did not cease teaching and preaching that the Christ is Jesus.
One-on-one	Acts 13:7—He was with the proconsul, Sergius Paulus, a man of intelligence, who summoned Barnabas and Saul and sought to hear the word of God. Philip & the Ethiopian eunuch in Acts 8.
Large crowds	Peter on the day of Pentecost in Acts 2. Paul at Lystra in Acts 14.
Entire cities	Acts 8:5-6—Philip went down to the city of Samaria and proclaimed to them the Christ. And the crowds with one accord paid attention to what was being said by Philip when they heard him and saw the signs that he did.
Public debate and preaching	Peter and John in the temple in Acts 3. Paul in Athens in Acts 17.
Media	John 20:31—These are written so that you may believe that Jesus is the Christ, the Son of God, and that by believing you may have life in his name. The gospels were the original evangelism tracts.

Paul seems to want to make it clear that evangelism in each context and to each audience is helpful and necessary:

How I did not shrink from declaring to you anything that was profitable, and teaching you in public and from house to house, testifying both to Jews and to Greeks of repentance toward God and of faith in our Lord Jesus Christ.
Acts 20:20-21

> **Theology Anchor**
> Power is a method, not a context. Find the context that works for you.

Likewise I commend to each of you to experiment with different contexts and find out what fits you the best. When I first began with power evangelism, I spent a lot of my time practicing a one-on-one type of evangelism that could be labeled as street evangelism. As I developed skills there and experimented with various contexts, I found that I do better in a more public form of evangelism. It is much more natural for me to hold an evangelism meeting than to engage with people one-on-one. This way evangelism partners with the teaching gift I carry. I can start off teaching then mix in power as the driving force for evangelism. It probably took me the better part of a year of practice to figure this out though. Only after having practiced a number of times in a number of different contexts did that become clear.

Now that I'm aware that public meetings are a more natural fit for me, I try to focus more of my efforts there. I began to look for contexts to practice this type of evangelism. One fruitful example was when we began to minister with healing meetings in the county jail. The first time we went in, we had hour-long meetings with about 20-25 attendees each. In both meetings, we experienced dramatic healings and had 4-5 first time commitments to the Lord and about that many rededications as well. In that one meeting I saw probably as much fruit as months of practice on the streets.

Likewise, I would encourage you to experiment with the contexts you can. Maybe house-to-house evangelism is the most natural context for you. Great! Then get to it in

that context! Whichever is the most natural fit is where you should be focusing your efforts; evangelism is supposed to be fun, not painful.

Power and Evangelism

Another facet of power evangelism is the realization that the order of power and evangelism isn't necessarily fixed. It's not always power then evangelism; sometimes it's evangelism then power. The power opens the door to evangelism, but it's also true that evangelism also opens the door to power. It goes both ways. On one hand, the power opens the door for the reception of the message:

> *It was declared at first by the Lord, and it was attested to us by those who heard, while God also bore witness by signs and wonders and various miracles and by gifts of the Holy Spirit distributed according to his will. Hebrews 2:3-4*

But on the other hand, the message opens the door for the demonstration of power:

> *For I am not ashamed of the gospel, for it is the power of God for salvation to everyone who believes, to the Jew first and also to the Greek. Romans 1:16*

If the gospel is the power of God for salvation, then to share the gospel is to share the power of God! Don't forget that the gospel is not just another message; it is actually a message that contains power.

This means that in our journey as growing power evangelists, our open doors are not just opportunities to demonstrate power, but also opportunities to share about the good news. We grab either one as an opportunity to share and lead to the other. Indeed biblically it seems that without power we're not actually witnesses. Remember Jesus' words to the disciples before the ascension:

But you will receive power when the Holy Spirit has come upon you, and you will be my witnesses in Jerusalem and in all Judea and Samaria, and to the end of the earth. Acts 1:8

Jesus instructs them to wait until power comes, and *then* they will be witnesses. This implication here is really profound; the disciples already had the message! They already could have shared about Jesus and his teachings, but by Jesus' own definition this isn't being a witness. According to Jesus, you can't be a witness without power!

This means we need to shift our understanding of evangelism. We tend to think of evangelism as sharing the news about Jesus, but it's clear that Jesus means more than that. We aren't witnesses to Jesus' message; we are witnesses to who he is. Jesus wants us to share who he is, not just the message of who he is, and to share who Jesus is with people requires power. Jesus is the most powerful guy around, so to represent him requires power.

Becoming a Power Evangelist

According to Robby Dawkins, there are four categories of power evangelism:

- Healing
- Prophecy
- Deliverance
- Ministry of the Presence of God

These are the four main "power tools" to power evangelism. There are, of course, others that could be used (dream interpretation, for instance, is popular as well), but these provide a fantastic starting point.

Becoming a power evangelist is a process, and it helps a lot to have a road map to get there. My road map to being a power evangelist is captured on the next page. I would suggest you assess where you are on this road map. What is the next stage to get to? What do you need to learn in your current stage before trying to move to the next? Power evangelism is a compound skill set; it requires the ability to do a number of different things and to know how and when to flow from one into another.

Power Evangelism Growth Process

Identity	•The bedrock for the practice of power evangelism •Every other step draws off of and feeds back into who you are in Christ
Activation in Spiritual Gifts	•Basic prayer training course
Practice in Created Spaces	•Small group •After service •Holy Spirit Night
Practice Outside Created Spaces	•Prophetic words to people anytime or place •Healing of physical conditions where prayer wasn't asked for
Use your Eyes Outside Church	•Start with healing conditions you can see •Work your way up in RISK with conditions •Start to get feedback and find out if they're healed
Add Revelatory Component	•Start with words of knowledge for healing only •Practice prophesying to people after prayer •Move into prophesy more generally
Lean into Evangelism	•Power comes first, then evangelism
Keep adding RISK	•Groups of people •Bolder claims about what Jesus will do
Train Others	•Introduce others to the process & start taking them through it

Identity is the bedrock of power evangelism. Once you know who you are, you are empowered to give away to others. Before that, you'll try to use power evangelism to figure out who you are. You'll be disappointed when people won't let you pray for them or when you do and people don't get healed. These reactions are a symptom that we're doing power evangelism for us, not for the other people. Once we do learn who we are and are empowered to self-differentiate (who I am doesn't depend on what you think of me), then we don't have anything to lose and we can truly give freely.

I started by focusing on the healing skill. I recommend starting with this skill because you can identify people in need of healing with your physical eyes. There are people with limps, casts, or canes everywhere, and you never have to guess about whether they could use healing. The other skill sets require a little more revelatory input. Because you can find people that already need healing, focusing on this category will help you with a number of skills to develop that support the encounter. Specifically, you'll get good at approaching people, learning how to ask to pray for people, and how to not come across like a salesman. All of those are important skills that can be honed; as we do, we'll get much more effective at power evangelism.

The truth is, when I got started, I wasn't even trying to get people healed. I wanted to see them healed, but the point when you start isn't to see healing, it's to learn how to talk with people and how to be a light. I got comfortable praying in public, and I learned how to not be nervous or feel as if I failed if the person didn't get healed. I learned how to approach "big" conditions such as wheelchairs and casts. To step into each of these skills and abilities is a victory.

Once I was more comfortable ministering to unbelievers, I started to try to mix in more prophetic and revelatory gifts into the encounters. I would prophesy to people after I had prayed for them, or I would try to identify a word of knowledge about healing. Again, choosing a focus (healing) for a word of knowledge helped me concentrate on a particular area, which was helpful to know where to start and to measure my growth. From there, I started being more comfortable just talking with people and prophesying to them in the course of our conversation.

Finally as I started to see power pick up, I leaned into evangelism more. Generally power leads to evangelism, so I didn't even make my focus the lost when I started. I'm getting better at evangelism that's probably my growth edge right now.

This process doesn't have to be the same for everyone, but I would recommend starting with a goal of this kind. Whatever it looks like for you, learn how to break it down into small, concrete steps and move towards them one at a time.

When I first got started practicing power evangelism, I tried to record how many people I prayed for (I used a website called 42goals.com). This helped me track how many people I prayed for, how many healings or prophetic words I would get, etc. I found seeing my progress helped me continue to stay invested through the discouraging times. I tracked:

- # of people I prayed for within ministry settings
- # of people I prayed for outside of ministry settings
- # of rejections of prayer offered
- # of words of knowledge given
- # of prophetic words given
- # of healings that occurred

This helped me see my consistency and my growth in a number of areas. It helped me realize where I'm growing (and thus need to be focusing my energy), and where I might be backing off my growth and should probably reengage. I don't know that I would say tracking data like this is for everyone, but by adding some quantitative measures to my goals allowed me to know whether I was improving or not.

Core Values of Power Evangelism

It can be very helpful to articulate some core values for power evangelism. Just like our Code of Ethics gives us a set of principles to help us make decisions and point us towards the person we want to become, pinning down some core values for power evangelism will help us make decisions about how to react in the moment and how to treat people as we evangelize.[65]

Love

If we have encountered the love of God and been changed thoroughly by it, then love will become the motivation we have to evangelize others. We will spread love because we have been loved. In a real sense, our love is the completion of God's love towards others:

> *Beloved, if God so loved us, we also ought to love one another. No one has ever seen God; if we love one another, God abides in us and his love is perfected in us.*
> *1 John 4:11-12*

If we do not evangelize out of love, then we probably will do it out of guilt and a sense of religious duty. We do not *have* to evangelize; we get to.

Honor

Honor is about celebrating the worth and value of a person, regardless of who they are or how they are acting towards you. We have been honored by God, and we honor others out of that as well. Honor prevents people from becoming projects. People with sicknesses aren't projects to be fixed, they are people to be valued and loved. We

---

[65] These core values are taken from Chris Overstreet's book *A Practical Guide to Evangelism—Supernaturally.*

appreciate and celebrate the person for who they are and the value they have regardless of whether they are open to us praying for them or not.

Honor also is about respecting the environment we are in. Often power evangelism happens in the marketplace: a store, mall, or company. We need to be respectful of location in which we are ministering to people. We want to bless *everybody*, even storeowners. If we are harassing customers or creating an environment where people are uncomfortable, then we need to learn to respect the environment. We can be radical without being dishonoring.

Presence

We are called to be people of the presence of God. This is what sets us apart as believers: the presence of God within us and among us. As we power evangelize, we should be operating out of a place of abiding in the presence of God. We are simply giving away what we are presently experiencing. When we experience the presence of God, we can give it away to people too. Ministry of the manifest presence of God involves asking the Holy Spirit to touch people in a concrete way they can feel in their bodies. This can be a powerful tool to open people's eyes to the reality of God and his intervention in our daily lives.

Power

Without power, we cannot witness to who Jesus is. Power is vital to displaying the reality of the gospel that we are advertising to others:

> *For the kingdom of God does not consist in talk but in power. 1 Corinthians 4:20*

We need to expect the power of God to be at our fingertips at any moment. The Holy Spirit lives within us and longs to get out and touch people through us. Jesus has

passed the commission of destroying the works of the devil to us, and we need his power to do that.

Joy

Joy empowers us to not be bothered by the fact that we are living under a different set of rules. It provides the strength to lean into the goodness of God in the face of opposition:

> *And do not be grieved, for the joy of the Lord is your strength. Nehemiah 8:10*

Joy also makes us attractive. Everyone wants to be happy; if we display a joy that allows us to laugh in the face of trials, others will want what we have!

Faith

Faith through the form of R-I-S-K creates a space for the power of God to be made manifest. As we demonstrate our faith in God, not only does God show up and powerfully impact people's lives, but also the reality of Christianity is on display. People are often stunned by the reality that people actually believe this stuff enough to act on it, and that can often be just as much a witness to someone else as a healing or prophecy.

As we practice power evangelism, try to embrace a *lifestyle* of risk. This isn't about developing a skill that we turn on and off; it's about transforming who we are to the point where we're willing to risk in any situation. Once we embrace a lifestyle of risk we open the door for God to use us at any time and any place.

Ministering out of Our Identity

Power evangelism, along with all other ministry, needs to flow out of our identity. Until we are grounded in a sense of who we are as believers and the value that God already has for us, there is a tendency to try to earn favor from God or with people using power evangelism. It is a way to try to *earn* value rather than walk in a heart posture of *receiving* the value that God has already demonstrated for us.

What are the symptoms that we aren't ministering out of our identity? The primary one is that we spend a lot of time *trying*. You don't have to try to be something you already are. If you really believe you're part of God's family, you will naturally act like you have access to his resources. You don't have to muster anything up because that's who you are. Effort is a hint that you're trying to perform at a value higher than your identity.

On the flip side, when we are walking in our identity as believers, power evangelism isn't difficult—it is simply responding to the situation in an appropriate and natural way. We've got a big Father God who loves us and has the power to change any situation for the better. There is still risk involved, but the sting of risk has been removed because failure does not mean I lose value as a person. If you pray for someone and he or she isn't healed or try to give a prophetic word that isn't accurate, that's okay. You're still loved, you're still accepted, and you're still valued. God is not upset, angry, or disappointed. We tried, we'll learn, and we move on.

Additionally, until we learn to carry our own identity, we aren't doing ministry for the right reason. If we do not accept the value given to us from God and we are trying to perform to earn our value, the truth is we're not actually loving people; we're *using* them. If my feelings are hurt when someone shoots me down for prayer, then I'm trying to get some of my value from their approval.

Paul is very clear that the ends do not justify the means in the kingdom:

> *If I speak in the tongues of men and of angels, but have not love, I am a noisy gong or a clanging cymbal. And if I have prophetic powers, and understand all mysteries and all knowledge, and if I have all faith, so as to remove mountains, but have not love, I am nothing. If I give away all I have, and if I deliver up my body to be burned, but have not love, I gain nothing. 1 Corinthians 13:1-3*

It's not okay for us to use other people to try to earn our value. That needs to be settled between us and God. Only once we have learned to love ourselves through God's eyes can we actually love others. This is why Jesus says we love others *as ourselves*. Power evangelism, like all ministry, needs to be out of an overflow of love from our heart. As we encounter the love of God and are filled with his presence, we need to be so full to overflowing with God that we leak his presence everywhere we go!

There is always a learning curve when we are practicing a new skill. There will be times when God pushes us to the edge of our comfort zone. All of that is okay, and God is honored by us stepping out to be obedient. This is part of the reason that in this class we practice power evangelism from the beginning of our school year; we just need to make sure that we don't turn power evangelism (or any other type of ministry) into something we are doing as works to try and get something from God. God has already given us everything through Jesus. We don't need to add anything more than that.

One last observation: I've found that power evangelism, as well as other power ministry, goes much better if I can keep a *learning* focus. I've not arrived with healing, prophecy, deliverance, or anything else. Any opportunity that comes up is then practice. I'm learning how to do this. I know the Bible says it's available, so it's up to me to learn how to do it with God. This takes the pressure off. Everything is a chance to try new things, to see what works and what doesn't. I've found that as I start to drift away from a learner's mentality, I tend to get more caught up in a performance mentality.

Moving from Love or "Sealing the Deal"

It is important to move away from a "seal the deal" mentality with evangelism. Most people have felt pressured by guilt into sharing the gospel with their friends and family in an attempt to make converts. There can be an underlying focus on getting people to pray a specific prayer or try to push people along a spiritual journey faster than they are ready or are interested. This again is a manipulative motivation to doing evangelism. If we really are moving from love, our goal is not to make converts, but to love people. Jesus himself said that with evangelism, one sows and another reaps. In other words, there is a process that needs to be engaged that results in life change and conversion. If our goal is to hit the end of the process, we can force people through too quickly and actually hurt people.

Don't settle for an "always be closing" type of evangelism. This type doesn't see people as people and doesn't move from love. Love people purely and bless them wherever they are and leave the process up to God. When people are ready, they'll want to have what they recognize in us.

Prophecy

Scripturally, prophecy is a gift that is available to every believer. This was foreshadowed by a statement made by Moses when the Spirit came upon two people in the Israelite camp and they began to prophesy. Joshua suggests that Moses stop them from prophesying, and Moses' response was:

> *But Moses said to him, "Are you jealous for my sake? Would that all the Lord's people were prophets, that the Lord would put his Spirit on them!" Numbers 11:29*

The very thing that Moses mentions in this verse, the descending of the Holy Spirit upon the people of the Lord, happens in Acts 2. Peter stands up and quoting Joel 2 explains that exactly what Moses had wished has now come true:

> *But this is what was uttered through the prophet Joel:*
>
> *And in the last days it shall be, God declares,*
> *that I will pour out my Spirit on all flesh,*
> *and your sons and your daughters shall prophesy,*
> *and your young men shall see visions,*
> *and your old men shall dream dreams;*
> *even on my male servants and female servants*
> *in those days I will pour out my Spirit, and they shall prophesy. Acts 2:16-18*

As the Spirit of the Lord descends on his people, one aspect is the empowering to prophesy. This is completed in Paul's perspective on the accessibility of prophecy in the gathering of believers:

Pursue love, and earnestly desire the spiritual gifts, especially that you may prophesy . . . For you can all prophesy one by one, so that all may learn and all be encouraged, and the spirits of prophets are subject to prophets.
1 Corinthians 14:1,31-32

As such, we should expect that prophecy can be part of every believer's life. There is never a question of whether a believer can prophesy, but rather whether he or she desires to.

What is Prophecy?

As we discussed earlier in the unit on the Holy Spirit, prophecy is more than just speaking out something God has revealed to you. It takes more than revelation to prophesy. Prophecy is connecting people to the heart of God. It is plugging them into who they are in the Lord and who the Lord wants to be for them right now.

Simply put, it's not just saying what you've heard God say, it's God saying through you what you've heard him say. Because it's actually God speaking through you, prophetic speech is fundamentally different than non-prophetic speech. The Bible makes it clear that our speech has power:

Death and life are in the power of the tongue, and those who love it will eat its fruits. Proverbs 18:21

But prophetic speech contains weight in the spiritual realm that surpasses our normal speech, powerful as that already is. Jesus mentions this in a passage where his followers had found one of his teachings offensive:

It is the Spirit who gives life; the flesh is no help at all. The words that I have spoken to you are spirit and life. John 6:63

Jesus says that only the Spirit can deposit life; without the Spirit it won't happen. The words he's spoken have substance in the spirit realm that release life in the person. When God speaks through Jesus (who only said what he heard the Father say), the words released are spirit. Likewise when God living in us speaks through us, the words released are spirit and can impart life. Peter makes it clear this is a power that goes beyond the power of other words:

> *Simon Peter answered him, "Lord, to whom shall we go? You have the words of eternal life." John 6:68*

Only Jesus had the words of eternal life,[66] so Peter knew that even if he didn't understand what Jesus said, or even was offended by it, he couldn't go anywhere else and get it. When God speaks, the words released are creative and dynamic in nature:

> *For as the rain and the snow come down from heaven*
> *and do not return there but water the earth,*
> *making it bring forth and sprout,*
> *giving seed to the sower and bread to the eater,*
> *so shall my word be that goes out from my mouth;*
> *it shall not return to me empty,*
> *but it shall accomplish that which I purpose,*
> *and shall succeed in the thing for which I sent it. Isaiah 55:10-11*

[66] Notice the text says that Jesus has the words *of* eternal life, not *about* eternal life. When Jesus speaks he releases life connected to eternity in us. This is exactly what he was saying in verse 63: only the Spirit has the ability to release the life of eternity in us *now*. Jesus felt it was important for his disciples to realize that even though his teaching was offensive to their minds they recognize that it released life to them through the Spirit.

Theology Anchor
Prophecy is God's word spoken through us.

Prophecy is God releasing his word *through* us. I believe that Paul is talking about this dynamic in a passage in Ephesians:

> *Let no corrupting talk come out of your mouths, but only such as is good for building up, as fits the occasion, that it may give grace to those who hear. Ephesians 4:29*

He indicates that our speech can *give grace* to those who hear. That's a really amazing statement; our speech can release the favor of God to people! Remember that grace is the means of the kingdom coming. Our speech has the ability to release the flow of the kingdom into people's lives. This is what prophecy is; it is speech that dynamically affects what is happening in the spiritual realm.

When we understand this, we can see why the nature of prophecy seems to change between the Old Testament and the New Testament. The prophetic books in the Bible (Isaiah–Malachi) tend to contain two major themes:

1. *The heart of God for his people.* God almost seems overly emotional in these books because of the pain and anguish that he is going through as a result of the choices of his people and at the same time the heavenly promises he still intends to lift them up to. The purpose of this was to reveal who God is and who the Israelites are. This function still exists largely today. Revealing the heart of God to a person in a personal way is a large part of prophecy.
2. *Instruction about what is coming in the future.* This has slightly changed in the New Testament. Remember in the Old Testament, the people of God were under an external covenant. Their relationship with God was based on what each of them would *do* for one another. By revealing what was going to happen, God would provide an opportunity for his people to prepare themselves to uphold their end of the covenant and to show how God is upholding his end of the

covenant. This has changed in the New Testament because now we are under an internal covenant; the concern is not what we *do* so much as what is the condition of our heart. For God to prepare us to uphold our end of the covenant here, there is a shift. No longer should we expect the default mode of prophecy to be prediction of the future (although that can certainly be a part), but rather we should expect a *relational* connection. Who does God want to be for us in the next season? What is the Lord growing in us and how can we position ourselves to experience what he has for us in this time?

As you can see, the purpose of prophecy is more or less unchanged across the divide between the Old and New Testaments, but the types of prophetic words delivered will differ under the two covenants. This is because each covenant has different terms and conditions, so the same purpose finds expression in different ways. In both covenants, it is about revealing the heart of God and positioning ourselves within our covenant relationship with Him. Because our covenant has changed, we can expect prophecy to be more related to our identity and our life in the Lord than is depicted in the Old Testament. This is the heart of prophecy.

Prophetic words tend to involve at least one of four aspects:[67]

- **Now words**: A now word provides perspective on where we are currently positioned in the Lord. It gives us a bit of map in terms of the terrain we're navigating.
- **Confirming words**: A confirming word provides strength to continue to fight. It reassures the person they are on the track God has put them on and to maintain their focus even though they may feel as if they have lost their momentum.
- **Future words**: A future word connects where we are with where we are going. It gives context to the present and may even help us chart the course for what direction to be moving towards.

---

[67] This list is taken from pages 116-118 in Graham Cooke's *Prophecy and Responsibility*.

- **New words**: New words indicate a shift in the spiritual winds. It indicates something that the Lord is preparing for us that may be something totally new and unexpected.

Methods of Prophecy

Prophecy tends to flow through one of two methods. In Kris Vallotton's book *Developing a Supernatural Lifestyle,* he defines prophecy as having both *foretelling* and *forthtelling* components.[68] These components are relevant in future directed prophecy; that is future words and new words as discussed above.

Foretelling is the dimension of prophecy that most people think of when they hear the word *prophecy*. It is seeing the future in advance and revealing what has been seen. Because the Lord exists outside of time, he can reveal to us what hasn't yet occurred. Graham Cooke is fond of saying "Prophecy is history written in advance." This captures the idea of foretelling prophecy quite well.

A clear example of foretelling captured in scripture is Jesus foretelling the destruction of the temple:

> *And as he came out of the temple, one of his disciples said to him, "Look, Teacher, what wonderful stones and what wonderful buildings!" And Jesus said to him, "Do you see these great buildings? There will not be left here one stone upon another that will not be thrown down." Mark 13:1-2*

Foretelling prophecy is often given to the end of encouraging someone and giving them an anchor point for moving forward. At the time it can look more like the exact opposite of the prophecy is happening before the prophetic word comes true. This is

---

[68] *Developing a Supernatural Lifestyle* by Kris Vallotton, page 187.

why, in fact, you were given the prophetic word. Without it you may not realize where you're going to wind up and may lose hope. Furthermore, as we hold on to the prophetic word by faith, the very essence of the prophetic word is formed in us. There is an interesting verse in the Psalms that refers to Joseph and the prophecy over his life while he was in prison:

> *until what he had said came to pass,*
> *the word of the Lord tested him. Psalm 105:19*

Often first you test a prophetic word, then it tests you. The grace released to you by the prophetic word is what empowers you through the testing, which actually forms the heart of the word in you.

One last comment on foretelling prophecy: we prophesy in accordance with our faith (Romans 12:6), and faith works through love (Galatians 5:6), so prophecy follows love. Don't primarily try to prophesy; try to love the person, and you may find that God gives you something that centers them and gives them hope for the future.

For example, one Sunday afternoon, I found myself thinking about a friend of mine. Recently, he and his wife had experienced the death of two close friends, the latter being just that week. I had talked with her and ministered to her that morning at church but hadn't had a chance to talk with the husband at all. That afternoon I was thinking about him and wanted to convey that I appreciated and valued him, so I sent him a quick text. Right after I sent that text I felt I heard the Lord saying that a week from that day his family was going to experience a shift in the spirit. The family had been experiencing a number of tensions, including financial pressure and a son that was walking apart from the Lord.

I sent him a follow-up text sharing what I felt I heard the Lord saying. Within the next month their son began to warm up considerably to the faith and to God and the wife got a significantly better job that not only paid better, but also allowed her to spend more time at home as well!

Notice though that only after I reached out to him in love did I begin to hear what the Father was saying about them. I didn't have that word before I sent the text. I wasn't even thinking about prophecy at all!

Forthtelling operates differently; instead of telling the future in advance, we actually cause the future to happen through our speech! In a sense, as we speak it creates a gap that opens the space for what has been spoken to happen. This mechanism is also referred to as "the kingdom announcement." Possibly the clearest example of forthtelling prophecy is Ezekiel in the valley of dry bones:

> *The hand of the LORD was upon me, and he brought me out in the Spirit of the LORD and set me down in the middle of the valley; it was full of bones. And he led me around among them, and behold, there were very many on the surface of the valley, and behold, they were very dry. And he said to me, "Son of man, can these bones live?" And I answered, "O Lord GOD, you know." Then he said to me, "Prophesy over these bones, and say to them, O dry bones, hear the word of the LORD. Thus says the Lord GOD to these bones: Behold, I will cause breath to enter you, and you shall live. And I will lay sinews upon you, and will cause flesh to come upon you, and cover you with skin, and put breath in you, and you shall live, and you shall know that I am the LORD."*
>
> *So I prophesied as I was commanded. And as I prophesied, there was a sound, and behold, a rattling, and the bones came together, bone to its bone. And I looked, and behold, there were sinews on them, and flesh had come upon them, and skin had*

covered them. But there was no breath in them. Then he said to me, "Prophesy to the breath; prophesy, son of man, and say to the breath, Thus says the Lord GOD: Come from the four winds, O breath, and breathe on these slain, that they may live." So I prophesied as he commanded me, and the breath came into them, and they lived and stood on their feet, an exceedingly great army. Ezekiel 37:1-10

> **Theology Anchor**
> Foretelling prophecy sees the future. Forthtelling prophecy creates the future.

Both foretelling and forthtelling require risk, although the result of taking the risk actually is quite different. If you choose not to step out on a foretelling word, the result will still happen even if we don't speak it. With a forthtelling word, if we choose not to speak the prophetic word, then what we see won't happen!

Forthtelling can sometimes be a useful tool to keep in mind while ministering to someone. There are times when for the ministry to move into another level the Lord allows us to participate in the process by releasing us to speak it into being. If we choose not to speak out, the ministry will level off.

I find that with forthtelling that I often do it in response to unction in the Spirit. I'll give you two examples:

A few years ago we were running our basic prayer training class, and I was talking with a young woman. She was sharing with me that in a few months she was moving to Redding to attend Bethel's School of Supernatural Ministry. I knew a little bit about her because she was the daughter of a Vineyard pastor not far from my location. As I was talking with her, she made it clear that she was excited to go to Bethel and was more or less ready to move on from the Vineyard. I began to feel almost a sense of injustice that people who are passionate about the supernatural need to be in the Vineyard and help us restore our birthright, so right in the middle of the conversation I put my hand on her shoulder and prayed a short prayer, "God, bring her back; we need people like her." She responded by saying something to the effect of "No! I don't want to come back!"

She moved to Redding and began to attend the school, and neither of us thought much more about it. I was busy with other things, until about halfway through the year she sent me a message telling me she was having dreams about the Vineyard and felt that she was hearing God say she should come back to our church to do an internship! She did wind up coming back and interning with me. I was always curious whether what I had said had changed her opinion about the Vineyard, so about halfway through her internship I asked her, at which point I discovered she had completely forgotten about the whole interaction until right then!

Another example happened as I was driving down the road one day. There is a private Christian school on one of the roads I frequently drive on to work and back. Right across the street from this Christian school was an eastern spirituality and medicine practice building that as far as I could tell had been abandoned for a long time, but it still had the sign and so forth up. As I drove down the street one day, the presence of this building made something rise up in my spirit. It wasn't right for the enemy to have a foothold, even if only a sign in my town! As this unction came upon me I spoke out something along the lines of, "[To the enemy] Your hold on that building is broken! [To the church] You will be a church, in Jesus name!" Literally two weeks later, I saw the sign on the building had been replaced as a Spanish speaking Pentecostal church that was opening shortly. I honestly don't know whether my forthtelling made a difference as to whether the church would meet there or not, but I do know I experienced a moving in my spirit and two weeks later the building was a church. That doesn't seem like a coincidence to me.

In both instances, the forthtelling was in response to something that was deposited in my spirit. As I spoke out what God put in my spirit, it released things in the spirit realm that caused events to come to pass.

The Three Phases of Prophecy

How then, do we prophesy? Prophecy tends to have three steps: *revelation*, *interpretation*, and *application*. (For more information on the practical aspects of prophecy, see the "The Process of Prophecy" in the skill development section.)

Revelation is the first step. It is the reception of supernatural information. Revelation comes in many forms. (To review that more concretely, see the "Receiving Revelation" part in the skill development section).

Revelation requires interpretation. Most revelations aren't a direct, meaningful message; they are wrapped in mystery and require an interpretation. Whether it is a picture, a sense, or some other method, we need to translate that into a meaningful message before we can do anything with it. Interpretation requires wisdom, and it requires continuing to seek God. Once God reveals something to you, then take that and hold it up to the Lord and ask what it means.

From interpretation we need to actually *do* something with what God has shown us. This is the application. Application can take many forms: we can speak it out to someone, we can write it down and give it to the person, we can even deliver the prophecy through an art form like song or dance. Ask the Lord what the proper means of delivery for this prophecy is and then act on it.

These three steps will apply to any form of prophecy, be it now words or new words. I'd suggest committing this process to memory and keep it in the back of your mind as you practice prophesying until it becomes second nature.

What Do I Do with Prophecy?

Receiving prophecy is an important part of prophecy. Prophecy is the *intention* of God, not the guarantee. A true prophecy does not guarantee the outcome, but rather it provides a road map for where God wants to take you.

The first thing you need to do with prophecy is *weigh* it.

> *Do not quench the Spirit. Do not despise prophecies, but test everything; hold fast to what is good. 1 Thessalonians 5:19-21*

Weighing prophecy means to test the validity of it. Obviously not everything that is described as a prophecy is accurate. There are two common ways that a prophecy can be off:

- Wrong Source: the person is either prophesying from a demonic source or from their own thoughts, feelings, or opinions. In this case, you just want to toss out the prophecy.
- Wrong Delivery: the person has legitimately heard from God (correct revelation), but has either an incorrect interpretation or is applying (delivering) the prophecy in such a way that the meaning of the prophecy is being obscured. In this case hold the prophecy up to the Lord and ask him what the correct meaning of the prophecy is.

How do you know if a prophecy is off? Hold the prophecy against these criteria:

- Is it Scriptural? Does it explicitly violate the Scriptures or the heart of the Father that is revealed in the Scriptures?
- Does it ring true in the spirit of the person the prophecy is intended for?
- Does the prophecy bring the person in closer relationship to God or his people?

If the prophecy passes all of these criteria, it's a pretty good bet that the Lord was speaking through it.

> **Theology Anchor**
>
> All prophecy should be true to the new covenant.

Once you've weighed a prophecy and believe that it is from God, you need to integrate it into your life. Prophecy isn't meant to be heard and then dropped; it is meant to be a directive toward the heart of the Father. The prophecy is like a seed of grace that has the power to grow in our life into what the prophecy declared. Here are useful steps to receiving and processing prophecy:

- Acknowledge the truth of it. Say "yes" to the heart of the Father for you in this season.
- Let the prophecy affect your prayer agenda. If this is the heart of the Father for you, take that prophecy back to God in prayer. Hold it up and turn it over. Examine it before the Father and ask what your next steps are.
- Declare the prophecy over you. Prophecy is God's perspective of you; align that with your own perspective and declare the will of the Father over your own life.

An amazing example in the Scriptures of processing prophecy comes up in the life of Mary, the mother of Jesus. When the shepherds come to see Jesus on the night of his birth, this is what we see:

> *And when they saw it, they made known the saying that had been told them concerning this child. And all who heard it wondered at what the shepherds told them. But Mary treasured up all these things, pondering them in her heart.*
> *Luke 2:17-19*

Mary stores the prophecies from the angels about who Jesus is in her heart. Twelve years later when Mary and Joseph take Jesus to Jerusalem and they find him teaching at the temple, this is the close of the account:

> *And he said to them, "Why were you looking for me? Did you not know that I must be in my Father's house?" And they did not understand the saying that he spoke to them. And he went down with them and came to Nazareth and was submissive to them. And his mother treasured up all these things in her heart. Luke 2:49-51*

Mary is storing up in her heart who Jesus is. Thirty years after his birth we see Jesus starting his ministry in the story of Jesus turning water into wine. Notice the beginning of this story:

> *When the wine ran out, the mother of Jesus said to him, "They have no wine." And Jesus said to her, "Woman, what does this have to do with me? My hour has not yet come." His mother said to the servants, "Do whatever he tells you." John 2:3-5*

Have you ever thought this is a really interesting interchange? Mary seems to already have an understanding that Jesus can solve the problem, even though Jesus had not done any miracles yet (see John 2:11). When Jesus tells Mary his time has not yet come, she seems to ignore him—but he does what she says!

Well, remember that Jesus only did what he saw the Father doing (John 5:19). So what has happened is that actually *God* has changed his mind here. When Jesus says it's not his time. That's because God isn't turning water into wine. But then a minute later He *is* turning water into wine! The only way I can put that together is to say that God was actually *waiting* for Mary to release the prophecies spoken over Jesus' life to release him into his ministry. Mary already knew who Jesus was; she'd been storing prophecies over Jesus up in her heart for 30 years! God is waiting for Mary to recognize

and release Jesus into miraculous ministry, and as soon as she affirms that's who Jesus is, his miraculous ministry is launched and his glory is manifest. The power of meditating on a promise and releasing it is powerful indeed.

Maturity in Prophecy

In his excellent book *Prophecy and Responsibility*, Graham Cooke identifies two types of prophecy: inspirational and revelational prophecy. I think these are useful categories that deserve a little more discussion.

Inspirational Prophecy

This type of prophecy is available to every believer. Paul discusses it in 1 Corinthians:

> *Pursue love, and earnestly desire the spiritual gifts, especially that you may prophesy. For one who speaks in a tongue speaks not to men but to God; for no one understands him, but he utters mysteries in the Spirit. On the other hand, the one who prophesies speaks to people for their upbuilding and encouragement and consolation. 1 Corinthians 14:1-3*

The core of inspirational prophecy is speaking by the Spirit for the purpose of their strengthening—building them up, encouraging them, or consoling them. It is a gift that every believer can move in and that Paul instructs us to desire to move in. The word translated "eagerly desire" here is actually a very strong word, translated as "covet" or "envy" in other places. In any case, this is a form of prophecy that is for everyone and that we should all aspire to.

One aspect that is important to realize about prophecy is that we only have the right to speak into someone's life to the point that we have relational equity with him or her. Inspirational prophecy is a fairly harmless form of prophecy, and so we can be fairly

liberal with whom we prophesy to in this form. As we're learning, it is a good idea to run things by a more experienced person until we grasp the fundamentals of protocol.

For example, a situation that often comes up when prophesying is called "flipping." Flipping is when the Lord reveals to us something negative about the person's life that he wants to speak into. In this case the information about a negative situation is the word of knowledge that provides the context God wants to speak into (see the "Process of Prophecy" section). We don't need to speak this negative revelation to them; often that will be hurtful and at times, it is flat-out inappropriate (particularly if ministering in front of people). What we need to do is ask God what He wants to do in this part of the person's life and reveal that to them. They already know their problems; what they need to learn is God's heart for them in their situation. Whenever we are upbuilding or consoling, we need to do it in the context of encouragement.

Revelational Prophecy

This form of prophecy is a "weightier" form of prophecy that requires considering the relational equity we have with people and the protocol we use to deliver the prophetic word. Revelational prophecy includes:

- Words of Correction
- Words of Direction—opening something new
- Words of Warning—a call to repentance of heart, lifestyle, or attitude
- Words Highlighting a Way Forward—defining a faith or prayer agenda

Revelational prophecy usually should not be given spontaneously. It needs to be prayed through, turned over, and rehearsed before delivery. It is too directive to be shared lightly.

There is higher level of anointing and power on revelational prophecy than there is on inspirational prophecy. There is a level of momentum on the word that provides an opportunity for spiritual alignment that can cause acceleration in a person's life. The grace on the word has a building power behind it.

> **Theology Anchor**
>
> Inspirational prophecy is for everyone. Revelational prophecy requires maturity and relational equity.

Conversely, the handling of the word is more important. If the timing is off or if we do not step into the revelatory prophecy, there can actually be damage caused in a person's life. For this reason, I don't recommend that people try to step into revelational prophecy. If God begins to reveal this type of revelation to you, my suggestion is to take it to your prayer closet. Before you begin to deliver revelational prophecy, it is important to have a bit of a track record and to have gleaned some experience. If God wants to begin to use you in revelational prophecy, he will inform you that what he's shown you needs to be shared. If that begins to happen, I would suggest reading Graham Cooke's book *Prophecy and Responsibility*, and align yourself with a prophetic mentor (approved by your pastor) before you begin to share revelational prophecy with anyone. This is a great book that discusses issues of protocol and timing in depth.

Prophecy and Prophets

Our discussion so far has revolved around prophecy mostly as it is available to every believer. What then is the role of the prophet? Biblically, prophets still exist, and their role is actually one of equipping:

> *And [Jesus] gave the apostles, the prophets, the evangelists, the shepherds and teachers, to equip the saints for the work of ministry, for building up the body of Christ. Ephesians 4:1-12*

The primary aim for the prophetic office (or the other offices listed) is not to do the ministry to which they have been gifted, but rather to equip the saints for the work of ministry. Rather than the prophecy being the gift (as it is with the gifts of the Spirit listed in 1 Corinthians 12), the prophet him or herself is the gift. The gift is not the ability to prophesy, but the person is the gift to the body of Christ for training and equipping.

To be a prophet is really a call from God; but even prophets need to grow into the prophetic gifting (and the same for healing or other ministries). Generally there are four levels of ministry as described in the Scriptures:[69]

- *Level 1: The Role of the Believer*—Jesus makes it clear in John 10 that as believers we know his voice. Every believer then has the ability to hear God and communicate to others as a form of prophecy.
- *Level 2: The Gift of Prophecy*—As we learn to move with the flow of the Holy Spirit, the gift of prophecy is something we can learn to flow in. As we learn to recognize and operate consistently in that gift, we are practicing the gift of prophecy. Paul seems to think that every Christian should strive to operate at this level.
- *Level 3: The Ministry of Prophecy*—People who don't have the call from God to be prophets but operate for a long time in prophecy successfully have a ministry of prophecy. They should have a strong relationship with church leadership and understanding of protocol and display enough maturity that the church leadership trusts them to move in revelational prophecy.
- *Level 4: The Office of Prophet*—This is a calling from God that involves ministry to the church as well as to individuals. This involves a high level of anointing and responsibility.

---

[69] This designation of four levels is a useful model for thinking about many kinds of ministry beyond prophecy. Healing, evangelism and so on can also be thought of in these terms.

It really is God's decision where he wants to put us within the body of Christ. Put in your part and leave where God decides to place you up to him.

Physical Healing

Physical healing was one of the characteristics of Jesus' ministry. Everywhere he went he healed people. He was passionate about healing, to the point where he repeatedly put his life in jeopardy by healing people even though it was the Sabbath. You can tell the importance of healing in Jesus' ministry by Peter's summary of Jesus' ministry to the first Gentile converts as described in the book of Acts:

> *[Peter described] how God anointed Jesus of Nazareth with the Holy Spirit and with power. He went about doing good and healing all who were oppressed by the devil, for God was with him. Acts 10:38*

Furthermore, it looks as if Jesus believed that healing was the validation of his message and purpose. Look at the response Jesus has when John the Baptist's disciples come and ask Him if he is the messiah:

> *In that hour [Jesus] healed many people of diseases and plagues and evil spirits, and on many who were blind he bestowed sight. And he answered them, "Go and tell John what you have seen and heard: the blind receive their sight, the lame walk, lepers are cleansed, and the deaf hear, the dead are raised up, the poor have good news preached to them. Luke 7:21-22*

If healing is that important to Jesus, I think it should be that important to us!

Healing and the Presence of God

Healing is a sign of the presence of God among his people. One of the promises Jesus makes to us as believers is eternal life, or a life connected to eternity.[70] In Romans 8:2, Paul refers to the Holy Spirit as the Spirit of life. To put it simply, when God is around there is life, and if you get close to that life, your body is likely to respond to that life and get healed. Wimber used to put it this way: "The power is in his presence." Here is another verse that captures this idea with an astounding word picture. This is in the closing chapter of the Old Testament, looking forward to the day the Lord will come and live among his people again:

> *For behold, the day is coming, burning like an oven, when all the arrogant and all evildoers will be stubble. The day that is coming shall set them ablaze, says the LORD of hosts, so that it will leave them neither root nor branch. But for you who fear my name, the sun of righteousness shall rise with healing in its wings. You shall go out leaping like calves from the stall. Malachi 4:1-2*

As the presence of God is made manifest in our lives, healing is in its wake. If you want to grow in healing, then learn to be a better steward of the presence of God on your life. There are three important steps that affect power ministry and healing that you want to pay attention to:

- Encountering the presence: How often do you encounter the manifest presence of God? How do you respond to his presence? Do you prioritize encountering who he is? Will you stop what you are doing and engage with his presence if you feel his presence come upon you at a random time?

---

[70] The word *eternal* in Greek is *aionios*, which comes from the word *aion*, or "age." *Eternal life* in Greek is literally "life of the ages." Jesus is referring to the age to come here. It is true that we do get to live forever, but that's not the sense in which Jesus is primarily referring when he is talking about eternal life. Rather, he's referring to life that has its root in the kingdom of God.

- Carrying the presence: How do you live your life when you are not encountering the presence of God? This will determine how much you're "leaking." Are you able to maintain a sense of identity and purpose when you don't feel anointed?
- Releasing the presence: Do you know how to release the presence of God on to someone else? Do your words have power or do they "fall to the ground"?

Which of these steps could you grow in? What could you do to gain some momentum in that particular area? As we really do learn to become people of his presence—people who live with a sense of stewarding the presence of God over our lives—healing will become much more commonplace. This is lifestyle practice for a ministry of healing.

Power and Authority

In healing, it's important to learn the difference between power and authority and how to function in both of them. When commissioning his disciples to go preach the gospel of the kingdom, Jesus lends them some of his power and authority:

> *And he called the twelve together and gave them power and authority over all demons and to cure diseases, and he sent them out to proclaim the kingdom of God and to heal. Luke 9:1-2*

After Jesus is resurrected, he commissions the Apostles to have their own authority and power.[71] Authority (to extend and withhold forgiveness) is given when they are commissioned, and the Holy Spirit seals them as proof of their belief (see Ephesians 1:13):

---

[71] This, of course, doesn't mean that their authority and power didn't come from God, but rather that before Jesus died and was resurrected, they were acting as an extension of his call; whereas after the resurrection, the disciples are commissioned with their own call. When acting under someone else's mission, you can step into the authority and power that comes with that mandate. When you have your own mission, you need to get your own power and authority (which, of course, come from God).

Jesus said to them again, "Peace be with you. As the Father has sent me, even so I am sending you." And when he had said this, he breathed on them and said to them, "Receive the Holy Spirit. If you forgive the sins of any, they are forgiven them; if you withhold forgiveness from any, it is withheld." John 20:21-23

And power is extended when the manifest presence of the Holy Spirit comes upon them:

But you will receive power when the Holy Spirit has come upon you, and you will be my witnesses in Jerusalem and in all Judea and Samaria, and to the end of the earth. Acts 1:8

Likewise, we need to learn to understand power and authority and know how to minister out of power and out of authority.

Authority

Authority comes as a result of being commissioned. The authority that we have access to is a result of the mission that we've been given. Authority is a result of being under someone else's authority:

For I have not spoken on my own authority, but the Father who sent me has himself given me a commandment—what to say and what to speak. John 12:49

The centurion understood this as well. In fact, he realized that Jesus was under God's authority, and because of that, Jesus had access to God's resources:

Therefore I did not presume to come to you. But say the word, and let my servant be healed. For I too am a man set under authority, with soldiers under me: and I say to one, 'Go,' and he goes; and to another, 'Come,' and he comes; and to my servant, 'Do this,' and he does it. Luke 7:7-8

It is the position the centurion has relative to his superior and to the people underneath him that allows him to use authority. Because of this, it isn't so much that the centurion has authority so much as it is that he stewards the authority of his superior officer. It is the authority of the superior officer acting through the centurion that we often think of as the centurion's authority.

Similarly the authority we wield isn't our authority; it's actually Jesus' authority acting through us. We act as an extension of him and as such his authority flows through us. Note the language in the great commission in Matthew:

> *And Jesus came and said to them, "All authority in heaven and on earth has been given to me. Go therefore . . ." Matthew 28:18-19*

Jesus says, "I have all authority, therefore you go," because we act as extensions of who he is and as such his authority is implemented through us.

Because the source of our orders is God, we can always point back to him. That is authority. This level of authority that comes as a result of being submitted to God's mission is something that God witnesses to. Notice the response of the people who heard Jesus' teaching (even before he cast out the demon in their midst).

> **Theology Anchor**
> We pray in Jesus' name because we pray as Jesus on this earth.

> *And they went into Capernaum, and immediately on the Sabbath he entered the synagogue and was teaching. And they were astonished at his teaching, for he taught them as one who had authority, and not as the scribes. Luke 1:21-22*

Authority literally means something like "permission." The authority we have is permission to affect change in the spiritual realm. It is freedom or power to choose things in the Spirit; it is influence.

Being sent under Jesus' authority means we have permission to enact his will. Because Jesus' authority is complete, we always have permission to release his will. We are sent out as embodiments of who he is to enforce his will.

> *And he put all things under [Jesus'] feet and gave him as head over all things to the church, which is his body, the fullness of him who fills all in all. Ephesians 1:22-23*

Paul says that everything was put under Jesus' feet (subjected to his authority) and given to the church. This means the head of the church is the head of all authority. The church is spoken of as the fullness of Jesus; we are the ones who bring that authority to fruition. The writer of Hebrews speaks about this process quoting the same Old Testament passage:

> *". . . putting everything in subjection under his feet." Now in putting everything in subjection to him, he left nothing outside his control. At present, we do not yet see everything in subjection to him. Hebrews 2:8*

God has put Jesus in the place of supreme permission; he has permission to do whatever he wants. Nothing is exempt from his will. Not everything has lined up with his will yet (sin, sickness, death), and the writer acknowledges this, but it does not mean that it is permissible, just possible. In other words the enemy's work is now illegal. The enemy is on Jesus' turf on earth now and none of his work is justifiable. He may still have influence, but it's illegal influence. All works of the enemy will be driven out eventually, and all things will be made new (Revelation 21:5).

Understanding the authority that we're under and we extend as believers empowers us to realize we have permission. The will of God can always be extended on this planet. No demon, angel, or human being can say, "You can't do that." They may say, "I don't want you to do that," or "I won't let you do that" (a power statement), but we always

have permission to release the will of the Father. We always have permission to influence the spirit realm for Jesus' glory.

Power

While authority refers to the permission to do something, power refers to the ability to do something. To minister out of power is to be the means that God uses to heal. As we discussed in the Spiritual Gifts section of our course, Paul is referring to power when he uses the term "working of miracles [power]" in 1 Corinthians 12. The power comes from God, but he gives it to us to work so we can be involved in the process.

As such, a prayer that ministers out of power may not always be appropriate. The power comes when the Holy Spirit comes *upon* us. We looked at the passage in the beginning of Acts where Jesus refers to this just a little earlier. Notice as well the language Jesus uses referring to that in the close of the book of Luke:

> *And behold, I am sending the promise of my Father upon you. But stay in the city until you are clothed with power from on high." Luke 24:49*

When the presence of the Spirit (often referred to as "the anointing") comes over us or another person, our words become a vehicle for the power of God to be released. We are "clothed with power," to use Jesus' words. This type of ministry actually works much like it is depicted in the opening account of creation in Genesis. Genesis 1 describes the situation of the earth before God began to speak things into creation:

> *The earth was without form and void, and darkness was over the face of the deep. And the Spirit of God was hovering over the face of the waters. Genesis 1:2*

As the Spirit hovered over the surface of the earth, what God spoke was catalyzed into a reality. What was said became what was. This is the method of power ministry. As we see the Holy Spirit hovering over a person's body, we speak to the condition and our words are catalyzed by the Spirit into a new reality. Our words really do become the means of the power of God being appropriated into another person's life.

By the way, the Scriptures say that Satan no longer has authority (Matthew 28:18), but they don't say that he doesn't have any power; in fact it seems Satan does still have power. Indeed Jesus himself said to Paul when he met him on the road to Damascus:

> *to open their eyes, so that they may turn from darkness to light and from the power of Satan to God, that they may receive forgiveness of sins and a place among those who are sanctified by faith in me.' Acts 26:18*

Satan doesn't have permission to do anything, but he does still have ability to do things. This means that everything the enemy does is illegal, but it doesn't mean he can't do it. Satan isn't interested in following the authority structure in the Spirit realm; he's interested in doing what he wants. No wonder Jesus attributes theft, loss, and destruction to the *thief*. Satan acts as a thief in the spirit realm; he acts according to his will, not what is legal.

Prayers of Authority and Power

Using these two ideas, it is helpful at times to think about whether we are praying out of authority or power at any given time.

Prayers of authority are prayers in which we access the permission we have in the spiritual realm. It is a prayer along the lines of "Stop, you can't go any further" (particularly appropriate when dealing with demons) or "I release you to . . . " (perhaps speaking restoration to a body part). Here is a clear example from Scripture:

> *Now he was teaching in one of the synagogues on the Sabbath. And behold, there was a woman who had had a disabling spirit for eighteen years. She was bent over and could not fully straighten herself. When Jesus saw her, he called her over and said to her, "Woman, you are freed from your disability." And he laid his hands on her, and immediately she was made straight, and she glorified God . . . "And ought not this woman, a daughter of Abraham whom Satan bound for eighteen years, be loosed from this bond on the Sabbath day?"* Luke 13:10-13,16

Jesus perceives that the disease is spiritual in origin and prays a simple authority prayer to release her. Apparently the demonic spirit had removed permission for the back to straighten. Jesus simply releases that and restores permission for her body to function normally.

A prayer of power is different in that rather than using our authority to adjust things in the spiritual realm, which then have physical results, we release things in the physical directly. Remember, to pray with power is to have the ability to put things right ourselves. In prayers of power we minister gifts of the Holy Spirit. We discern a gift of healing, faith, etc., and then we release it directly ourselves. The perception of the gift is the sensing of the power (ability) to minister, and we step in and use the tool directly.

Authority and power fit together. There are times when we are to affect a transaction in the Spirit that will result in the person's healing, and there are times when we're supposed to get our hands behind God's and work the healing right then and there. They're both good, they're just different. Personally I usually start to pray out of authority because I know that since I'm on God's team, I always have the authority of being under his call on my life. As I pray out of authority (sometimes even using that authority to release the power of God), I try to follow to see if God is releasing the power to see it accomplished right there.

Always remember that if you didn't see anything happen in the moment, that doesn't mean anything specifically. I would estimate that probably for about 50% of the healings that I see, there isn't anything remarkable that happens during the prayer time (not any improvement or any manifestations of the Holy Spirit that point towards healing). Later in the day or week, they notice their condition is starting to improve or has disappeared. Remembering this helps me not get discouraged when I pray, and it doesn't seem like anything is happening. Authority will work a spiritual effect that may take time to work its way down to physical symptoms.

The Will of God and Healing

God's will and healing is a subject of much disagreement within the body of Christ. Since there is controversy about healing and many different views about the will[72] of God, this is not surprising. I will not explore the many different viewpoints but will only present the viewpoint that has been consistent with the theological view I have been taking throughout these notes.

The first question of discussion is: When is it God's will to heal? The nominal position on this subject is that God generally wants to heal in the sense that God likes to do good things, but that healing is a grace that God extends or withholds from each situation. The practice that is developed out of this theology is that we attempt to discern whether it is God's will to heal in a specific situation, then if we perceive a green light on healing, to pray for God to heal the person.

The problem with this practically is that if my belief that God's will to heal in this situation is up to my perception of his will, that can leave me in a rather dubious place. What if I'm having an off day in terms of my spiritual sensitivity? Where does that leave

[72] The subject of the will of God is wrapped up with the discussion of the sovereignty of God, which has come up a few times throughout our study of various topics.

me then? Biblically this runs into a bit of trouble because it doesn't really seem as if Jesus operated this way. It is true that Jesus did only what he saw the Father doing and said only what he heard the Father saying, but it's also true that everyone who came to Jesus got healed; so in Jesus' life the answer to the question if it's God's will to heal in any given situation was always yes. If God is the same yesterday, today and forever, then it seems as if there is a bit of a contradiction there.

Finally, this understanding is really rooted in a precept that God is micromanaging the universe. If I take this as my starting point, when my prayers for healing are not answered, it follows that God is withholding healing, which means it's not always his will to heal. This premise leads to the conclusion that things (like healing) do or don't happen because it is or isn't God's will in that given situation.

The problem is that Biblically this isn't true. The Bible never says that God's will always happens; in fact, it says the opposite:

> *The Lord is not slow to fulfill his promise as some count slowness, but is patient toward you, not wishing that any should perish, but that all should reach repentance. 2 Peter 3:9*
>
> *So it is not the will of my Father who is in heaven that one of these little ones should perish. Matthew 18:14*
>
> *This is good, and it is pleasing in the sight of God our Savior, who desires all people to be saved and to come to the knowledge of the truth. 1 Timothy 2:3-4*

The Bible is unambiguous that God's will is for everyone to be saved, yet clearly that doesn't happen, so biblically, just because something is in God's will does not mean it will necessarily happen.

Again, the problem here really is our starting point. The picture of God as the "king of the hill" of the decisions that determine what happens in the universe simply is not correct. This comes out of a misunderstanding of sovereignty. Sovereignty doesn't mean that everything that happens is God's will; it means that everything can be turned for God's will. It means God is so powerful and good that things never get so out of control that He loses the ability to move them to where he wants them. He's not controlling the universe, but it isn't out of his control.

This distinction is subtle but important, and I believe it mostly comes from a human model of sovereignty. For humans, there is no distinction between being in control and controlling things. If I'm really in control, then I have a yes-or-no check on everything that's happening. Does this mean it works like this when God is in control? I don't think so. Jesus makes it pretty clear that in the kingdom, leadership is not top-down, but bottom-up:

> *And [Jesus] said to them, "The kings of the Gentiles exercise lordship over them, and those in authority over them are called benefactors. But not so with you. Rather, let the greatest among you become as the youngest, and the leader as one who serves. For who is the greater, one who reclines at table or one who serves? Is it not the one who reclines at table? But I am among you as the one who serves. Luke 22:25-27*

Jesus just said that leadership in the kingdom means coming underneath others, not exercising lordship over them. But that's exactly how we often picture God running the universe: by exercising lordship over everything that happens. Clearly, there is some inconsistency here.

So what is the solution? Well, let me ask another question: has God already answered the question? If God has already given us a yes or a no on healing, then we don't need

to ask if healing is God's will in any given situation. We need to listen to what he's *already said*. The best place to start is definitely Jesus because Jesus is God's will revealed. Jesus came to put a face on God—to make clear who he is and what His will is for the world:

> *Long ago, at many times and in many ways, God spoke to our fathers by the prophets, but in these last days he has spoken to us by his Son, whom he appointed the heir of all things, through whom also he created the world. Hebrews 1:1-2*

> *For the law was given through Moses; grace and truth came through Jesus Christ. No one has ever seen God; the only God, who is at the Father's side, he has made him known. John 1:17-18*

God *has spoken* by his Son; Jesus *has made* the Father known. There is no question anymore about who God is. If we want to know, we can just look at Jesus because to see Jesus is to see the Father (John 14:9). Jesus is the complete story: to look at him is to catch the entirety of the picture of who God is:

> *[Jesus] is the radiance of the glory of God and the exact imprint of his nature. Hebrews 1:3*

> *For in [Jesus] the whole fullness of deity dwells bodily. Colossians 2:9*

Furthermore, God's will has been revealed in Jesus:

> *In [Jesus] we have redemption through his blood, the forgiveness of our trespasses, according to the riches of his grace, which he lavished upon us, in all wisdom and insight making known to us the mystery of his will, according to his*

purpose, which he set forth in Christ as a plan for the fullness of time, to unite all things in him, things in heaven and things on earth. Ephesians 1:7-10

What Jesus has done has made God's will known to us. If we look to Jesus' life, the mystery of God's will is solved. We don't have to ask ourselves that question anymore, and as we know, Jesus healed everyone who came to him! Jesus' life clearly demonstrates that God's will is to heal. In fact, if we read the Bible with a perspective that wasn't as westernized, this would be clear to us:[73]

This is good, and it is pleasing in the sight of God our Savior, who desires all people to be saved (sozo-ed) and to come to the knowledge of the truth. 1 Timothy 2:3-4

The Greek word *sozo*, which is the word translated "saved" here, actually means something along the lines of "to rescue, protect, keep well, restore to health or heal."[74] It is generally rendered as "save," "make whole," and "heal" throughout the New Testament depending on the context.

Scripture clearly says God wants this holistic sense of salvation, which includes both the soul and body for everyone. We can pray with confidence that healing is God's will.

This definitely seems to be the mentality that Jesus commissioned the disciples with:

These twelve Jesus sent out, instructing them . . . "Proclaim as you go, saying, 'The kingdom of heaven is at hand.' Heal the sick, raise the dead, cleanse lepers, cast out demons. You received without paying; give without pay." Matthew 10:5,7-8

---

[73] Here I'm specifically referring to our focus to prioritize saving the soul over healing the body.
[74] Blue Letter Bible, accessed 1/24/12.
http://www.blueletterbible.org/lang/lexicon/lexicon.cfm?strongs=G4982

Jesus gave them a general call. Heal which sick? *The sick*. Not some of them. Not the ones God leads you to, the ones who are sick! This understanding gives us permission; it puts us on the offensive. Jesus' life and practice make clear that God's will for us is wholeness—for every one of us. Let's not make God's will any more complicated than Jesus said it was:

> **Theology Anchor**
>
> It is unequivocally God's will to heal—no exceptions. Otherwise Jesus did not reveal the Father.

> *The thief comes only to steal and kill and destroy. I came that they may have life and have it abundantly.* ***John 10:10***

If it looks like theft, death, or destruction, it comes from the enemy and is not God's will. If it looks like abundant life, it is God's will.

Faith

Faith is often linked with healing. Jesus almost always seemed to be on the lookout for faith. There are times when he indicated that a person's faith was involved with their healing. We see this specifically with blind Bartimaeus and the woman who grasped Jesus' robe:

> *And Jesus said to him, "What do you want me to do for you?" And the blind man said to him, "Rabbi, let me recover my sight." And Jesus said to him, "Go your way; your faith has made you well." And immediately he recovered his sight and followed him on the way. Luke 10:51-52*

> *She had heard the reports about Jesus and came up behind him in the crowd and touched his garment. For she said, "If I touch even his garments, I will be made well." And immediately the flow of blood dried up, and she felt in her body that she*

was healed of her disease . . . And he said to her, "Daughter, your faith has made you well; go in peace, and be healed of your disease." Mark 5:27-29,34

On the flip side, when Jesus was debriefing his disciples about why they couldn't cast out the demon from the paralytic boy, He pointed to their lack of faith:

Then the disciples came to Jesus privately and said, "Why could we not cast it out?" He said to them, "Because of your little faith. For truly, I say to you, if you have faith like a grain of mustard seed, you will say to this mountain, 'Move from here to there,' and it will move, and nothing will be impossible for you." Matthew 17:19-20

So apparently it can help when someone you are praying for has faith; but if they do not, it looks like Jesus expects us to have it.

Speaking of faith, there is a common teaching that unbelief has the power to stop faith. This is based on passages such as this from when Jesus went to Nazareth:

And he could do no mighty work there, except that he laid his hands on a few sick people and healed them. And he marveled because of their unbelief. Mark 6:5-6

The standard teaching about this verse goes something like this: Jesus wasn't able to do dramatic miracles because unbelief shut down the corporate faith element. This is a pretty big jump from this text. The text only says that he couldn't do miracles except for a few healings. It does not say there wasn't faith to do miracles. In fact, the verses above say:

Is not this the carpenter, the son of Mary and brother of James and Joseph and Judas and Simon? And are not his sisters here with us?" And they took offense at

him. And Jesus said to them, "A prophet is not without honor, except in his hometown and among his relatives and in his own household." Mark 6:3-4

So we have a city where people are offended at Jesus and dishonor him. In a city filled with people of offense and dishonor, how many people are going to allow Jesus to pray for them? Not many. The truth is we know that Jesus healed everyone he prayed for:

God anointed Jesus of Nazareth with the Holy Spirit and with power. He went about doing good and healing all who were oppressed by the devil, for God was with him. Acts 10:38

If Jesus healed all who were oppressed by the devil, then there couldn't have been anyone who came to him in Nazareth who wasn't healed. This is important because otherwise we'll believe that other people's unbelief has the power to stop our faith based on this passage. That's not the case. The text even says that Jesus did heal the few people who came to him; there just were very few!

Recognizing Faith

So faith is important for healing. But how do we know when we have faith? Let me compare a few verses that are interesting:

"For truly, I say to you, if you have faith like a grain of mustard seed, you will say to this mountain, 'Move from here to there,' and it will move, and nothing will be impossible for you." Matthew 17:20

And Jesus answered them, "Have faith in God. Truly, I say to you, whoever says to this mountain, 'Be taken up and thrown into the sea,' and does not doubt in his heart, but believes that what he says will come to pass, it will be done for him. Mark 11:22-23

Looking at the two of these in parallel, I notice a few things:

1. The object of our faith is God. The mustard seed of faith is faith in God. As we come to know God, our faith grows.
2. Even a mustard seed of faith is signaled by not doubting in our heart.

This second point is important. Faith is observed by the reaction of our heart. Our heart response is our first, subconscious response. If our response to a situation is one of rest and joy and security in the goodness of God, we probably have faith. If our response is one of fear, doubt, or something along those lines, we don't have faith.

> **Theology Anchor**
>
> Faith is about the perception of the heart, not the acknowledgement of what is true.

In light of this, it becomes clear that if you're trying to muster up faith, you don't have it! If you need to muster up faith, it's already too late. The very fact that you're trying to find faith makes it clear that faith doesn't exist in your heart. No amount of trying to summon faith will change that heart response. At that point, what people are looking for is emotional stability; they're looking to find a confidence or lack of worry, figuring that feeling confident is faith. Faith means trust, it's not a feeling.

The time to get faith is before you are in the disaster. When the trial comes, you find out what you have built upon. The time to build is not during the storm, but beforehand:

> *"Everyone then who hears these words of mine and does them will be like a wise man who built his house on the rock. And the rain fell, and the floods came, and the winds blew and beat on that house, but it did not fall, because it had been founded on the rock. And everyone who hears these words of mine and does not do them will be like a foolish man who built his house on the sand. And the rain fell,*

and the floods came, and the winds blew and beat against that house, and it fell, and great was the fall of it." Matthew 7:24-27

The storm brings to the surface what you've built your house on. If you've been building your house on what Jesus has said, then it will be clear in the time of adversity, and you will have faith in God.

The fact is you do not have to try to believe what you believe, and you do not have to try to be who you are. If you have really understood who you are and really believe what you believe, faith is the most natural response you can have. If not, then recognize where you don't have the natural response of faith and begin to meditate on the truth. This dynamic is captured in an amazing passage in 1 John:

> *By this we shall know that we are of the truth and reassure our heart before him; for whenever our heart condemns us, God is greater than our heart, and he knows everything. Beloved, if our heart does not condemn us, we have confidence before God; and whatever we ask we receive from him, because we keep his commandments and do what pleases him. 1 John 3:20-22*

Here, John tells us that when our heart condemns us, we need to take God's perspective and reassure our hearts before him by building our lives around the truth that God knows better than our hearts do. When our heart shifts and we have confidence before God, we'll find faith there and we'll receive what we ask from him. This is why the writer of Proverbs says:

> *Keep your heart with all vigilance,*
> *for from it flow the springs of life. Proverbs 4:23*

Guarding our heart is a lifestyle. It is hearing Jesus' words and doing them.[75] It is watching what we are listening to and what we are focusing on—where we are deriving our life from. It is involving God in every facet of our lives until our lives begin to be lived in step with him.

Biblical Observations on Healing

These are a few practical things seen in Biblical accounts, which resulted in greater success in praying for healing when I began to put them into practice.

Prayers of Command

Biblically, prayers for healing are commands of healing:

> *And Jesus stretched out his hand and touched him, saying, "I will; be clean." And immediately his leprosy was cleansed. Matthew 8:3*
>
> *And Jesus said to him, "Recover your sight; your faith has made you well." And immediately he recovered his sight and followed him, glorifying God... Luke 18:42-43*
>
> *When he had said these things, he cried out with a loud voice, "Lazarus, come out." The man who had died came out... John 11:43-44*
>
> *And Peter said to him, "Aeneas, Jesus Christ heals you; rise and make your bed." And immediately he rose. Acts 9:34*

---

[75] Remember Paul says "Faith comes through hearing, and hearing through the word of Christ" (Romans 10:17). *Word* there is *rhema*—a freshly spoken now word from God (as opposed to logos which is more like teachings of Jesus).

He listened to Paul speaking. And Paul, looking intently at him and seeing that he had faith to be made well, said in a loud voice, "Stand upright on your feet." And he sprang up and began walking. Acts 14:9-10

In fact the only example of a prayer for healing (sometimes there was not even speaking at all, just a prophetic action), is followed by a command for healing:

But Peter put them all outside, and knelt down and prayed; and turning to the body he said, "Tabitha, arise." And she opened her eyes, and when she saw Peter she sat up. Acts 9:40

So the Biblical example is not to ask God for healing, but to allow God in you to speak a command of healing through you. If you don't believe you have the faith to issue a prayer of command, that's fine. Pray until you do, and then command the healing.

I've found that while it seems odd when you start, you'll get much better results overall when using the prayer of command for healing. You always want to follow the lead of the Holy Spirit; but when it comes to healing, I default to a prayer of command because that's the Biblical precedent. If the Holy Spirit leads me to pray in some other way, then I'll do that.

Point of Contact

Oral Roberts used to talk about a "point of contact"—an action that people would take to release their faith for healing. Remember faith without works is dead (James 2:17), so faith leads to action. As people take an action, it can be the means of the release of their faith for healing. Probably the clearest scriptural example of this is the woman who grabbed Jesus' garment:

She had heard the reports about Jesus and came up behind him in the crowd and touched his garment. For she said, "If I touch even his garments, I will be made well." Mark 5:27-28

Notice her process: she had faith that if she could touch his garments she would be healed. When she does touch his garment, she is instantly healed; and when Jesus hears the whole story, he says that her faith has healed her.

Other possible Scriptural examples include Peter's shadow in Acts 5 and Paul's handkerchiefs in Acts 19, as well as many examples of prophetic actions that led to healing—for example Jesus spitting in a blind man's eyes in Mark 8, Jesus putting mud in a blind man's eye in John 9, and Elisha sending Naaman to wash in the Jordan river seven times.[76]

An important aspect of the point of contact is that it can help release your faith just as well as it can help release theirs. Remember faith in either of you can contribute to their healing.

A very useful point of contact is to have the person begin to walk out their healing. Often I find that a person won't get healed until they begin to try to do what they couldn't do before they were healed. In the process of acting in faith the healing begins to come. You see this dynamic in Scripture as well:

Then [Jesus] said to the man, "Stretch out your hand." And the man stretched it out, and it was restored, healthy like the other. Matthew 12:13

---

[76] I can't prove to you from these scriptural passages that the action released their faith, but the principle that taking action is a part of healing is true in all of these.

But Peter said, "I have no silver and gold, but what I do have I give to you. In the name of Jesus Christ of Nazareth, rise up and walk!" And he took him by the right hand and raised him up, and immediately his feet and ankles were made strong. Acts 3:6-7

Notice in both cases action was taken as if the person was healed before they were. As the action was taken, the healing came.

When praying for people I use this often. If the problem results in pain, limited motion, or something else that can be tested after some prayer, I'll have them try it out to see if there is any improvement. Often for someone with a knee problem, I'll tell them to walk to the end of the room and back or something like that. I've also had the experience that when they begin to act, their healing begins to come.

Secondly, if there is any improvement, you want to focus the person's attention on the improvement. This can help build their faith (and yours too). If a person feels better, I'll ask them to quantify it. I'll usually say, something like "So how much better does it feel? 25%? 50%?" When they say something, I'll usually restate it to them in a way that helps to build their faith: "30% - so you're saying that God's healed almost 1/3 of it already? Great, let's pray again!" Often I find that as I shift their focus on to what God is doing and build their faith the rest of the healing comes quickly after that.

Causes of Disease

Scripture depicts diseases as having many different causes: structural, emotional, and spirits of infirmity are three broad categories we'll examine here. It's important to be aware of all three of these causes and to learn to discern between them because you'll have to handle each of these causes differently.

Structural Problems

Many physical healing issues are simply physically rooted. Most of the time a broken bone is simply a broken bone. Praying for this kind of condition is ministering to the person's body. Problems that have a clear physical cause often fall into this category. To pray for this kind of situation, I use the methods and ideas discussed in the previous few sections.

Emotional Problems

Negative emotions also have an impact on our bodies. Harboring negative emotions is bad for our health and can result in many different conditions. The Scriptures point to this kind of healing in many different passages:

> *He heals the brokenhearted*
> *and binds up their wounds. Psalm 147:3*
>
> *A tranquil heart gives life to the flesh,*
> *but envy makes the bones rot. Proverbs 14:30*
>
> *A joyful heart is good medicine,*
> *but a crushed spirit dries up the bones. Proverbs 17:22*
>
> *There is one whose rash words are like sword thrusts,*
> *but the tongue of the wise brings healing. Proverbs 12:18*
>
> *Gracious words are like a honeycomb,*
> *sweetness to the soul and health to the body. Proverbs 16:24*

Often this kind of a problem can be traced back to a negative relationship or a trauma that happened to the person, at which point they began to agree with negative

emotions such as jealousy, envy, bitterness, hate, or similar emotions. Unforgiveness is almost always mixed into the situation as well. These types of issues result in a physical condition in which the body starts to break down or turn against itself. Examples of such conditions are arthritis, fibromyalgia, ulcers and so forth. They usually come on gradually as well.

Dealing with this kind of an issue you will want to help people release their negative emotions to God. Guide the person in forgiving whoever needs to be forgiven and have them break their agreement with his or her negative emotions. Once the emotional stuff is dealt with, then you'll pray for his or her physical healing.[77]

Spirits of Infirmity

In the Bible you also see that demons can affect people's bodies and cause different types of disease:

> *And behold, there was a woman who had had a disabling spirit for eighteen years. She was bent over and could not fully straighten herself. When Jesus saw her, he called her over and said to her, "Woman, you are freed from your disability." And he laid his hands on her, and immediately she was made straight, and she glorified God. Luke 13:11-13*

> *And when they came to the crowd, a man came up to [Jesus] and, kneeling before him, said, "Lord, have mercy on my son, for he is an epileptic and he suffers terribly. For often he falls into the fire, and often into the water. And I brought him to your disciples, and they could not heal him." And Jesus answered, "O faithless and twisted generation, how long am I to be with you? How long am I to bear with*

[77] This order is just what I've found works well in my experience. You don't have to necessarily do it in that order, but I've found once the emotional stuff is taken care of the physical healing comes quite a bit quicker.

you? Bring him here to me." And Jesus rebuked the demon, and it came out of him, and the boy was healed instantly. Matthew 17:14-18

Demons can cause diseases or handicaps in people's bodies. When a spirit is causing the issue, the spirit needs to be dealt with for healing to flow. Notice in both of these accounts, freedom is ministered to the person before healing.

Dealing with a spirit of infirmity does not need to be a long and complicated process. Deliverance is a bit of a complex issue we'll talk about later, but you can just rebuke spirits of infirmity. They may not leave immediately, but keep after them and they will eventually leave. They have to listen to Jesus speaking through you.

One almost dead giveaway that you are dealing with a spirit of infirmity is when you're praying for someone and his or her pain leaves where you're praying for and appears somewhere else. Pain moving around is almost always a spirit of infirmity. When this happens deal with the spirit, and you'll probably find there isn't anything left to pray for after that.

When Healing Doesn't Stick

One thing you'll probably see when you move in the healing ministry is people who get healed, and then their healing doesn't stick. They may be better for a few days, but then the problem comes back. This is a useful thing to know how to deal with. While healing fundamentally involves much mystery, there are a few views that are helpful to be aware of with regards to this problem.

As we discussed in the section above, there are many causes to physical problems. Many problems are simple physical issues, but there are also emotionally and spiritually rooted problems. I believe what often happens when someone's healing doesn't stick is that you have treated the symptoms and not the cause of the problem.

For example, if someone has an ulcer because they are holding on to anger and unforgiveness towards their boss at work, if I just pray as if the problem is only physically caused, what will happen? Well, probably their ulcer will go away because I prayed, but then it will come back because the real cause has not been dealt with.

So when you pray for someone and their condition goes away and then comes back, ask God what is really going on behind the scenes. What aren't you seeing? Lean into his guidance, and he'll help you chop off the condition at the root.

Another common view is that healing doesn't stick because people don't have faith to keep their healing. Essentially, when we pray, there is enough faith to get the person free from their symptoms, but when the enemy comes back to try and reclaim his ground in the person's body, they lose the healing if they are unable to stand on their own faith. This is an application of Jesus' discussion of what unclean spirits do after they've been cast out in Luke 11:24-26.

Scripture seems pretty silent on the matter by and large. We don't have examples of people losing their healing in the Bible, so we're on theorizing grounds. We have to hold our opinion loosely when it comes to this question. I can see making a good case for either explanation in different cases because I've seen people move from temporary healing to lasting healing with both of them. My admonition would be to ask God and listen for his guidance with each specific situation.

Emotional Healing and Deliverance

Emotional healing and deliverance are two topics that are so closely tied together that I feel it only really makes sense to address them together. Rather than separating them in our discussion and study, we'll just hit them both at the same time.

The reason both of these issues sit next to each other is that the process of ministering to each of these situations involves ministering truth. Truth is the key to freedom in both of these areas:

> *So Jesus said to the Jews who had believed him, "If you abide in my word, you are truly my disciples, and you will know the truth, and the truth will set you free." John 8:31-32*

The cause of the lack of freedom in both areas is different, but a truth encounter is the key to freedom.

Emotional Healing

What do I mean by the term "emotional healing"? I don't mean the healing of negative emotions. Scripture seems pretty clear that negative emotions aren't actually a bad thing:

> *It is better to go to the house of mourning*
> *than to go to the house of feasting,*
> *for this is the end of all mankind,*
> *and the living will lay it to heart.*

Sorrow is better than laughter,
for by sadness of face the heart is made glad. Ecclesiastes 7:2-3

So our negative emotions aren't bad. In fact, they actually work for our good, and as such, we need to learn to respond to them appropriately. There are times, however, when we lose control of ourselves to our negative emotions. This is the difference between sadness and depression. When negative emotions become a lifestyle, we're getting stuck. This is the type of situation where emotional healing is a useful tool.

The way that truth empowers us to freedom in an emotional healing situation is that it shifts our perspective. Our emotions are a result of a combination of our beliefs and our circumstances. Our circumstances are directed by our beliefs to result in emotions. The reality is that our emotions come about due to the interplay between our circumstances and our beliefs. We view the circumstances we're in through the lens of our beliefs and our emotions point to what conclusions we arrive at.[78]

Let me illustrate this with an example. Let's say that you've fallen on some difficult times financially and you have to ask your parents to borrow some money. Given your history with your parents, your feelings as you approach them are going to be different:

- Suppose in the past your sibling had to ask to borrow money from your parents, but when he or she asked your parents they had such a large fight about it they haven't talked about it in the years since. How are you going to approach your parents? Probably with a sense of dread and concern.
- Suppose instead that when your sibling approached your parents he or she was met with warm enthusiasm, and they lent him or her more than was needed in

[78] Allow me to again bring up the reality that what we believe is not always what we think is true. We can acknowledge truths but still view our lives through a lens that doesn't line up with the truth we profess. The lens you use to see life is what you *really* believe (remember our discussion on worldviews).

case something else came up. In this case, you'd probably approach your parents with confidence and expectation.

The example may be a bit silly, but I think the point comes across. Our emotions are a product of the circumstances and our beliefs. This is where emotional healing differs strongly from counseling, because Christianity has some very specific beliefs that don't really allow room for long-lasting negative emotions. Even under the old covenant, it says:

> *For his anger is but for a moment,*
> *and his favor is for a lifetime.*
> *Weeping may tarry for the night,*
> *but joy comes with the morning. Psalm 30:5*

God is simply too happy to hold back joy for very long, and he wants us as his kids to walk in that as well! Our faith is meant to take us to the place where we are not bound by our emotions, but free to experience God's rule within our being:

> *For the kingdom of God is not a matter of eating and drinking but of righteousness and peace and joy in the Holy Spirit. Romans 14:17*

Our goal with emotional healing then is to shift people's paradigm to a more accurate one, where they can properly process their circumstances without their emotions spinning out of control. As we minister truth, if it begins to take root in their heart, freedom begins to displace pain.

Deliverance

The other side of the coin is deliverance. Deliverance is ministering to people to get them free from demonic oppression. Ministering deliverance is similar because the root of demonic influence in a believer's life is belief in demonically inspired lies. The Bible is clear that we already have been delivered from under the power of the evil one:

> *He has delivered us from the domain of darkness and transferred us to the kingdom of his beloved Son, in whom we have redemption, the forgiveness of sins. Colossians 1:13-14*

> *Since therefore the children share in flesh and blood, he himself likewise partook of the same things, that through death he might destroy the one who has the power of death, that is, the devil, and deliver all those who through fear of death were subject to lifelong slavery. Hebrews 2:14-15*

This is important; Jesus has already defeated Satan and delivered us from his bondage. Let's be clear that we don't need to do what Jesus has already done. The reason believers are in need of deliverance is not that the enemy has legitimate control or access to them. Jesus made it very clear that the enemy has no authority (permission) anymore:

> *And Jesus came and said to them, "All authority in heaven and on earth has been given to me." Matthew 28:18*

Any work the enemy does, he does without permission. Our job is to teach people how to live free. The enemy's main tool now is deception:

> *[Satan] was a murderer from the beginning, and does not stand in the truth, because there is no truth in him. When he lies, he speaks out of his own character, for he is a liar and the father of lies. John 8:44*

If we don't recognize and know how to deal with the voice of the enemy, we can give him influence in our lives he shouldn't have. Jesus makes it clear in our walk of following him that we need to recognize and follow his voice, as well as recognize and not follow the enemy's voice:

> *The one who enters by the gate is the shepherd of the sheep. The gatekeeper opens the gate for him, and the sheep listen to his voice. He calls his own sheep by name and leads them out. When he has brought out all his own, he goes on ahead of them, and his sheep follow him because they know his voice. But they will never follow a stranger; in fact, they will run away from him because they do not recognize a stranger's voice. John 10:2-5*

It is important to recognize the voice of the enemy as a stranger and not follow him! The enemy works hard to hide himself in the shadows; he would like us to believe he doesn't exist because then we begin to assume that the thoughts and feelings he puts in our minds come from us, and through that deception, he leads us. We need to learn to recognize the voice that is a stranger's and learn to deal with it appropriately.

This is why deliverance is the other side of the coin of emotional healing. In both situations the ministry is one of truth because truth leads to freedom. On one side, it is freedom from our own emotions run amuck; in the other, it is freedom from the bondage the enemy tries to lure us into through his voice.

> **Theology Anchor**
>
> Emotional healing and deliverance are both ministries that focus on rooting the person's life in truth.

Living by Faith

Here is an important aspect of the Christian faith; we are saved *to* something—living by faith. The faith that saves us is the same faith that keeps us on the road:

For in the gospel the righteousness of God is revealed—a righteousness that is by faith from first to last, just as it is written: "The righteous will live by faith." Romans 1:17

Some translations word this as "a righteousness from faith to faith." The point is this: we were saved by faith, and we are to live by faith now. Paul believes that our continuation in faith is critical:

But now he has reconciled you by Christ's physical body through death to present you holy in his sight, without blemish and free from accusation— if you continue in your faith, established and firm, and do not move from the hope held out in the gospel. Colossians 1:22-23

Here's the thing: the Christian life is meant to be lived as a continual walk of faith through dependence on the Holy Spirit. This is really what we're doing in this arena; we are teaching people to live by faith that's anchored in truth.

As faith becomes something we live from, our circumstances cease to carry the weight in our lives. In a sense, we no longer live in our circumstances. We begin to live above them because in every situation our faith is established and truth is established in us. Our circumstances become the stage on which we live our lives with God. Our internal experience of the kingdom continues uninterrupted and is actually reinforced through our external circumstances. In this way, all things begin to work for our good. Whether we find ourselves in good or bad circumstances, righteousness is established in us:

When [Paul and Barnabas] had preached the gospel to that city and had made many disciples, they returned to Lystra and to Iconium and to Antioch, strengthening the souls of the disciples, encouraging them to continue in the faith,

and saying that through many tribulations we must enter the kingdom of God. Acts 14:21-22

This is the discipline of the Father; not that God punishes us, or even corrects us—but that we are formed in all things by Him. Discipline from God tends to be a subject that there is much confusion about. Let me say one thing clearly: God's discipline has nothing to do with us messing up. It can't be; God doesn't even remember what we've done![79] He can't see our wrong doing now; it's covered by the blood of Jesus. We tend to think that God's discipline is about us learning right from wrong because that's how we were disciplined as we were raised.

God's discipline is not about us doing wrong; it's about us being formed in who we are:

For [our earthly fathers] disciplined us for a short time as it seemed best to them, but he disciplines us for our good, that we may share his holiness. For the moment all discipline seems painful rather than pleasant, but later it yields the peaceful fruit of righteousness to those who have been trained by it. Hebrews 12:10-11

God disciplines us so that the fruit of righteousness, which is holiness, may be in our lives. That is why the "discipline" section in Hebrews comes right on the tail of the "hall of faith" section. God is holding up the discipline process, which comes from living by faith. If God is bringing us through this process of living by faith, it is what leads to our increase and is how he treats his sons.

It is for discipline that you have to endure. God is treating you as sons. For what son is there whom his father does not discipline? If you are left without

---

[79] Indeed, that word translated "discipline" means literally "to train children." Blue Letter Bible, accessed 2/15/12. http://www.blueletterbible.org/lang/lexicon/lexicon.cfm?Strongs=G3811&t=KJV

discipline, in which all have participated, then you are illegitimate children and not sons. Hebrews 12:7-8

As we go through the process of discipline from Father God, we learn to live by faith. Living by faith empowers us to thrive through the process of facing lies, whether they come from the enemy or our emotions.

Count it all joy, my brothers, when you meet trials of various kinds, for you know that the testing of your faith produces steadfastness. And let steadfastness have its full effect, that you may be perfect and complete, lacking in nothing. James 1:2-4

The Downward Spiral of Demonic Assault

Emotional healing and deliverance then are really two sides of the same coin, both ministering truth to the work of the enemy. Sometimes the devil ties us up with our own emotions, and other times a demon personally stays to continue the torment. In this sense, a person in need of deliverance is just further along in a process of the work of the enemy than a person just in need of emotional healing. For this reason from now on, I'm going to just refer to both of them together as deliverance.[80]

How does the enemy work in our lives? As we discussed before, his main tool is deception. He tries to take us through a process of deception in which he has increasing leverage over our experience, and through that he seeks to control us.

Here's how it works: as we discussed before, our Christian life is meant to be a walk of faith. Faith isn't part of the journey; it **is** the journey. Through faith, what has already been bought becomes our experience. Faith appropriates what is available:

---

[80] I choose the term deliverance instead of emotional healing because that is the term used in the Bible.

And we desire each one of you to show the same earnestness to have the full assurance of hope until the end, so that you may not be sluggish, but imitators of those who through faith and patience inherit the promises. Hebrews 6:11-12

For good news came to us just as to them, but the message they heard did not benefit them, because they were not united by faith with those who listened. For we who have believed enter that rest, as he has said,

"As I swore in my wrath,
They shall not enter my rest,'"

although his works were finished from the foundation of the world. Hebrews 4:2-3

As the truth is met with faith, it becomes our experience. What happens when we don't see things clearly? What happens when what we think is true isn't actually true? Well, unfortunately, what happens is our belief appropriates to our experience (often with assistance from the enemy) what we think is truth. We talked about this in the earlier section about emotional healing. A good example is this: how many of us have felt condemnation at some point since we became Christians? Romans 8:1 makes it clear that condemnation doesn't exist for us as believers. It isn't there to be had, but our belief that we are condemned creates an experience of condemnation.

This is the negative side of what Jesus talked about with the eye passage we've looked at many times:

The eye is the lamp of the body. So, if your eye is healthy, your whole body will be full of light, but if your eye is bad, your whole body will be full of darkness. If then the light in you is darkness, how great is the darkness! Matthew 6:22-23

When our eye—our perspective—is wrong, an experience of darkness is the result! The enemy knows this, and so his starting point is our perspective, or what we believe to be true. He works to snatch up truth that will make us whole:

> *The ones along the path are those who have heard; then the devil comes and takes away the word from their hearts, so that they may not believe and be saved [sozo—literally restored or made whole]. Luke 8:12*

He attacks truth because he knows if truth takes root in belief, we are released into freedom. Likewise, the enemy speaks to us lies constantly hoping they will take root in our belief.

Once his lies begin to take root in our belief (many of which we often believe without much convincing because we don't understand the gospel), our experience begins to reflect those lies. These lies take root where? (See the passage above.) In our *hearts*. In the deepest place of identity and belief, the lies of the enemy begin to take root.

Now here's the trick: what exists in our heart will come out from within us and begin to manifest in our lives:

> *The good person out of the good treasure of his heart produces good, and the evil person out of his evil treasure produces evil, for out of the abundance of the heart his mouth speaks. Luke 6:45*

> *But what comes out of the mouth proceeds from the heart, and this defiles a person. For out of the heart come evil thoughts, murder, adultery, sexual immorality, theft, false witness, slander. These are what defile a person. Matthew 15:18-20*

At this point, the person is in a destructive downward spiral. What they believe in their heart is destructive and results in destructive behavior, which the enemy heaps back on them. This reinforces the belief in their heart, and the cycle repeats.

The overall process looks like this:

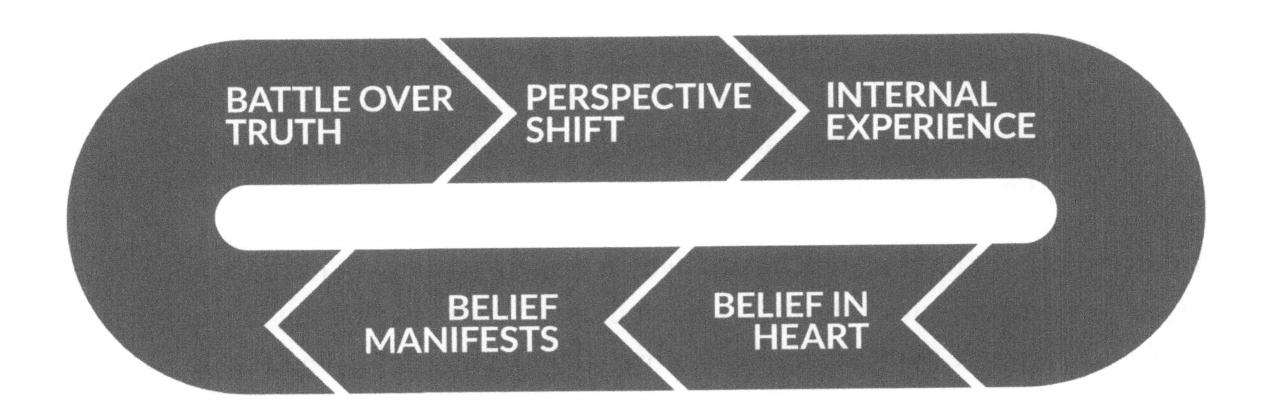

What's happening, essentially, is a methodical attack on increasingly internal aspects. First, Satan attacks what we think is true, which shapes our perspective (notice the shift from external truth to an internal perspective), then that leads to an internal experience which then affects our heart, a more internal place of belief. From there, what we believe begins to come through us, which serves to reinforce the identity that Satan has been working to cultivate in us.

Scripture refers to the process of building your life on truth through the metaphor of a house:

Everyone then who hears these words of mine and does them will be like a wise man who built his house on the rock. And the rain fell, and the floods came, and the winds blew and beat on that house, but it did not fall, because it had been founded on the rock. And everyone who hears these words of mine and does not do them will be like a foolish man who built his house on the sand. And the rain fell, and the floods came, and the winds blew and beat against that house, and it fell, and great was the fall of it. Matthew 7:24-27

According to the grace of God given to me, like a skilled master builder I laid a foundation, and someone else is building upon it. Let each one take care how he builds upon it. For no one can lay a foundation other than that which is laid, which is Jesus Christ. 1 Corinthians 3:10-11

Scripture speaks of the way we live our lives as building a house. The foundation is laid in truth (remember Jesus is the truth), but it must be truth that is caught; truth that apprehends us to the point where our actions fall into line with it. This is the foundation of the house that is built through the life we live.

Whatever we build apart from the foundation of truth creates a house that is unstable to the pressure of this world. In this place our circumstances get the better of us and we collapse (a fitting metaphor for how a person in need of emotional healing often feels). On top of that, it is also a house that a demon finds habitable. Notice that the scriptures speak of demons having a house in a person:

When the unclean spirit has gone out of a person, it passes through waterless places seeking rest, but finds none. Then it says, "I will return to my house from which I came." And when it comes, it finds the house empty, swept, and put in order. Then it goes and brings with it seven other spirits more evil than itself, and

> *they enter and dwell there, and the last state of that person is worse than the first.* Matthew 20:43-45

> *Or how can someone enter a strong man's house and plunder his goods, unless he first binds the strong man? Then indeed he may plunder his house.* Matthew 20:29

This cycle is demonic, but it's actually not always directly caused by demons. Demonic influence in the world has created systemic structures of false belief that will guide people through this process without direct demonic influence. In that case, the person usually winds up in a place of bondage to their own emotions that are running amuck because of their incorrect perspective. For the case where a demon is involved, the demon usually tries to directly take advantage of this process and facilitate it by messing with the person's mind and body. The real source of the conflict, though, is the person's belief system. Paul calls this a stronghold:

> *For the weapons of our warfare are not of the flesh but have divine power to destroy strongholds. We destroy arguments and every lofty opinion raised against the knowledge of God, and take every thought captive to obey Christ, being ready to punish every disobedience. 2 Corinthians 10:4-6*

A stronghold is simply a place where demonic beliefs have taken root in our lives. They wind up resulting in the kingdom of darkness manifesting through our lives. Remember the progression we discussed in the Identity unit:

1. Destroying arguments and lofty opinions raised against the knowledge of God. This addresses the issue of what our truth and what our perspective is.
2. Taking every thought captive to Christ. This addresses the belief that is formed in our heart. Every thought that we have must be brought into submission to Jesus so that we only meditate on the truth and the truth is continually formed in us.

3. Punishing every disobedience. This addresses when our belief manifests through actions that aren't in line with the truth. When this happens we have to cut our actions off immediately and stop the cycle of reinforcement.

Through this whole process we are guarding our hearts from the enemy sowing into them. It is what is in our heart that determines our ability to receive the life of God and live from that place:

> *[Unbelievers] are darkened in their understanding, alienated from the life of God because of the ignorance that is in them, due to their hardness of heart. They have become callous and have given themselves up to sensuality, greedy to practice every kind of impurity. Ephesians 4:18-19*

From this point of view, it becomes clear why intense struggle with sin, emotional healing, and deliverance all go together; they are all manifestations of a house that's not built on truth.

It may not be obvious how this downward spiral actually results in a person in bondage to a demon to the point where a demon can control their body. As the cycle progresses and reinforces itself, there is a gradual blurring of the voice of the demon and the thoughts and impulses of the person to the point where the person begins to listen to the demon even at the subconscious level. The thoughts are so aligned with demonic thoughts that the thought processes begin to run along those rails without conscious awareness.

I recently ministered deliverance to a young woman. Someone called me over to her and when I got to her, she was lying on the ground hissing like a snake. I brought the situation under control and began to ask her what was happening. She shared with me about struggling with this process over a number of years and how recently it had

intensified over the last few months to the point where she would often find herself on the ground slithering and hissing like a snake for a few hours at a time.

I wanted to learn from her experience, so I began to ask some questions to get a sense of what her experience was like when she manifested like this. I found her response very illuminating. These were her words as she described her experience: "Well, I'm sitting there listening to the voice of guilt in my head speaking over and over again that at some point the natural thing to do is to get on the ground and slither like a snake to try and deal with it." At some point, the demonic thoughts become so engrained and the person is so used to listening to their voice, that their actions begin to bleed over as well.

So the starting point of the war is in the mind. Demons will work hard to establish places where our thinking runs on their rails. When they have, they have an anchor for powerfully influencing our behavior. At times, their influence grows so strong a person loses control over himself or herself completely.

The critical observation to make here is this: any place a person's life isn't fully in submission to Jesus is a place where the enemy is empowered to build a house. When we choose to live a sinful lifestyle, that is a place where we've elected to let the enemy's influence and thinking be more important to us than God's. We've let the enemy begin to form our thinking. When we don't live with our money in submission to God, that is a place where the enemy has the ability to control us. When we choose not to forgive but hold on to bitterness and anger instead, we empower the enemy's attempt to make our thinking line up with his own. Remember Paul's words to the Ephesians:

> *Be angry and do not sin; do not let the sun go down on your anger, and give no opportunity to the devil. Ephesians 4:26-27*

We can choose to submit our anger to God and deal with it his way (see Matthew 18:15), or we can choose to hold on to it and deal with it the devil's way. What is the result? We sin and empower the devil to influence our thinking.

So an important question to ask ourselves and the people we minister to is this: how free do we want to live? We are free, but we don't all live in *freedom*.

> *For freedom Christ has set us free; stand firm therefore, and do not submit again to a yoke of slavery. Galatians 5:1*

The first step is to submit every aspect of our lives to God. This is what we mean when we say "Jesus is Lord." What does Lord mean? It means he calls the shots! It means what he says goes, not what we say.

Keys to Freedom

So how do we reverse the process of demonic attack and bring the person freedom? Well first of all, what do we mean by freedom? Freedom is not that the enemy doesn't bother us. If Satan messed with Jesus, he'll mess with us. Freedom is knowing how to handle the voice of lies so it doesn't disrupt our lives.

When ministering to someone with these types of issues, what we're trying to do is equip them to move towards the walk of faith. The opposite of the downward spiral of the attack of the enemy is walking by faith. To give the person true freedom, then, you need to not only break them out of their current bondage, but also empower them to begin to reverse the process for themselves to begin to walk in strength. The following are some keys that I've found are incredibly helpful for helping people to begin to handle the enemy's lies in constructive ways.

Key 1: Know the Gospel—Addresses the Battle over Truth

This might even sound a little too obvious, but it is clearly important to know the gospel. Paul says

> *For I am not ashamed of the gospel, for it is the power of God for salvation to everyone who believes, to the Jew first and also to the Greek. For in it the righteousness of God is revealed from faith for faith, as it is written, "The righteous shall live by faith." Romans 1:16-17*

The gospel is the power of salvation. Why? Because it reveals who we are (righteousness) and how to walk (by faith). Very often people don't understand who they are because they don't understand the gospel as it pertains to our identity as we've already discussed. Know the gospel and be prepared to teach people who they are. When people know who they are because of the gospel, the lies of the enemy are exposed and recognized. Without that grounding lies can be passed off as the truth.

This is really important because one of the major lies the enemy tries to pass off on many people is that we are what we've done. He tries to trick us into defining our identity on our actions, rather than on Jesus' actions. The amazing thing about repentance is that is actually changes us into new people! The very act of turning to the Lord about what we've done actually releases us in our heart to be a new person that isn't who we were!

Key 2: Live under Grace, Not Law—Addresses the Battle over Truth

Living under the law is not how we're meant to live, but many believers don't know that. As believers, we are to live by faith, not the law, and you can't mix the two. You can't try to live by grace in most areas of your life but revert back to the law in regards to morality. Paul makes it pretty clear that to accept the littlest bit of the law is to accept it completely and cut ourselves off from grace:

> *Look: I, Paul, say to you that if you accept circumcision, Christ will be of no advantage to you. I testify again to every man who accepts circumcision that he is obligated to keep the whole law. You are severed from Christ, you who would be justified by the law; you have fallen away from grace. Galatians 5:2-4*

So it's either law or grace; you can't do both. Additionally if it's law:

> *For all who rely on works of the law are under a curse; for it is written, "Cursed be everyone who does not abide by all things written in the Book of the Law, and do them." Galatians 3:10*

So if we live by the law (doing things to please God), we actually put ourselves under a curse! It gets worse if we share this way of living with others; we move to a double curse (see Galatians 1:8-9). Furthermore, grace is what liberates us from the dominion of sin:

> *For sin will have no dominion over you, since you are not under law but under grace. Romans 6:14*

Living by the law puts us under a curse and the dominion of sin! Add to that condemnation, (Romans 8:1-2) and you're in really sad shape. The enemy is ready to have a heyday with you.

Key 3: Don't Let Your Circumstances or Feelings Define Your Truth—Addresses Shaping Our Perspective

Another common catch point is that people take cues about truth from their feelings and circumstances. We are to live by faith, not feelings. It doesn't really matter how I

feel if I am rooted in truth. Take your truth from the word of God and don't let your feelings sway your opinion. This doesn't mean you deny what you feel or your circumstances, but you know there is a higher truth-God's word.[81] This is critical because what happens otherwise is that our feelings get mixed up in our perception. The enemy comes along and throws a thought in our head that stirs up feelings because he's cultivated them in our heart! Just because a lie feels true doesn't make it true!

This is important because the enemy will always try to attack us where we're not established in the truth, which will feel like the lies are true. That's his strategy because he knows that if he attacks us in places where we're already established in the truth, the lie stands out as ridiculous! It doesn't stick to us because the truth is formed in us, and the lie is exposed immediately. In places where the truth isn't established in us, our emotions get stirred. That doesn't mean the lie is true; it just means that we know a place where the truth needs to be built in our lives. We need to perfect this process, of seeing our weak points as opportunities for strength. If we don't know how to process the case where our emotions get away from us, we often try to find something to do to alleviate them, which is actually playing into the enemy's hands because we're reinforcing our tendency to live by our feelings.

Key 4: Don't Internalize the Voice of the Enemy—Addresses Our Beliefs Leading to Experience

The enemy works very hard to convince us that his voice is ours. He does this with temptation, and he does this with condemnation and accusation. Until we realize that the voice of condemnation, accusation, temptation, shame, guilt, fear, doubt, torment,

---

[81] The distinction here is vital. There is something that looks like faith that is denial. Faith doesn't deny the problem, but holds to the fact that God is bigger than the reality of the problem. If we're living to achieve rather than receive, we'll try to manufacture faith. This leads to denial, not true faith.

and so on are his voice and not ours, we're very likely to internalize what he says, and that's exactly what he wants! Many times I have ministered to people, and they have quickly gone from inner turmoil to freedom in just minutes by realizing the voice was coming from the outside, not the inside.

Perhaps the most common place this comes up is with temptation. The enemy loves to tempt us and then turn around and accuse us for having the thoughts he just put in our mind. Don't buy that lie! Hearing his voice is not sin. Jesus was tempted as well.

His tactic here is to get us to turn inwards and begin to look at ourselves. This is a trap and leads to taking our eyes off of Jesus. Remember, we always look to Jesus for our salvation, not to ourselves. If we feel insecure about our motives, we need to look to Jesus for the answer, not step aside and examine ourselves. Jesus says it's his job to keep us:

> *Now to him who is able to keep you from stumbling and to present you blameless before the presence of his glory with great joy, to the only God, our Savior, through Jesus Christ our Lord, be glory, majesty, dominion, and authority, before all time and now and forever. Amen. Jude 24-25*

Key 5: Don't Let the Enemy Make You Feel Guilty for Hearing His Voice—Addresses Our Beliefs Leading to Experience

This one affects so many believers. The enemy's first tactic is to sell his thoughts to us as our own. If we know enough truth to recognize his voice as separate from ours, then his second tactic is to turn around and accuse us of hearing him. He speaks to us and suggests something and then turns around and harasses us for hearing him.

We need to realize that hearing the voice of the enemy doesn't mean anything is wrong. Many believers feel that if they can hear a demon that must mean they're demonized.

(Notice what happened there? The circumstances became an identity very quickly.) This is not true. To hear the enemy is to hear the enemy. It doesn't mean there is something wrong with you. It doesn't mean you've "opened a door" that if you closed you wouldn't hear the enemy. It is a fact of being a Christian—we hear from God and from the enemy. In fact, what Jesus promised as followers of him is that we would recognize that his voice is different from the enemy's voice:

> *When he has brought out all his own, he goes before them, and the sheep follow him, for they know his voice. A stranger they will not follow, but they will flee from him, for they do not know the voice of strangers.* John 10:4-5

What's the implication? You'll hear Jesus' voice and the enemy's voice! Jesus didn't promise we wouldn't hear the enemy's voice, but that we'd recognize it.

The fact is that if you never hear the enemy's voice, he'll also never be able to tempt you. Jesus himself went through a temptation in which the enemy talked with him directly, and we don't think there was anything wrong with Jesus. If the enemy can speak to Jesus, he can speak to you. Don't let him make you feel guilty for hearing his voice, indeed be encouraged that you can discern his voice. That's what Jesus promised!

I believe there are a lot of good believers out there who are oppressed because they are living under the law. The law is the ammunition the enemy uses to condemn and accuse us. Notice the language used for the way Jesus dealt with the law and how it relates to the enemy:

> *by canceling the record of debt that stood against us with its legal demands. This he set aside, nailing it to the cross. He disarmed the rulers and authorities and put them to open shame, by triumphing over them in him. Colossians 2:14-15*

By setting aside the legal demands (read law) that resulted in a record of debt, which was cancelled, Jesus *disarmed* the rulers and authorities. The law is the enemy's weapon; to continue to live under it is to give him a tool to use against you.

Key 6: Know the Enemy Always Lies—Addresses Beliefs Forming in Our Hearts

The enemy is the father of lies; when he lies, he's just speaking out of whom he is. When we recognize his lies, how should we receive them? As lies! What does that mean? *It means the opposite is true.* When the enemy whispers guilt to us, rather than feeling guilty, we can receive this knowing that it's a lie and that we are so spotless and so far from guilt it's not even funny. Every time he provokes our feelings to be condemned, we can rejoice that we're not condemned but completely free!

This is critical because often what happens is that when the enemy lies, we recognize that it is a lie, so we try to resist the lie rather than meditating on the truth. The problem is that if the lie has been sown in our heart and we don't turn our thoughts towards the truth when the lie is provoked, we never displace the lie with truth in our hearts.

> *Keep your heart with all vigilance,*
> *for from it flow the springs of life. Proverbs 4:23*

This process of guarding our heart sits right next to the biblical practice of meditation. I find it interesting that when Moses died and God passed the fulfillment of Moses' mission to bring the Israelites into the Promised Land to Joshua, he gave him some very specific instructions, including:

> *This Book of the Law shall not depart from your mouth, but you shall meditate on it day and night, so that you may be careful to do according to all that is written in*

it. For then you will make your way prosperous, and then you will have good success. Joshua 1:8

God instructed Joshua to meditate on the Law day and night by not letting it depart from his mouth. He instructed Joshua to speak as a meditative practice. Likewise, we would do well to learn to guard our hearts through speaking meditation. Don't just think about the truth; speak it out over your life. Remember, life and death are in the power of the tongue.[82]

If we realize that every time a lie lands on us and stirs up our hearts, it is an opportunity to meditate on the truth and the reality of the situation and receive truth into our hearts. Then every time the enemy comes after me, he actually provokes me to get stronger! The very fact that his arrows are hitting me reveals the places that I immediately begin to exercise my faith towards to receiving the grace to change. It's amazing—the devil actually reveals where truth is to be formed in us!

Key 7: Understand Freedom Is a Process—Addresses the Cycle of Reinforcement

Just as the enemy attacks us in a process, so our growth is a process as well. We learn to walk by faith over time, not instantly. This perspective is important because often people are in so much pain or torment, they want a quick fix; when something isn't a quick fix, they feel it's not working and give up hope. God wants to establish us in the truth and build something in us, and that takes time. Sometimes we may see dramatic improvement over a short period of time, and that's great, but that doesn't always mean strength has been built. Expect freedom to be something you have to grow into to keep. Notice what God said about the Promised Land to Moses:

---

[82] Proverbs 18:21

I will not drive [the other nations] out from before you in one year, lest the land become desolate and the wild beasts multiply against you. Little by little I will drive them out from before you, until you have increased and possess the land. Exodus 23:29-30

Paul speaks directly of many of these keys in his discussion about putting on the armor of God:

Put on the whole armor of God, that you may be able to stand against the schemes of the devil…Therefore take up the whole armor of God, that you may be able to withstand in the evil day, and having done all, to stand firm. Stand therefore, having fastened on the belt of truth, and having put on the breastplate of righteousness, and, as shoes for your feet, having put on the readiness given by the gospel of peace. In all circumstances take up the shield of faith, with which you can extinguish all the flaming darts of the evil one; and take the helmet of salvation, and the sword of the Spirit, which is the word of God, praying at all times in the Spirit, with all prayer and supplication. Ephesians 6:11,13-18

The parts of the armor that Paul lists are:

- Belt of truth—in Roman armor the belt was the first part of the armor to go on. It is the foundation of our defense (Keys 1 - 3).
- Breastplate of righteousness—this piece would actually hook into the belt in Roman armor. Our identity is rooted in the truth and protects our heart (Keys 2 - 5).
- Shoes of readiness from the gospel of peace—In combat your footing is critical. It determines how much force you can exert resisting your enemy. The more we are prepared to resist the enemy through the gospel and submit to God by receiving his grace, the harder we can push him back (Keys 1 & 2).

- Shield of faith—notice Paul commends us to take up this tool in all circumstances. As we exercise our faith towards the darts of the enemy, they are extinguished (Keys 5 & 6).
- Helmet of salvation—what protects our mind and shapes our thinking is an understanding of the wholeness that God has for us. This protects our thinking from wandering (Key 3).
- Sword of the Spirit—Paul explains this is the "word of God," where *word* is *rhema*, a freshly spoken word from God. Paul instructs us to pray over us at all times what God speaks over us to counter what the enemy speaks over us (Key 6).

Symptoms and Manifestations of Demonic Operation

It is quite useful to have a sense of the types of behavior that demonic influence heads towards. Many of these symptoms can be caused by other circumstances as well, but with demonic activity, you can expect to see at least some of these:[83]

- Inability to live a "normal" life and breaking down of sociability
- Extreme, erratic behavior often trending towards violence
- Rapid personality changes
- Restlessness, possibly leading to insomnia
- Inner anguish that persists through life
- Self-inflicted injury that might lead towards suicide
- Unexplained illness with no obvious medical cause
- Compulsive and addictive behavior
- Abnormal sexual behavior
- Defeat, failure, and depression in the Christian life
- Occult involvement and behavior
- Speech difficulties

[83] This list is drawn from Ron Phillips' book *Everyone's Guide to Demons and Spiritual Warfare pp 99-103.*

- Doctrinal error
- Religious legalism

These are symptoms that occur during the person's life. They are sort of *lifestyle* symptoms; the demon trying to direct the person into living the same quality of existence they have. There are also manifestations that happen in the moment, often during worship or prayer. Here are some of the more common manifestations:[84]

- Cold
- Pungent smells
- Trembling or shaking
- Falling to the ground, often violently
- Sudden onset of feeling ill, faint, headaches, pressure or other physical pain
- Contortions or other unnatural movements
- Pupils dilating
- Squints or eyes rolling back or looking two different directions
- Trying to run away
- Sudden catatonic state
- Swearing and other foul language
- A number of animalistic noises, including hissing, snarling, barking, roaring and bellowing
- Animalistic motions, including clawing and slithering like a snake

This is by no means a complete list; one time I had a demon manifest by freaking my cell phone out!

Here is a useful rule of thumb to remember; a demon prefers *not* to manifest. When demons manifest, particularly in dramatic ways, they risk giving up their cover. As

[84] This list is taken mostly from a more extensive list in Peter Horrobin's *Healing Through Deliverance,* pp 480-483.

agents that act through deception, it is much safer for them to maintain a low profile and not be seen. Why do they manifest then? Well, for two reasons:

1. They can't hold it back. Demons don't like the presence of God. It is intensely uncomfortable to them because they know that God brings judgment on them. This is seen in the demon's reaction to Jesus' presence in the synagogue as Jesus taught:

   And immediately there was in their synagogue a man with an unclean spirit. And he cried out, "What have you to do with us, Jesus of Nazareth? Have you come to destroy us? I know who you are—the Holy One of God." Mark 1:23-24

- Remember that the Holy Spirit comes to bring conviction of judgment because the ruler of the world is already judged (John 16:11). The presence of the Spirit of God creates a conviction of judgment in demons. Basically they start freaking out and can't control it!

2. As a threatening tactic. Demons know that their manifestations cause fear. They know we freak out when things happen that we can't see the cause for. They manifest then to put us in a state of fear, so we will capitulate to their control further.

So know when a demon starts to manifest, it's probably a good thing! It means God is already there and putting pressure on the demon. Our response then shouldn't be fear, but confidence. God already has our back, and the demon is already seeing its influence on the person loosening.

What should you do when you're ministering to a person that begins manifesting a demon? Well, remember that we minister to people, not to demons. Don't let your focus change from the person to the demon. The *person* is to whom we're ministering, and the manifestation is meant to frighten and embarrass him or her. For this reason, we want to shut down manifestation and bring the situation under control as quickly as possible. If a person is manifesting, quickly bind manifestation (see the prayer below) and call the person back to you. Use their name and ask them to look you in the eyes. The eyes really are the windows to the soul, so with eye contact most people regain control of themselves.

When I'm in a situation like this where a demon begins manifesting, or a situation where a person is asking for prayer for deliverance (and nothing has manifested yet), I will usually pray something like this:

In Jesus' name right now I bind all demonic influence. I forbid you from manifesting and I silence your voice while we are praying for this person. I cover [person's name] with the blood of Jesus right now and forbid demons from affecting him/her.

The specific words of the prayer obviously aren't terribly important, but my goal is to block the demons from interfering with our process, whether it is due to outward (manifestation) or inward (the demonic voice) torment through the authority we have in Jesus. Demons know the name of Jesus is the name they must bow to and that the blood of Jesus buys our freedom, so it's important to bring those up. They actually have substance in the spiritual realm.

I find that most of the time the manifestation is shut down almost completely immediately. Sometimes the demon will thrash around a little bit before complying. Just keep the pressure on. Jesus actually had a situation like this as well:

> *And crying out with a loud voice, he said, "What have you to do with me, Jesus, Son of the Most High God? I adjure you by God, do not torment me." For [Jesus] was saying to him, "Come out of the man, you unclean spirit!" Mark 5:7-8*

Jesus was commanding the demon to leave, and it was resisting him. Deliverance often isn't a one-command solution; demons often don't comply without resistance. Know your authority and keep at it.

Moving Towards Freedom

So what specifically do we do when dealing with an emotional healing or deliverance issue? The first thing to keep in mind is that we have kind of a two-fold problem: there is the presenting problem and the "house" of the problem. True healing involves addressing both issues.

First of all, the end goal of the process is the freedom of the person, which means we need to empower the person to reverse the demonic downward spiral we talked about before. If the demon leaves or the current emotional pain is relieved but the person is still caught in the downward spiral, they're not free; the process has just been temporarily set back. On top of that, we probably want to give them a bit of a running start in the process, so we'll want to break down the strongholds that have been built as much as we can.

Additionally, you want to make sure that you choose the battlefield. There are times when a person is manifesting or in emotional turmoil and you have the choice as to whether to deal with the situation right away or whether to just try and ease the situation somewhat immediately and choose to meet again later. Don't let the enemy choose the terms of battle; the person has had this problem for quite a while, they can handle dealing with it for another few days. Pay attention to time constraints and the degree of public exposure, as well as your current level of stamina. You want to go into this refreshed and confident in the authority you have in Jesus. Ministering in teams is usually best in this type of ministry as well; it's good to have both an extra set of ears and eyes, as well as prayer support during the process.

Here a general path that I follow for these situations:

Step 1: Bring the Situation under Control

Often when someone comes to you, it is because the situation is already out of control. Sometimes a demon is already manifesting; other times the person is already out of control emotionally and in a downward spiral. The first thing I do is try to pull the person out of their current downward spiral.

This is important because it empowers the person to take responsibility. Often when a person is dealing with an issue this prevalent in their lives, they switch to victim mode. The first step towards healing is taking responsibility for the problem and for the journey of getting out of where they currently are. Getting control of the situation, then, looks a little different depending on the situation:

- If the person has a demon manifesting, stop the manifestation as described in the section above.
- If the person is in debilitating emotional pain, minister the peace and love of Jesus until they regain their composure.
- Be very intentional about connecting with the person and getting their cooperation. The more centered in themselves the person is, the more they will be able to help with the process and continue to walk it out on their own.

Step 2: Assess The House

Talk with the person and begin to get a sense of the problem. As you do, ask questions that help uncover the thoughts and beliefs of the person. Remember the real problem

here is the assault on their belief through the process we discussed earlier. You want to get a sense of where the enemy has built strongholds in their thinking. Look for the signs of the enemy: killing, stealing, and destruction in their thought patterns. These often start through fear, condemnation, or guilt. You can often trace those backwards to an identity deficit due to a lack of understanding of the gospel that demons are taking advantage of to sell lies to the person as truth.

As well as looking for what direction the person is having struggles, it's also helpful to assess how far along the person is on the downward spiral we discussed earlier.

While working through this step, definitely ask Holy Spirit for his direction as well; he knows the situation better than either of you and wants the person free more than either of you!

Step 3: Minister Truth to Activate Their Faith

Our goal here is to activate the person's faith and empower him or her to break out of the downward cycle. At this point we want to share some of the keys discussed earlier. Different people need different keys; so depending on what you learn in step 2, you'll share different keys. Walk them through how the gospel secures who they are, and in light of that how to process the voice of the enemy and turn it into a tool for strength in their life. I almost always talk with the person about at least keys 1 and 4.

Our goal here is two-fold. First, we want to empower the person to stay free and conquer the accusations the enemy slings at them. Secondly, the more we speak truth, the more their faith will be activated. This makes the next step easier as well. Don't rush through this step. This is probably the place you should spend the most time.

Step 4: Break Strongholds

Once you've equipped the person to begin to establish truth in his or her life, you also want to break down some of the work of the enemy and give the person a bit of a running start. Each person's life is different, and you'll need to address different things depending on what you've been gathering from the process so far. Here are some of the common things you may want to help them work through:

- Sin issues—One of the common teachings in deliverance is that sin gives the enemy access to us as believers. I don't believe that at all. Nothing gives the enemy permission or access to us as believers. He's an illegal intruder regardless of whether we've sinned or not. Furthermore, sin ought to have no power over us anymore:

  For sin will have no dominion over you, since you are not under law but under grace. Romans 6:14

- The problem isn't that sin gives the enemy access to the believer; the problem is that sin gives the enemy ammunition to fire at us. It is grounds for the enemy to lobby guilt and shame at us. If we're not rooted in a deep understanding of the gospel, we are actually feeling as if we should feel guilty or shameful. It creates in us an expectation of hearing the enemy's voice and an understanding that we deserve the condemnation we're hearing.

  The truth is that we've already been forgiven, but relationships are based on honesty. So, in our relationship with God, we need to own what we've done. In this kind of a situation, I'll lead the person through a prayer owning their actions before God and thanking him for the provision that has been provided through the Cross both for their forgiveness and their transformation to not be that person anymore.

- Forgiveness—Forgiveness issues with other people or themselves is another common topic that comes up. Choosing to not forgive people puts us in the same place as the devil. God forgives everyone; only the devil is bitter and has unforgiveness. When we choose to hold on to hurt (usually because we don't know who we are), we are actually aligning our thoughts and beliefs with Satan's. It is actually an express choice to choose to believe the devil's perspective instead of truth and hold in our heart something that doesn't belong there. The power of forgiveness is often dramatic in people's lives. Choosing to form our truth based on the hurt in our heart puts a large platform of ungodly belief in our worldview.

  Often people don't want to forgive people because of the hurt that the other has caused in their life; forgiving them feels like letting them off the hook. The opposite is actually true; one of the lies the enemy sells to us is that unforgiveness somehow makes the other person pay for what they've done. That's pretty much never true! The other person is probably somewhere else not even thinking about what they did, and the person in front of you is the one paying! Giving them this perspective often helps them see that unforgiveness only makes them worse off.

Both of these are ways that people actually align the way they live their life with the kingdom of darkness. There are many others as well. My goal isn't to provide an exhaustive list, but to point out a few common ones. Essentially what you want to start with is doing demolition to any place the person is living the way the enemy wants them to live. Pay attention to what comes up in the process and deal with it.

Theology Anchor

Activating faith and destroying strongholds is the binding and loosing Jesus referred to.

After going directly after what comes up, I'll often pray a prayer that is aimed at breaking down the work the enemy has built in the person's life. Something along the lines of:

Father, I thank you for [person's name], and I bless him/her right now in the name of Jesus. I ask by the power of Holy Spirit that every way the enemy has tried to form his/her thinking be broken right now. I release a grace for renewing the mind and being free from the voice of the enemy. I dismiss feelings of guilt, condemnation, and fear and release this person into the freedom that Jesus bought for him/her with his blood.

Once you've spent some time breaking the house down, then if there is a demon, you probably want to confront the demon directly and tell it to leave. Usually demons leave more quietly when you've broken things down more. If they know they have a platform to affect the person, they'll use that to resist leaving. My goal is usually to make deliverance as minimally traumatic to the person as possible, so I usually try to do as much demolition as possible before confronting the demon directly. At this point the prayer is somewhat direct. I'll pray something along the lines of:

Demon, in the name of Jesus I command you to leave [person's name]. I release him or her from your bondage.

Often the demon will leave quickly and quietly. Sometimes there is a physical manifestation; other times there isn't, but the person almost always knows when the demon has left. It's very clear to them.

If the demon doesn't leave right away, I'll usually keep the pressure on for a little bit. If after a minute or two the demon doesn't submit, I'll go back and do some more demolition before trying again.

Step 5: Aftercare

After the prayer session is over, direct the person to the process of building truth in his or her life based on the keys you've shared. Remind him or her that this is a big step on the road of healing, but that he or she will need to continue to move forward on their own, too. I give him or her the "Staying Free" document at the end of this chapter. If possible, I like to check in with him or her after a week or two and see how he or she is doing.

Often the enemy will come back and attack him or her a few times at a later time. This is really the person's chance to establish his or her healing. Most of the time the enemy comes back a time or two, but after getting beaten back he starts to give up the fight.

Deliverance and Unbelievers

The subject of deliverance to unbelievers is a bit tricky. If the person isn't a Christian, they don't have the means to keep themselves free, so deliverance isn't a good idea. On the other hand, you never really know when God is going to use deliverance to free someone and show them his love and power so that they want to be saved![85]

Generally, these are my guidelines regarding deliverance to unbelievers—of course, subject to Holy Spirit's guidance:

- If they really ask for it, I tell them that I can get them free, but without knowing Jesus they won't be able to stay free. If they are willing to become a Christian when they see it gets them free, I'll proceed with deliverance and pray for salvation between steps 2 & 3.
- If an unbeliever is in need of deliverance and doesn't want to be free, I'll just release the peace of Jesus over them. This kind of calms the storm around them.

---

[85] None of the people Jesus ministered deliverance to were born again.

One time I prayed for a lady in a grocery store who God gave me a word of knowledge about having trouble sleeping. She said she did, and I immediately saw a lot of darkness around her. I prayed the peace of God over her, and she said she felt a shift as I prayed. Her countenance changed dramatically and afterwards she thanked me profusely and said that I had probably made her year![86] Even if we don't bring the person to know Jesus, we can still sow powerful seeds in people's lives by bringing the peaceful presence of God into their lives.

Staying Free

After the battle to get free there is a battle to stay free. In Matthew 12:43-45 Jesus informs us that demons will come back and try to occupy the territory they used to. This sheet is intended to equip you with some tools to fight the continuing fight of freedom more effectively.

- **Take responsibility for your freedom**. This is probably the single most important factor. Take ownership of the fight and responsibility for your actions. Holy Spirit will keep you free, but usually not without your cooperation.

- **Stay connected to the church**. The enemy tries a divide-and-conquer tactic against us. If we are separate from the fold, we become easy targets. Stay in community and fellowship with believers, and find some people you can be honest with about the process you're in right now. Keeping things in the light is the road to freedom—see 1 John 1:7.

- **Hearing the enemy's voice doesn't mean something is wrong**. Satan loves to speak to us and then accuse us of hearing him. In John 10:5 Jesus actually says that his followers will hear the voice of the enemy. Learn to process the voice of the enemy when you hear it, instead of feeling like there is a problem with you.

[86] I've often wondered if I should have pressed in further and offered her to pray for her salvation. I had a feeling she was into new age spirituality and might have been a witch or a channeler. This was one of my earlier encounters with power evangelism and I wasn't quite as forward as I've grown to be.

- **Don't internalize the voice of the enemy**. Another common tactic the enemy does is speak to us and then try and convince us those thoughts are coming from ourselves. He always tries to subvert our identity as sons and daughters of God and convince us we're less than that. John 10:10 gives us the criteria—anything that sounds like death, loss or destruction comes from the enemy. Don't buy the lie it's coming from you. It's not.

- **Remember that our feelings are often not true**. This dovetails with the last one—the enemy tries to use our feelings against us. Regardless of whether you feel like the lies of the enemy are true, they're still lies! John 8:44 says he is the father of lies. The devil can't attack you with truth; he doesn't have access to it.

- **Understand the enemy always lies**. If the enemy can only attack you with lies, then realize the opposite is always the truth. If the enemy attacks you with fear the truth is you're not fearful! Take what he says and recognize the truth. Meditate and pray over that truth with God and let it be formed in you. In this way even the enemy is strengthening our walk with Jesus.

- **Don't let him distract you**. The enemy loves nothing more than to get us to focus on him and distracted from our pursuit of Jesus. We don't need to rebuke or resist the enemy—keep your focus on God and truth. Every time the enemy speaks take it and turn it around to focus on God with. If every time he presses you it pushes you closer to God he's not going to want to stick around very long.

- **Expect a process**. We all want to have a deliverance where the enemy is pushed back in our lives and never comes back and bothers us again, but the reality is that freedom is most often a process. That's okay though, because the process strengthens us and establishes truth in us (see Exodus 23:29-30). Don't get discouraged—every time the enemy comes against you he's giving you resistance training; you're only getting stronger!

Stewarding a Deposit

Jesus tells a very interesting parable towards the end of Matthew:

> *"For [the Kingdom of God] will be like a man going on a journey, who called his servants and entrusted to them his property. To one he gave five talents, to another two, to another one, to each according to his ability. Then he went away. He who had received the five talents went at once and traded with them, and he made five talents more. So also he who had the two talents made two talents more. But he who had received the one talent went and dug in the ground and hid his master's money. Now after a long time the master of those servants came and settled accounts with them. And he who had received the five talents came forward, bringing five talents more, saying, 'Master, you delivered to me five talents; here I have made five talents more.' His master said to him, 'Well done, good and faithful servant. You have been faithful over a little; I will set you over much. Enter into the joy of your master.' And he also who had the two talents came forward, saying, 'Master, you delivered to me two talents; here I have made two talents more.' His master said to him, 'Well done, good and faithful servant. You have been faithful over a little; I will set you over much. Enter into the joy of your master.' He also who had received the one talent came forward, saying, 'Master, I knew you to be a hard man, reaping where you did not sow, and gathering where you scattered no seed, so I was afraid, and I went and hid your talent in the ground. Here you have what is yours.' But his master answered him, 'You wicked and slothful servant! You knew that I reap where I have not sown and gather where I scattered no seed? Then you ought to have invested my money with the bankers, and at my coming I should have received what was my own with interest. So take the talent from him and give it to him who has the ten talents. For*

to everyone who has will more be given, and he will have an abundance. But from the one who has not, even what he has will be taken away.'" Matthew 25:14-29

In this parable, Jesus presents a kingdom principle that what you have been given is given for a reason, and the key to increase is stewardship. Whatever God gives us that we don't steward properly isn't something we can expect to keep. On the flip side, when we steward correctly we upgrade from the little that God gives us, and He turns it into much!

The last eight months we've been on a journey. God has deposited unique things in each one of us, and we've grown and been changed in the process.[87] The question we want to ask ourselves now is where do we go from here? What's next for us? If we want to continue moving forward in the kingdom, we need to turn our attention to stewardship. How do we steward the deposit that God has made in us during our journey?

One of the most important ways to steward the deposit we have is to give away what we've experienced. Wimber would say it this way: "We only keep what we give away." This is the nature of the kingdom: grace can't restrain itself from giving away. This is captured well in a passage that we often apply towards financial giving, but we forget that this is actually in a context of spiritual behavior:

Judge not, and you will not be judged; condemn not, and you will not be condemned; forgive, and you will be forgiven; give, and it will be given to you. Good measure, pressed down, shaken together, running over, will be put into your lap. For with the measure you use it will be measured back to you. Luke 6:37-38

---

[87] If you've ever taught, you know that the teacher learns at least as much as the students do!

If we receive something and keep it to ourselves, we're not stewarding through kingdom understanding. On the flip side, when we receive something with thankfulness and give it to others, it multiplies:

> *Jesus then took the loaves, and when he had given thanks, he distributed them to those who were seated. So also the fish, as much as they wanted. And when they had eaten their fill, he told his disciples, "Gather up the leftover fragments, that nothing may be lost." So they gathered them up and filled twelve baskets with fragments from the five barley loaves left by those who had eaten. John 6:11-13*

If we want to learn to steward the momentum of the Spirit on our life, we need to learn to give it away to others.

Pulling Others into Your Momentum

Jesus brought his disciples through a process to pull them into the momentum he had on his life. Crowds of people were following Jesus, and at some point Jesus chose twelve people from among those following him around and sent them out to do the same thing that he was doing:

> *And he called to him his twelve disciples and gave them authority over unclean spirits, to cast them out, and to heal every disease and every affliction...These twelve Jesus sent out, instructing them, "Go nowhere among the Gentiles and enter no town of the Samaritans, but go rather to the lost sheep of the house of Israel. And proclaim as you go, saying, 'The kingdom of heaven is at hand.' Heal the sick, raise the dead, cleanse lepers, cast out demons. You received without paying; give without pay. Matthew 10:1,5-8*

By inviting and commissioning the disciples, Jesus was beginning to pull them into his momentum. He does this by pulling them into his mission. There is authority and power that are available to complete the commission Jesus has; by pulling the disciples into his mission, Jesus makes available to the disciples the resources necessary to complete the call. Jesus even informs them of this dynamic as he sends them out:

> *Whoever receives you receives me, and whoever receives me receives him who sent me. The one who receives a prophet because he is a prophet will receive a prophet's reward, and the one who receives a righteous person because he is a righteous person will receive a righteous person's reward.* Matthew 10:40-41

Jesus does the same later with seventy-two:

> *After this the Lord appointed seventy-two others and sent them on ahead of him, two by two, into every town and place where he himself was about to go.*
> *Luke 10:1*

After pulling these others under his call, Jesus mentored them and taught them how to steward what they now had access to. You can see examples of how to posture yourself in light of success (Luke 10:17-20), and rejection (Luke 9:54-55), reasons for failure (Matthew 17:19-20), as well as a wealth of teaching about how the kingdom works.

By pulling the disciples into his mission, Jesus is both more effective in completing his task,[88] but also he is teaching the disciples how to maintain momentum on their own lives. Likewise we need to learn to pull others into the mission that God gives us in our lives, as well as we need to learn to be pulled into someone else's mission and be taught by them. The disciples didn't receive their own call until they had been under

---

[88] Note that Jesus specifically sent the seventy-two to places he was about to go. Jesus was mentoring them in the context of completing his own call. He had a specific mission to complete before Calvary (see John 17:4), and the disciples helped him complete that mission.

Jesus' call for three years. Likewise, only as we demonstrate faithfulness in the context of someone else's call can we learn to be faithful to the call that God gives us.

Bill Johnson teaches about the fact that there are actually many giants listed in the Bible that were killed. David killed the first and his mighty men killed the others. If you want to be a giant killer, find one to learn from!

Owning Your Own Call

After being pulled into Jesus' momentum by coming into his call, and through that experience learning how to maintain momentum on their own lives, Jesus releases to the disciples a call of their own:

> *Jesus said to them again, "Peace be with you. As the Father has sent me, even so I am sending you." And when he had said this, he breathed on them and said to them, "Receive the Holy Spirit. If you forgive the sins of any, they are forgiven them; if you withhold forgiveness from any, it is withheld." John 20:21-23*

There is a time of being mentored and pulled into someone else's momentum, and there is a time to step into your own call from God and develop your own momentum behind that. Notice that their own call comes with authority (over sin) and power (to come on the day of Pentecost).

This concept is important not only for us personally, but also for the whole body of Christ. Elisha is a great example of this. When Elijah left for heaven, Elisha asked for a double portion of what Elijah had:

> *When they had crossed, Elijah said to Elisha, "Ask what I shall do for you, before I am taken from you." And Elisha said, "Please let there be a double portion of your spirit on me." 2 Kings 2:9*

> **Theology Anchor**
> What doesn't get stewarded gets lost.

Elisha gets the double portion of what Elijah had and performs exactly twice as many miracles as Elijah did. Elisha failed to pass on what he carried, though, and he took it with him to his grave, literally:

> *So Elisha died, and they buried him. Now bands of Moabites used to invade the land in the spring of the year. And as a man was being buried, behold, a marauding band was seen and the man was thrown into the grave of Elisha, and as soon as the man touched the bones of Elisha, he revived and stood on his feet. 2 Kings 13:20-21*

Likewise, if we do not pass on to others what God has given us, it will die with us. It is my opinion that in a large way this happened to the Vineyard with John Wimber. Wimber brought a breakthrough in healing and the ministry of the Spirit, and the Vineyard as a movement stepped into Wimber's breakthrough. The tragedy, though, was that by and large there wasn't ownership of what was passed on. Many were content to ride off of Wimber's breakthrough; as a result, when Wimber passed away, much of the healing dropped off in the Vineyard.[89]

Jesus is clear, though, that being able to ride someone else's momentum is no substitute to having your own momentum:

> *On that day many will say to me, 'Lord, Lord, did we not prophesy in your name, and cast out demons in your name, and do many mighty works in your name?' And*

[89] I often pray that the same thing doesn't happen with Bethel and other moves of the Spirit happening right now.

then will I declare to them, 'I never knew you; depart from me, you workers of lawlessness. Matthew 7:22-23[90]

> **Theology Anchor**
>
> We're meant to be trained under someone else's call and then stand on their shoulders for our own.

Likewise, if we want to make a lasting impact, we need to learn to take ownership of what has been passed down to us and learn to pass it down to others. In this, what we pass along multiplies; and our impact increases dramatically. Not only is our momentum growing, but we are influencing more people as well.

Compared with stepping into someone else's momentum, creating your own can often feel like hard work, and it is! It is much harder to walk in your own call, but you're developing something that can be built upon. Learning to maintain your own momentum is like laying a foundation; it's not glamorous work, but it does hold everything else up, and it will eventually determine the extent of your impact and what you pass on.

An inheritance gained hastily in the beginning
will not be blessed in the end. Proverbs 20:21

A good man leaves an inheritance to his children's children,
but the sinner's wealth is laid up for the righteous. Proverbs 13:22

Even Jesus went through the process of developing momentum. When Jesus' family moves back to Nazareth from Egypt, the Scripture records this:

---

[90] Of course I'm not saying that people who didn't own what Wimber brought us aren't saved, I'm just making the point that you can ride off of someone else's moment without even being saved!

And the child grew and became strong, filled with wisdom. And the favor of God was upon him. Luke 2:40

After the temple incident when he was twelve, there is a similar statement:

And Jesus increased in wisdom and in stature and in favor with God and man. Luke 2:52

What Do We Steward?

The shift of focus to stewarding the momentum on our life is an important one for all the reasons described above. What is it that we're stewarding though? There is a really interesting sleeper verse in Deuteronomy that addresses this:

The secret things belong to the Lord our God, but the things that are revealed belong to us and to our children forever, that we may do all the words of this law. Deuteronomy 29:29

The things that are revealed belong to us and to our children forever. They are to be passed down, stewarded from generation to generation. This is the inheritance that we pass on: revelation! What has become real to us in our hearts and what we live from internally is meant to be a treasure that we impart.

You may remember in our discussion about Matthew 16 in the beginning of the Relationships chapter that we talked about how Jesus teaches that what we have a revelation of we have permission to give away. This ties directly into what we're talking about here, but takes it a step further. Not only do we have permission to pass on whatever revelation the Father has given us, but we have a responsibility to do so!

As we steward revelation God wants us to step into it in increasing measure. Revelation gives us access to something in the Spirit, but as we continue to grow into

revelation we can come into a place of ownership of the revelation God has given us. This is a place of established faith based on God's faithfulness. The revelation has formed something in us that gives us consistent access to a realm in the Spirit.

Probably the most obvious example of this is people who move in the prophetic gift consistently. People who walk in a sense of ownership of this realm in the Spirit have access to hear God's voice consistently. They can pretty much get a word from God for anyone as long as they listen. These people have a revelation of God's desire to speak that has become a place they have access to at any time. It's like their faith is always there for hearing God's voice because they have seen the reality of his wanting to speak.

This same principle applies to people who pray in tongues. Most people make a practice of praying in tongues using this principle; there is an established faith for it, so they can step into that place at will and pray in tongues without a specific leading of the Spirit leading them into it. Likewise this principle applies to other gifts as well. Personally I'm moving into increasing ownership of a revelation based on activation, specifically activation of healing. This also happens with healing, although it tends to be with specific conditions; people will have a specific condition of which they will have a very high success rate of healing.

As we step into ownership of an area in the Spirit we can use that as a building block to step into something else. For example I've been knocking on the door of broken bones being healed for a while now, and as I've begun to see success there that's begun to grow my faith in other areas as well. In my head it works like this: *Well, I've prayed for people and had their bone fractures go away, so that's not very different than praying for this guy's bones to grow in his leg.* The faith that's been established is a springboard to a new realm.

Likewise we pass all of this down to others when we pull them into our momentum. The realms we have access to we open to them so our breakthrough becomes theirs as well. In this way the revelation we walk in is passed on and continues to grow.

So the takeaway is that whatever you've gleaned this year, you're now empowered to give it away. Whatever revelation, whatever breakthrough you've experienced, find some people and share it with them. Bring it into your small group or another ministry you serve in.

This is actually the story of this school. After returning from China in November 2008, I was so rocked by what I experienced that a friend and I decided to get a small group together and study power ministry and intimacy with God. For more than two years I practiced teaching and activating people in that group. People were healed, learned how to hear God's voice, and were empowered to live a supernatural lifestyle. As I continued to give away what I had, God continued to multiply it back to me. Eventually that group became a class called the School of Kingdom Ministry at our home church; then it grew to multiple churches.

What began as a small group with me sharing the little bit of breakthrough I experienced has grown to something impacting many more people in multiple churches. I couldn't have guessed that would be the result—nor was that what I was trying to accomplish, but that's what God did.

So find somewhere you can give away and start doing it. Don't look for the big; be faithful with the small. When we first started meeting, we had two co-leaders and two other people—and it stayed small for a long time! As I faithfully invested in that small group of people, God began to bring people to me (there were some incredible stories here), and the group grew and multiplied.

The question I have to ask you is this: what do you have to give away? What has gripped your heart this year? What do you find yourself thinking about because you can't help it? What brings a smile to your face every time you have the opportunity to talk about or practice it? Whatever that is, find some people and begin to give it away.

In Closing: A Commission

I want to close with the verses that I believe God gave me to be the mission for this school. As you read them, realize this is your call—a call to a radical state of being that is a visual demonstration of who God is. Step into ownership of it and give it away to others.

> *Arise, shine, for your light has come,*
> *and the glory of the Lord has risen upon you.*
> *For behold, darkness shall cover the earth,*
> *and thick darkness the peoples;*
> *but the Lord will arise upon you,*
> *and his glory will be seen upon you. Isaiah 60:1-2*

school of
KINGDOM
MINISTRY

Theology Anchors

Theology Anchors

We're well aware that experiencing the School of Kingdom Ministry teaching is often a total paradigm shift for the students. We've put the list of "theology anchors" here as a summary of the major anchor points of the view of life presented in the School of Kingdom Ministry. They're sprinkled throughout the reading notes. The complete list is given here:

- Worldviews filter our perception and determine what we see.
- Repentance means changing our worldview—learning to think and see differently.
- The kingdom is what we're sent to bring. We bring the now to the not-yet.
- God wants the new covenant. He's tired of the old one and he's not interested in going back.
- Sin rules over humanity in the old covenant. Grace rules over sin in the new covenant.
- The gifts of the Holy Spirit are given *situationally*. We can learn to flow in all the gifts because we have the giver living inside of us.
- The gospel saves us from sin to righteousness. It is about the image of God being restored. Jesus died as us so we could live as him.
- Worldviews give us the grid of explanations we use to understand the world.
- This world exists on the battleground between two opposing kingdoms.
- God's goodness is simple and his sovereignty is complicated. Not everything God wills happens and God is never the bad guy.
- When the kingdom doesn't come, keep your focus on Jesus, not your situation.
- The Spirit is in us to transform us; he comes on us to release His power through us.
- God speaks to us from the inside, not from the outside.
- Jesus is 100% of the truth about God and 100% of the truth about man.
- Our sin nature is completely killed at the cross. We struggle now because we think like our old selves, not because we are old.

- We never have to draw life from the world around us; we can always draw it solely from Jesus.
- We can always respond and remain in control ourselves. The situation never has control us.
- The only motivation in relationships the kingdom recognizes is love.
- The message educates. Power creates interest.
- Prophecy is God's word spoken through us.
- All prophecy should be true to the new covenant.
- We pray in Jesus' name because we pray as Jesus on this earth.
- It is unequivocally God's will to heal—no exceptions. Otherwise Jesus did not reveal the Father.
- Emotional healing and deliverance are both ministries that focus on rooting the person's life in truth.
- What doesn't get stewarded gets lost.
- Our revelation gives us access to release the kingdom. Our relationships determine how much capacity we have to do so.
- The more we honor each other and each other's gifts, the more we gain access to their breakthrough.
- Power is a method, not a context. Find the context that works for you.
- Foretelling prophecy sees the future. Forthtelling prophecy creates the future.
- Inspirational prophecy is for everyone. Revelational prophecy requires maturity and relational equity.
- Faith is about the perception of our heart, not the acknowledgement of what is true.
- Activating faith and destroying strongholds is the binding and loosing Jesus referred to.
- We're meant to be trained under someone else's call and then stand on their shoulders in our own.

school of
KINGDOM
MINISTRY

Developing Ministry Skills

This portion of the school materials is oriented toward skill development. Skills are grouped into categories that we will explore as we make our way through the school year. Some of the activations listed are activations we will practice; others are there to help develop the skills on your own.

Please read the ministry skills sections according to the schedule that is given in the class. This material will form the basis of understanding for many of the clinic and activation times that will be part of this class.

Power Evangelism

Power Evangelism is simply using the power of the Holy Spirit to evangelize—to spread the good news of the gospel. In practice, it usually means praying for people as a means to show them the love of Jesus.

There are many facets to practicing power evangelism. One of them is the ability to just talk with people. It's amazing how socially fragmented our society has become. People seldom actually talk to people they know, much less people they don't know! The ability to begin the conversation (approaching) is a key part of the process of power evangelism.

Another critical element is being able to engage with the person without coming across as if you have an agenda. Many people will be suspicious that you're trying to get something out of them or trying to convert them (which you shouldn't be—you should be trying to *love* them), so learning how to posture yourself in the midst of the encounter so you're perceived accurately is important as well.

Finally, knowing how to handle success is important as well. People aren't used to a supernatural God; so when they encounter him, they're in unfamiliar territory. Helping them walk through the encounter (and possibly to salvation) is a skill as well.

Approaching

When taking the supernatural outside the building, how you approach people and how you carry yourself in the moment often determines how many people will allow you to pray for them. Fortunately, this is a skill that can be *learned*. With intentional practice and reflection, I've found that my success rate for asking has dramatically improved. Because I've learned better methods to talk with people, I've learned to be more natural and to use supernatural as well as natural cues.

When practicing the approach, your primary goal is to build *rapport*. You want to develop trust with the person and give the person the message that you genuinely care about and want the best for him/her. Most of these decisions are made largely subconsciously, so the manner in which we approach and dialogue with people is very important.

The best way to make people feel loved and cared for is simply to love and care for them. If we genuinely do love and care for them, then it isn't manipulation to try to send this message on multiple levels. If we just want to pray for the person to satisfy our sense of religious duty or our current excitement, we are using the person and more than likely they will pick up on that and feel manipulated.

So your goal when you start power evangelism is to practice loving people. If you do truly love people, then you'll want to offer the help you can, which involves the supernatural.

> *For in Christ Jesus neither circumcision nor uncircumcision counts for anything, but only faith working through love. Galatians 5:6*

Visible Need

The visible need is the easiest approach in my opinion, so I recommend beginning there. There are plenty of people who need physical healing (or have another visible need) which you can clearly see with your eyes. I've found that if I just go for people in casts, in wheelchairs, or with canes, and those who have limps or just generally look uncomfortable while walking, I've often got plenty to keep me busy.

The advantage here is that you know there is a need. They may not be interested in prayer or may not believe that God heals, but none of that matters because in the beginning, you are just practicing talking with and engaging with people who are quite possibly not believers in a God who heals.

The approach for a visible need might look something like this:

- "Excuse me sir, but I noticed you're limping as you walk. Is your knee the problem?"
- "Hey—sorry to interrupt, but I see you have a cast on your arm; what happened?"
- "You look a little uncomfortable as you're walking. Do you have an injury?"
- "Excuse me, ma'am. I was just wondering why you have to be in a wheelchair?"

There are a few key points here I've found very helpful:

1. Start very politely. People will respond more positively.
2. Direct the discussion towards the person, and specifically his/her injury. This accomplishes two goals: first, you direct the conversation back towards the person. People love to talk about themselves, and they love to complain about their health problems. Instantly, you'll get interest. Secondly, you can probe a little more and get more information about the problem—this is just the interview portion of the five-step prayer model!
3. Don't mention healing or God yet. You generally want to spend some time building trust before you bridge that gap. Otherwise, you run the risk of becoming a salesperson (see the next skill).

One last thing—it can be intimidating to approach a blind person or a person in a wheelchair to offer prayer. I've actually found it is quite a bit easier than I expected; it's really not any different than approaching anyone else. The point when you're getting started isn't even to get people healed or saved specifically as much as it is to learn to talk with people and learn how to ask them what's going on and if you can pray for them. When I made the *decision* not to be intimidated by others' health problems and just practice on anyone I could, I found I not only got a lot more practice, but it also pushed me to grow significantly as well.

Some people are afraid to approach someone with a big health issue because they don't want to probe in a sensitive area in another person's life. It is true that disabilities can be a sensitive issue for people; regardless, the truth is that if we really believe that God can heal such people, we still need to learn to approach them in a sensitive and caring manner. We cannot write off people with disabilities because they are the ones who really need God's healing. To not approach them because their feelings might be hurt is to prioritize their feelings about their disabilities above God's. Their reaction is their own business; bringing Jesus to them is our business. Let us focus on that truth rather than whether or not bringing the healing Jesus commanded us to bring to them might be offensive.

Word of Knowledge

Another type of approach is when we have a word of knowledge about something in their life. I recommend not trying to lead with words of knowledge until you're comfortable approaching people with visible ailments. Once you're comfortable talking with people and making the transition to prayer, you're ready to start trying to lead with a word of knowledge. In that case, I recommend starting by narrowing the field to healing words. This gives you a specific range in which to focus, which is helpful. Once you get good at healing words, you can start opening it up to more general words of knowledge.[91]

Here are a few helpful suggestions for how to lead with a word of knowledge:

- "Excuse me, sir. Do you happen to have a headache right now?"
- "Sir, do you have a problem with your neck?"
- "Hey, by any chance do you happen to suffer from vertigo?"

You're going to get one of a few responses. If the person says no, then you have a few options:

- If they just say no and nothing more:
    - You can say, "Oh, I'm glad to hear that." Then smile and excuse yourself.
    - If you want to try to flip their response, you can say, "That's great. Hey, I really want to bless you right now. Do you have anything wrong with your body I can ask God to heal?"
- If they say no and ask why:
    - If you don't feel comfortable pushing further, you can just say, "Oh, just a hunch. I guess I was wrong." The truth is that if you were wrong, it was just a hunch!
    - If you do want to try to flip the encounter, you can say, "Because if you did, Jesus would have healed you. Do you have something else that needs healing?"
- If they just say yes, then continue to ask questions and build rapport.
- If they say yes and ask why:
    - If you feel favor, you can say, "Well, I felt like I heard God say that was a problem for you. I'd really like to pray and ask God to heal you from that. Is that okay?"
    - If you don't feel favor, you can either describe it as a hunch, or a sense, or you can say you got that vibe from them.

[91] I'll add that if you ever get a word of knowledge, you can always act on it, but I'm talking about *trying* to get a word of knowledge and using that as the approach.

It takes wisdom to try to figure out which approach will be received best by the person. I find that often the bolder approach is received a lot better than you might expect. If you have a bold response, you stand out and it looks like you really believe it, which you do! *Don't* just choose a less bold response because you're afraid; choose it because you don't want to push the other person away.

One final note on approaching with a word of knowledge: I find that if I don't have a specific sense, generally it is better to say things like "do you have a problem with . . . " rather than "do you have pain in your . . . " because many ailments don't actually cause *pain*, but are still a problem and still could require healing.

Nothing Specific

Sometimes there is a person that you just feel led to pray for (or you just want to pray for), but you don't have anything to go on. You have two main options here: you can either go straight for asking about prayer, or you can indirectly start a conversation and work your way towards prayer.

Direct Approach

- Offer prayer or blessing. "Is there anything I can pray for you about right now?"
- It can be helpful to list categories to give people an idea of what you're talking about: "Relationships, financial issues, physical problems, anything else?"
- If you want to, you can hint at the fact that you feel directed by God to pray for them. I'd say something like "You kind of stood out to me." or depending on the vibe you get from the person you can use more direct language: "I felt God pointed you out to me."

Indirect Approach

- Start talking to the person and try to work your way to some need they have, and offer prayer.
- Start with some commonality with them if there is something you can see, or ask a question they have to answer.
- This is the approach Jesus used in John 4 with the woman at the well, so there is nothing wrong with this approach, even though it may seem as if it requires less faith.

Praying

When you pray for people in a public place, pray short, non-religious prayers. This is not the time to spend a lot of time waiting on God or getting very emphatic. Remember that however awkward you feel the other person probably feels even more uncomfortable! I've found that keeping my prayers quick and to the point is most effective in this context. Remember, it's not long prayers that heal people anyway!

Once you're done praying for the person, ask them to try it out. This is important; *oftentimes, people don't get healed until they start to try it out.* Get some feedback, and ask if they are feeling better. Depending on your read on the situation, you may offer to pray again.

It's always useful to try to be as measurable as possible when praying for healing. One thing I've found helpful is when I ask the person how it feels, I'll phrase it like this: "So if we started at 100% pain before we prayed, where is it now—80%, 50%, 25%?" I know other people like the 1-10 scale, but I've just found that's a little hard to explain

in the moment. The percentage improvement seems to get the same point across more quickly.

If the person has experienced some healing, I'll almost always ask if I can pray again. You can simply just reiterate that God has started healing them and tell them the more you pray, the more likely it is they'll experience more healing. Once things happen, many people become a lot more receptive.

How to Not Be a Salesperson

One of the hardest parts of power evangelism is not coming across as a salesperson. This comes up critically in at least two steps: the approach and the transition.

The truth is that if your agenda is to pray for the person, you are a salesperson. If your agenda is to love the person, then you can love them freely. This is the biggest goal overall. The reality is that we're not comfortable expressing love to people we don't know. As we learn to do that openly and over the top, that disarms people, and they see our heart.

Here are some suggestions for diffusing the salesperson impression:

The Approach

- Don't rush the approach. Convey that you really care about the person.
- Listen when people talk; don't just wait for them to shut up so you can ask to pray for them.
- If you have any common ground with a person, build on that. If you've had a similar injury or know someone who has, express your sympathy and that you have some idea of what the person is going through.

The Transition

- Don't pass the buck when asking to pray for the person. Don't mention your church, group, or your beliefs.
- Point to yourself instead. Say something like "I'd really like to pray for you about that right now. May I do that?"
- Don't try to pressure the person into getting prayer if the person seems hesitant. Tell the person it'll just take a second and provide them a chance to opt out if desired.

Remaining Present

When doing power evangelism, one of the most important skills we can learn is to stay present and fully engaged in the moment. This practice will benefit our spirituality as a whole because it is only as we engage with the present that we can meet Jesus. The only time you can experience God is *now*.

What I've discovered is that power evangelism is awkward for both sides. It is often at least as awkward for the other person as it is for us! They have the same tendencies we do—to shut down and try to minimize the discomfort because of the social situation.

Furthermore, there tends to be a thrust that undergirds social interactions, which is that *the person who remains most present tends to be deferred to*. If you are fully present in the moment and others are uncomfortable, they subconsciously recognize that where you are is healthier and in some way better than where they are, and they tend to go along with you, *as long as they don't feel as if you are using them.*

Let me suggest these tools to try to remain fully engaged in the moment:

Teamwork

- Encourage each other as a team and build each other up both naturally and prophetically in between encounters.
- This helps each team member remain centered in their identity, which is a large part of staying fully present.

Remain Spiritually Open

- Continually open yourself spiritually to the Holy Spirit, almost as if you're receiving ministry.
- This helps maintain a constant readiness to receive revelation.
- Furthermore, it forces you to remain in the moment.

Loving People

Displaying radical love should be our goal throughout any power evangelism we undertake. Our responsibility is to love people; God's responsibility is to show up in power. It takes some time to learn to display love in an "over the top" kind of way without feeling uncomfortable. Like everything, as you practice, it gets easier. Here are a few helpful suggestions:

- Don't *just* say, "Jesus loves you." It is a true statement, but that statement by itself passes the buck. Say, "I love you." Jesus lives in you, so these two statements go together. I realize it is hard to say this to a stranger. Learn how to say it.
- I love to hug people if it's appropriate. Of course, there are many times you can't do this, but there is nothing I love to do more than pray for people, see healing, and then give them a hug as I tell them I love them. It blows people away.
- The antithesis of love is manipulation. I try to never manipulate or coerce people into getting prayer or anything else.

Handling Success

When things go right, you'll almost always have to help the person understand what just happened. Whatever just happened is almost certainly outside the other person's worldview, so they probably won't know how to handle it. They very often won't come to the same conclusion that we do while processing the events that just occurred.

It's helpful to walk them through the process. When someone gets healed, reiterate that you prayed to Jesus and that he healed him or her. When a prophetic word is accurate, explain that God told you that about the person because he loves him or her. Describe the events and explain why God did what he did. If you provide the context for understanding, you can guide people to the right conclusion.

Evangelism

As you improve at approaches, prayer, etc., you'll likely see power come through before evangelism. Once you start to see power increase, you can start to lean into evangelism more. Start by taking advantage of what just happened. When people got healed, tell them that Jesus just healed them because he wants them to know him. Just ask if they know Jesus personally.

When it comes to praying for salvation, there are three things you want to hit:

Making Jesus Savior

- Communicate to the person that everybody has been marred by sin, and because of that, everyone has sinned.
- Jesus is the answer to the problem; he is God and died to take care of sin.
- Have the person turn to Jesus and accept his forgiveness.

Making Jesus Lord

- Communicate that Jesus is the boss of everything and that knowing him requires following his lead.
- Have the person put his/her life in Jesus' hands.

Filling with the Holy Spirit

- Pray for the Holy Spirit to fill the person and empower the person to live a life victorious over sin and full of the supernatural.
- If you feel led or the person wants it, you can ask the Holy Spirit to give him/her the gift of tongues.

If the people ask what church I go to, I'll tell them; but I don't usually volunteer that information. Again, that would make me a salesperson, which is absolutely the opposite of what I want to be doing.

Studying

One thing I found very helpful when I started pressing into power evangelism more was to watch videos of others doing power evangelism and studying them.[92] How did they approach? How did they pray? What are they doing differently than I am and how does the effect differ? Each person will develop a method of doing power evangelism that is unique to him or her. If you begin to think critically about your methods, you'll find it very helpful.

---

92 There are lots of videos of Todd White on YouTube. I found them very helpful as I started practicing and trying things on the streets.

Shining

Your goal in power evangelism is to be a demonstration of the gospel. It isn't so much to bring signs and wonders as it is to *be* a sign and wonder. The gospel of the kingdom is that we get to live by a different set of rules. When we do power evangelism, we want to *look* like we live by a different set of rules. Jesus puts it this way:

> *You are the light of the world. A city set on a hill cannot be hidden. Nor do people light a lamp and put it under a basket, but on a stand, and it gives light to all in the house. In the same way, let your light shine before others, so that they may see your good works and give glory to your Father who is in heaven. Matthew 5:14-16*

Jesus commands us to put ourselves on display and demonstrate our light. He tells us to put ourselves at the center of attention. As we do that by *our* good works, they will see the Father in heaven. As you get more comfortable, step further and further outside the box of what's normal. The point isn't to be normal. You want the person to walk away from you thinking, "What is wrong with that person?" The truth is that *God* is what is wrong with you! Put yourself on display and show how outrageous the love of God is and how completely different we can be once we've been saved.

Revelatory Information

Receiving revelation (that is, direction from God) is one of the most fundamental skills in kingdom ministry. It is the foundation of the prophetic, which is the gateway to moving in other spiritual gifts. Words of knowledge, words of wisdom, and prophecy all flow through revelation.

Words of Knowledge

Words of knowledge tend to be the starting point for moving in revelation. A word of knowledge is simply information (knowledge) that has been revealed to you by the Holy Spirit. Revelation tends to come in a few different channels:

Seeing

- A mental picture of something
- Often requires interpretation
- For healing, it can often be a body part or an injury

Feeling

- The same emotions as someone else
- Physical sensations of pain in your body that are not your own

Hearing

- Words that pass through your mind

Reading

- Word(s) written on or above a person

Knowing

- An inner feeling or knowing about a specific issue
- Feels very similar to a conviction or a hunch

Speaking

- Words that just tumble out of your mouth as you are speaking
- Words that seem to bypass your mind - often you're surprised you've even said them

People tend to have some of these that are usual and others that are more occasional. My brother is very much a seer—he sees pictures when praying for people, during worship, and so forth. I tend to be a knower. As you practice receiving revelation, you'll probably find some types of revelation more natural for you than others.

The *quality* of these types of revelation often feels very similar to the quality of the senses or thoughts you have in your imagination. You see spiritually very similarly to the way you can see someone you had a conversation with recently just by thinking of them. It works the same with hearing or reading as well. Because of this, many people hear God and just dismiss it as their own imagination or subconscious.

As you learn to recognize these subtle promptings, practice stepping out to develop your ability to hear God speaking to you. As you practice, you will learn to recognize when it is God and when it is you.

Activating Words of Knowledge

Variation 1:

Partner with someone you don't know particularly well to practice trying to share words of knowledge. We're going for words of knowledge, not prophecy, *so don't transition past the direct information that God shows you* to praying, encouraging, or anything else. Choose one person to share first. You'll take turns—one minute each.

Have a group leader pray an activation prayer, then have the first person look at his/her partner. The sharing partner will then speak out whatever thoughts, impressions, feelings, or anything else they have received. After one minute, the recipient gives some feedback, and then trades roles.

Variation 2:

Split your group into two. One group will keep their eyes open; the other will keep them closed. Have one person with his/her eyes open approach one of the people with his/her eyes closed and place a hand on that person's shoulder. When the partner with closed eyes feels the hand on his/her shoulder, he/she immediately says the first thing he/she thinks, feels, hears, or whatever else is perceived. Then the person with his/her eyes open gives feedback if it means anything.

After repeating a number of different times with different partners, switch the roles of the two groups so that everyone gets a turn to do both roles.

Variation 3:

Break up into groups of four and label four pieces of paper A, B, C, and D. Take turns passing the paper around and asking God for a word of knowledge to share. Write down whatever you get. When everyone has written something on all four pieces of paper, mix them up and have each group member draw a sheet of paper at random. Evaluate as a group the accuracy of the words given.

Variation 4:

Partner people with one small piece of paper each. Have the leader pray and ask God to show everyone a biblical name for his/her partner. Have each person write the name down; and when both people have a name, have them share the paper with their partners and evaluate the accuracy of that name applying to them. If you don't remember where that person is in the Bible, look it up!

Other Modes of Revelation

There are many other kinds of revelation:

Scripture

- God highlights Scripture such that it speaks to you in a profound way.

Dreams

- God gives dreams during your sleep.
- These usually require interpretation, which is another spiritual gift.

Open Visions

- These are like watching a movie superimposed on to real life.

Physical Sensations

- Can indicate spiritual phenomena.
- Sometimes you may feel the presence of angels as winds that blow across your hands or face without an apparent source.

Scents

- It is possible to smell in the spirit realm.
- You can smell both the presence of the demonic as well as the presence of God.

Pay attention to what happens during times of worship. You may find different sensations happening in your body, soul, and/or spirit that are signals of your response to the presence of the Holy Spirit. As you experience these skills on a semi-regular basis, you'll begin to learn what is normal for you. When you do, lean into it, and develop an understanding of how it works, what information you can obtain from it, and how to use that information.

The Process of Prophecy

Prophecy is much more than just revelation. Revelation is supernatural *information*; prophecy takes it to the next level by revealing the heart of God to an individual. It is revelatory, but it involves a more thorough process than speaking a word of knowledge.

Generally, there is a process of gifts that contribute to the formation of prophecy. Each gift contributes a different dimension; and as they all come together, a prophecy is forged.

The process develops like this:[93]

Word of Knowledge

- Sets the stage for a prophecy.
- This is God establishing the *context* in which He wants to speak.
- Often when you get a negative word of knowledge about someone, that is God starting up a prophetic process in which he wants to speak life to the brokenness that person is experiencing.

Prophecy

- Speaks into that context and releases *where God wants to go* with that person in that part of his/her life.
- It provides a direction forward and often relates to a person's destiny and/or identity.
- It is the answer to the question raised by the word of knowledge.

Word of Wisdom

- This brings the prophecy into the practical realm.
- It shapes *how the prophecy should be delivered* and *what the person should do* in agreement with the prophecy.

[93] I take this process from Graham Cooke's excellent book *Approaching the Heart of Prophecy*. I recommend it as the best introductory book on prophecy that I know of.

So, when we obtain a word of knowledge about someone, we need to consider leaning into it and seeing if the Lord wants to release a prophecy about this area into a person's life. Sometimes we are just to share what we've been given; not only is not every word of knowledge the beginning of a prophetic process, but sometimes the Lord won't release the prophecy until you've shared the word of knowledge.

Activating Prophecy

Partner up with someone you don't know very well. Choose one person to practice prophesying first. Have the person prophesying first walk through these steps:

1. Ask the Lord for a word of knowledge about something he wants to speak about to your partner.
2. Share with your partner the word of knowledge you receive.
    a. Confirm its accuracy.
    b. If you heard incorrectly, go back to step 1.
3. Now ask God what he wants to do with that part of your partners' life. Sample questions could be:
    a. Where is he taking the person?
    b. What is he revealing to the person?
    c. What is he growing in the person?
4. Ask God how to share that with the person.
    a. What is the most important part of what God showed you that the person needs to hear?
    b. How can you deliver it in a way that imparts hope and grace instead of focusing on the negative?
    c. Does your partner have a role in this growth process?
    d. How should your partner respond?
5. Deliver the prophecy and ask for feedback on the accuracy of the prophetic word as well as the quality of the delivery.

When you're done, switch roles so both people get a chance to practice.

Drafting off Another's Gift

One useful dynamic when getting started or trying to press into receiving revelation is the fact that you can draft off another's gifting. While working with a person who moves strongly in a particular gift, it is common to start to pick up that same kind of revelation. For example, sometimes I start to see pictures if I'm praying with my brother for someone else.

This is useful because by using this principle we can start to learn to recognize the different methods of revelation for words of knowledge. Because I have learned to recognize pictures better, I have noticed that I can trust them when I get them.

Try partnering in a group of three in which each of you gets revelations in different channels. Take turns praying for each group member. While you are praying, pay attention to see if you pick up anything that is the other person's normal mode of revelation.

Revelatory Perception

A second kind of revelation is revelatory perception. This differs from the gifts we discussed in the last section because of the nature of the information received. In the last section we discussed revelatory information; it is information gathered from the spiritual realm.

Revelatory perception differs because it is information gathered about the spiritual realm. Rather than the spiritual realm communicating to us, we are surveying what is happening in the spiritual realm directly.

Most people find revelatory perception more difficult than revelatory information. I believe this is because it is more sensory oriented. With revelatory information, we're learning how to recognize revelation that primarily flows to us through our thoughts; if we can learn to pay attention to our thoughts, we can recognize this kind of revelation. With revelatory perception, we have to look at the movement of our senses and affections. It isn't as mental in nature, so it is harder to recognize. Yet, like all other ways of ministry, it can be learned. Keep practicing, and it will come.

Seeing the Presence of God

Learning to see the presence of God is a very valuable skill in ministry. It can be helpful to use when deciding whom to minister to first if there is a group of people. It can give us confidence as we minister in healing or the prophetic. It is an invaluable skill because we are quite literally doing what we see the Father doing. I found a dramatic increase in effectiveness when I started to minister out of this skill. When you see the presence of God, you partner with what God is doing, knowing that the power of God is there because the power is in his presence.

There are a number of ways that people perceive the presence of God. There are a whole host of physical symptoms (see the unit on the Holy Spirit). In addition to those, there are spiritual eyes as well:

Highlighted

- A person looks more real than real in some way.
- They almost seem like they have a soft glow.
- The atmosphere around them seems kind of shimmery or like a mirage.

Feeling Drawn

- You feel drawn to a person, or compassion rises in you when you look at the person.
- This is your emotions responding to the presence of God.

Repeated Looking

- You find that you keep coming back and looking at the same person even though you don't know why.
- This is your spirit's response to something your eyes can't see.

Activating Your Spiritual Eyes

Do this activity in a group of at least 20 to 30 people.

- In a large group, have the leader of the group choose someone whom they see the presence of God upon. The leader will ask that person to stand up.

- Have the leader describe why he or she chose that person in as much detail as is possible.
- Have the other participants look at the person standing and describe if they see or feel any of the descriptions listed above. (Don't try to make something happen, just let it happen if they do.)
- Have the leader pray to activate people's spiritual eyes, and then have them look again.
- Have the leader choose another three or four people he or she sees the Spirit of God on, and have the others repeat the exercise.

As you learn to recognize the presence of God on someone, you can grow in your ability to recognize what God is doing. Is God releasing something in that person's life? Is his power on the person right now? Is he presently healing them?

Learning to minister based on seeing the presence of God is very useful when you have to minister to groups. I usually start with whomever I see the Lord moving on and then move on to the next person.

Discerning Atmospheres

Another dimension to revelatory perception is developing a sensitivity to the atmosphere. There are times that atmospheric effects interact with the way we minister. Faith can be in the atmosphere, and power can be in the atmosphere too:

> *On one of those days, as he was teaching, Pharisees and teachers of the law were sitting there, who had come from every village of Galilee and Judea and from Jerusalem. And the power of the Lord was with him to heal. Luke 5:17*

Satan is called the "prince of the power of the air":

And you were dead in the trespasses and sins in which you once walked, following the course of this world, following the prince of the power of the air, the spirit that is now at work in the sons of disobedience. Ephesians 2:1-2

Much of spiritual warfare exists in the atmosphere around us. What applies to the devil applies to the angels as well. They influence the atmosphere we are in at any given time. As we learn to read the atmosphere, we can discern what is happening in the spiritual realm around us.

As we learn to grow in this, we can begin to learn to discern what anointing is present in the atmosphere. When the Lord sends his angels to work, he sends them with things to do. As we learn to discern what that task is, we can direct our work accordingly to partner with his intentions.

To detect the spiritual atmosphere, we need to still ourselves for long enough to differentiate what is in us from what is coming from outside of us. As you do that, begin to sense what your attitude is. What are you drawn towards? What do you feel is rising up inside you? This is the activity of the Spirit within you. Anointing is the presence of the Spirit to do something. You see this in Jesus' mission statement—he has been anointed for a number of tasks:

"The Spirit of the Lord is upon me,
because he has anointed me
to proclaim good news to the poor.
He has sent me to proclaim liberty to the captives
and recovering of sight to the blind,
to set at liberty those who are oppressed,
to proclaim the year of the Lord's favor." Luke 4:18-19

Likewise, when the anointing of the Lord comes into the room, it also comes to accomplish specific things. As we learn to tune into the atmosphere and discern that the anointing is present, we can partner more effectively with the Lord.

Activating Discerning the Atmosphere

Try this in a large-to-medium sized group.

- Take some time as a group to wait on the presence of the Holy Spirit.
- When you can sense the manifest presence of the Spirit in the room, begin to try to discern what anointing is in the room.
- Have a few people share what they felt the anointing was and how they observed it.
- Minister to people who have the need the Lord is intending to address.

Shifting the Atmosphere

Once we learn to attune ourselves to the spiritual atmosphere, we can recognize not only the presence of the Lord but also the work of the enemy. Sometimes we need to shift the atmosphere when the enemy has created an atmosphere of division or unbelief. The Lord wants to teach us how to break through for others; one way we can do that is to learn to shift the atmosphere. The following is a list of methods through which I've seen the atmosphere shift:

Shifting the Spiritual Atmosphere

- Worship
- Speaking in tongues followed by interpretation
- Prophetic declaration of the will of the Lord
- Intercessory prayer
- Releasing your internal environment (Mark 4:35-40)
- Waiting on the Lord
- Sharing testimony of what God has done

As with all things, as we develop a sensitivity to the Holy Spirit and a knowledge of the ways of God, we will begin to develop an understanding of when and how to shift the environment.

Recognizing Demons

The other side of the discerning of spirits gift involves learning to ascertain the presence of the kingdom of darkness. Recognizing the demonic is invaluable, and having some spiritual tools to do so is quite useful. Demons can be wrapped up both in physical and emotional issues, so it definitely takes some discernment to tell when demons are the source of the problem.

The gift of discerning of spirits helps us recognize the demonic. I think of discerning of demonic spirits as our spirit's reaction to the presence of the demonic. As we learn to recognize that reaction in our spirit, we can learn to realize when the demonic is around. Common responses to the demonic are:

Spiritual Recoil

- This is a reaction in your spirit to something distasteful.
- It kind of feels internally like what your face looks like when you smell rotten food.

Unusual Temptation

- A demonic influence in someone else is kind of reaching out and sliming you.
- You find yourself struggling with sin that you don't usually struggle with.

Mental/Emotional Reactions

- Confusion and difficulty thinking.
- Restlessness and/or a desire to leave.

Physical Sensations

- Cold temperature.
- Smell of rotten food.

As you grow in your ability to discern the presence of the demonic, you may start to develop an ability to distinguish what type of demon it is as well.

Manifestation Symptoms

There are a number of physical symptoms that are common manifestations of the demonic in a person:

Physical Movements

- Demons often contort people and affect their physical motion.
- Sometimes they are quite dramatic and violent.
- Other times they can be subtle such as hiding from you or closing themselves off.

Voice

- The tone of voice can change when demons are manifesting. Listen for both changes in pitch as well as a difference in accent.
- The content of the speech often changes as well. People may become more vulgar or change how they refer to themselves (plural or third person).

Face

- The emotional state of a person is betrayed by facial expressions. When a demon is manifesting, you can usually see a change in a person's face.
- Pay attention to the eyes specifically. The person's eyes take on a different quality, sometimes even an icy stare.

Knowledge

- Demons have access to knowledge the person can't have access to. They may know personal information about you there would be no other way to know.

Not every source of some of these manifestations is demonic, so it is best to proceed slowly, assuming it isn't demonic until you're confident the source is a demon. It can be pretty damaging to people to be told they have a demon; then if nothing is cast out of them, they are left wondering what is wrong with them.

Ministry of the Holy Spirit

Another ministry skill set is learning how to minister the Holy Spirit. All the gifts could be called the ministry of the Holy Spirit, but we can also learn to minister the Holy Spirit *himself* to a person. Being filled with the Holy Spirit (sometimes called "baptized in the Spirit") is the promise of the Scriptures. As we are filled with the Spirit, we are empowered to live the Christian life.

What Does Filling Mean?

Being "filled with the Spirit" is a somewhat loaded term; it means different things to different people depending on their backgrounds. In some Christian traditions, it seems to be the only thing that matters; in others, it seems to be an afterthought. Almost every group would claim they're filled with the Spirit, although they would mean completely different things by that statement.

Biblically, being filled with the Spirit doesn't mean you didn't already have the Holy Spirit living in you. This is made clear by the order of two passages that occur shortly after Jesus is resurrected. The evening of the first Easter Sunday, we see Jesus passing the presence of the Holy Spirit to his disciples:

> ***Jesus said to them again,*** *"Peace be with you. As the Father has sent me, even so I am sending you."* ***And when he had said this, he breathed on them and said to them,*** *"Receive the Holy Spirit..."* ***John 20:21-22***

Fifty days later on the first Pentecost, we see the first time the language "filled with the Spirit" is used:

When the day of Pentecost arrived, they were all together in one place. And suddenly there came from heaven a sound like a mighty rushing wind, and it filled the entire house where they were sitting. And divided tongues as of fire appeared to them and rested on each one of them. And they were all filled with the Holy Spirit and began to speak in other tongues as the Spirit gave them utterance. Acts 2:1-4

So being filled with the Spirit does not mean a person did not have the Holy Spirit before. Actually, as the term is used in the Bible it appears to be more consistent with the Holy Spirit coming *on* a person than the person receiving the Holy Spirit, which they did not have previously. When the Holy Spirit comes on a person, what happens is described as being filled with the Spirit. It is that presence of the Holy Spirit coming upon us that fills us with power:

But you will receive power when the Holy Spirit has come upon you, and you will be my witnesses in Jerusalem and in all Judea and Samaria, and to the end of the earth. Acts 1:8

But Saul, who was also called Paul, filled with the Holy Spirit, looked intently at him [Elymas the magician] and said, "You son of the devil, you enemy of all righteousness, full of all deceit and villainy, will you not stop making crooked the straight paths of the Lord? And now, behold, the hand of the Lord is upon you, and you will be blind and unable to see the sun for a time." Immediately mist and darkness fell upon him, and he went about seeking people to lead him by the hand. Acts 13:9-11

So being "filled with the Spirit" is our response to when the Holy Spirit comes on us. It comes with a heightened awareness of God's presence that tends to produce an almost ecstatic state. This meeting of the Holy Spirit's presence upon us with the presence of

the Holy Spirit within us produces a two-way Holy Spirit deluge that the Bible calls being filled with the Spirit.

With this perspective, it becomes clear that being filled with the Spirit is not a one-time deal. You are not filled once and for all with the Spirit; rather it is a meeting of God and man in a unique and powerful way that can and should be sought after repeatedly. In fact, Paul commends us to this in such a way that almost makes one think that being filled with the Spirit is a unique form of Christian entertainment:

> *And do not get drunk with wine, for that is debauchery, but be filled with the Spirit. Ephesians 5:18*

Praying for Holy Spirit Filling

Praying for someone to be filled with the Holy Spirit is not complicated. In fact, the most critical ingredient is the person's hunger to be filled with the Spirit. The Holy Spirit *wants* to fill his people.

> *If you then, who are evil, know how to give good gifts to your children, how much more will the heavenly Father give the Holy Spirit to those who ask him!*
> *Luke 11:13*

When a person's desire to be filled with the Spirit becomes stronger than the desire to remain in control, you're in a very good place. The biggest hindrance occurs when a person wants to maintain control; in this case a person will only let the Holy Spirit go so far, then he or she will shut down in order to remain in control.

Praying for a person to be filled with the Spirit is pretty straightforward:

- Have the person position themselves in a comfortable receiving posture.

- Ask the Holy Spirit to come and fill the person. Watch the work of the Spirit and bless his work.
- Sometimes you will sense there is somewhat of a barrier that is keeping the Holy Spirit from going deeper. In that case, you may sense some direction from the Lord as to how to "uncork" the person.

Receiving prayer to be filled with the Spirit is also a very common time for a person to receive the gift of praying in tongues. I like to ask people if they want to receive the gift of tongues when they ask to be filled with the Spirit. If so (and some don't, which is totally fine), then I instruct:

- If you feel something is bubbling up from inside of you, just allow that process to happen. For some people, speaking in tongues comes erupting out of them.
- For other people, sometimes you will hear a word or a sequence of words in your head that isn't in English. When that happens, just speak out what you hear in your head.
- It is common as well to have some physical sensations that accompany the gift of tongues. Sometimes the mouth feels strange—almost like your tongue is enlarged or you sense the power of the Spirit on your mouth. When this happens, sometimes you just have to speak out by faith. Open your mouth and let whatever comes, come.
- Activation in speaking in tongues requires acting in faith. In my experience, it often seems remarkably nondramatic and questionably supernatural. It might almost seem as if you are just making something up in your head. It's okay if it feels like that. Sometimes people have the idea that there is only one way to experience a particular spiritual gift. Putting stipulations on how the gifts are to operate can cause you to miss them when they come in a different guise.

As you pray for the person, coach them through speaking out whatever way the gift of tongues comes. Often they'll get just a few words or a simple phrase to repeat. I then

instruct the person to practice praying in tongues every day. Encourage the person to practice the gift to begin to experience the benefits.

Waiting on the Presence of God

I love waiting on the presence of the Spirit because it is a through-and-through Vineyard practice. It actually comes from the Quakers (John Wimber was saved in a Quaker church), who run their meetings by sitting in a circle and waiting for the presence of God to be made manifest among them. They were nicknamed Quakers because the Lord would manifest his presence among them in such a way that their bodies would shake.

I believe it was largely Wimber who introduced this practice of waiting on the presence of the Spirit to the modern day church. From what I understand, it wasn't really practiced in the charismatic movement before Wimber; and other modern day renewal movements don't put as much emphasis on it as there was in the early days of the Vineyard. In my opinion, it is an important contribution to the church as a whole that the Vineyard has made and something we need to get back to practicing more regularly.

Training Ourselves to Recognize the Presence

There are many benefits of waiting on the presence of God. High on the list is that it teaches us to recognize the presence of the Lord. It is entirely possible to have the manifest presence of the Lord in the room with you in a powerful way and have no idea He is there. We must learn to discern the presence of God.

As we practice waiting on the presence of God, two things happen. The first is that any internal clamor we have begins to become stilled. Within us, below the surface of our conscious thoughts, most of us carry a sea of internal thoughts and feelings that have not been expressed or processed. Because of this, when we try to bring ourselves to stillness, we find our thoughts jumping around from one thing to another and an inability to quietly focus our minds on God. The practice of waiting on God gives an opportunity of expression to that deeper level of ourselves; as we continue to practice, we find an internal stillness develops within us. We can access that place within ourselves more quickly, and our inner being begins to exist at rest rather than restlessness.

Second, the presence of the Lord is made manifest among us. This happens in two ways. First, we tune into the presence of God within us. The presence of God lives within us, but most of us are completely unaware of that on an experiential level. As we wait on the presence of the Lord, it is common to feel the presence of the Holy Spirit rising up within us. The Quakers speak of an "inner light"; practicing a "silence that is active" causes your inner light to "glow." This is exactly what they are speaking of. Additionally, we begin to sense the presence of God externally. The environment shifts, and we become aware that we are in an environment pregnant with the presence of God. We often feel a weight resting on us or an atmosphere that feels electric. Often the presence of God comes in waves—increasing in strength in a pattern of advancing and then dropping off.

The Practice of Waiting

Waiting on the Spirit is a practice that can be done by ourselves or in groups. The basic format is more or less the same.

Position Yourself

- Find a body position that you can remain in for a while comfortably without moving.
- Make sure your body position doesn't inhibit your breathing at all (no slouching).

Wait on the Presence

- Invite the Holy Spirit to come.
- Still your thoughts and direct them towards the Lord. Don't force your thoughts. If they wander, don't force them back too quickly; try to remain still internally.
- Keep an expectancy of experiencing his presence.
- When you start, sometimes it is helpful to focus lightly on your breathing. This will keep your mind from wandering too much.
- As you start to experience the presence of the Spirit, don't focus on what you're experiencing; just keep directing your thoughts towards the Lord and a quiet expectation of meeting him.
- Thank the Lord for what he's doing and ask for more.

When the Power Comes

- Sometimes the Lord will begin to move on you in such a way that you'd have to shut the Lord out to stop something from happening (laughter, crying, falling over, etc).
- When that happens, try not to disengage but stay engaged with the Lord. Try not to be self-conscious about it; the Lord is using you to minister to the group.
- Sometimes the Lord will give a prophecy or a tongue to be spoken out over the group. Feel free to speak it out, but don't speak out unless you feel a strong prompting to. Remember the goal is not to share prophetic words but to experience the presence of the Lord, so only speak out if you feel it will contribute to others' experiencing the presence of the Lord.

Imparting Gifts

The Bible teaches that through prayer we can impart a gift to another person:

> *For this reason I remind you to fan into flame the gift of God, which is in you through the laying on of my hands. 2 Timothy 1:6*

> *Do not neglect the gift you have, which was given you by prophecy when the council of elders laid their hands on you. 1 Timothy 4:14*

Gifts Are Grace

How are we to understand impartation? Do we literally have a gift that we are giving to a person? I don't think that is the case. A clue comes from an interesting passage in 1 Peter:

> *As each has received a gift, use it to serve one another, as good stewards of God's varied grace: whoever speaks, as one who speaks oracles of God; whoever serves, as one who serves by the strength that God supplies. 1 Peter 4:10-11*

Peter describes the different spiritual gifts we have as varied grace that is given us. This, of course, is also reflected in the term *charismatic*, which comes from the word *charis*, meaning grace. Spiritual gifts actually are grace flowing. You can think of the different spiritual gifts as different flavors of grace.

This grace that we have and that we use by serving one another tends to follow a few principles. One of them is that as we honor other people, we can enter into the grace that is on their lives:

> *The one who receives a prophet because he is a prophet will receive a prophet's reward, and the one who receives a righteous person because he is a righteous person will receive a righteous person's reward.* Matthew 10:41

Another principle is that what starts out small grows into more:

> *He put another parable before them, saying, "The kingdom of heaven is like a grain of mustard seed that a man took and sowed in his field. It is the smallest of all seeds, but when it has grown it is larger than all the garden plants and becomes a tree, so that the birds of the air come and make nests in its branches."* Matthew 13:31-32

Impartation functions on these two principles. Remember, the Holy Spirit already lives inside of every believer. We already have the giver of all the gifts resident inside of us, so impartation isn't so much giving a gift that the person did not have before as much as it is activating the person to move in a gift he/she may not be moving in, or giving the person an extra measure of grace on a gift he/she already is moving in. It is about smearing some of the grace that is on our lives onto someone else's. As people honor us, they can enter into the grace that is on our lives and that gives the grace that is on their lives a bit of a kick-start. *Impartation* may not be quite as accurate a word as *activation* is.

You Only Keep What You Give Away

Another kingdom principle is that if you keep what you have to yourself, it stagnates. The spiritual gifts are meant to be used in community; the various types of grace that are on our lives are meant to be shared with others. We should desire to impart the gifts that we have to others for their benefit and the benefit of those to whom they will minister. Grace grows stronger when it is given away:

For I long to see you, that I may impart to you some spiritual gift to strengthen you— that is, that we may be mutually encouraged by each other's faith, both yours and mine. Romans 1:11-12

Praying Impartation Prayers

When we pray for impartation then, we simply ask God to take what is on us and share it with other people. We ask for the grace on our life to be smeared (the word "anointing" means "to be smeared with") onto someone else. The grace that is on our lives will then activate the other person in a gift he or she may not be proficiently functioning in yet.

Try this activity in groups of 8-10:

- Discuss among the group and determine which of the methods of receiving revelation (as listed on the "receiving revelation" section) are uncommon for most of the people in your group.
- Choose one or two people who move in one of those methods of revelation and have them pray impartation over each person in the group.
- Choose another person in the group and practice prophesying to them. Pay attention to the revelation you receive and try to tune yourselves in to receiving revelation in this new way. If you have time, choose another person and prophesy again.

Activating Faith

It seems that Jesus was always looking for faith. While it is true that we should not use a lack of faith as an excuse not to pray for someone or as a reason to blame someone for not being healed, it clearly is a powerful force that we need to learn to recognize and utilize when we see it.

Gifts of Faith

Hebrews 12:2 informs us that faith belongs to Jesus. If we have faith, it is because Jesus gave us faith. We don't have to muster up faith. Faith is not trying to believe something. If we have to try to create something, that's already proof we don't have faith. If we pray for healing and a person isn't healed, it is not faith to say they are healed. Faith is pure and simple trust in who God is.

This is the nature of a gift of faith: it is an ability to trust in God beyond where we normally would be able to trust. It is clarity in being able to see who God is. A gift of faith is a relational gift; it is pointed at God. As soon as faith ceases to have God as its target, it ceases to be faith.

Hebrews 11:1 tells us that faith is the substance and foundation of the miraculous. In order for that faith to be appropriated into the miraculous, action is often required. James 5:17 informs us:

> *So also faith by itself, if it does not have works, is dead. James 2:17*

If we think we have faith but it never works itself into our actions, we are wrong. The end of faith is always action. Otherwise, it may be our confession—what we say—but it is not faith. If we really have faith, it comes out through our actions. The presence of faith is always revealed by action.

Prophetic Acts

Many of the healings described in the New Testament happened as a result of *prophetic acts*. A prophetic act is a physical action that becomes a means for a spiritual effect. A prophetic act is a common channel for the release of faith. Here are some examples:

> *On another Sabbath, he entered the synagogue and was teaching, and a man was there whose right hand was withered... And after looking around at them all he said to him, "Stretch out your hand." And he did so, and his hand was restored. Luke 6:6,10*

> *But Peter said, "I have no silver and gold, but what I do have I give to you. In the name of Jesus Christ of Nazareth, rise up and walk!" And he took him by the right hand and raised him up, and immediately his feet and ankles were made strong. Acts 3:6-7*

Notice the sequence of timing on both of these prophetic acts. Only after doing the prophetic act (which is tantamount to acting as if they were already healed) were their bodies healed. This is R-I-S-K at its finest!

At other times, the prophetic act tends to have a more immediate result:

> *"But that you may know that the Son of Man has authority on earth to forgive sins"—he said to the paralytic— "I say to you, rise, pick up your bed, and go home." And he rose and immediately picked up his bed and went out before them all. Mark 2:10-12*

> *She had heard the reports about Jesus and came up behind him in the crowd and touched his garment. For she said, "If I touch even his garments, I will be made well." And immediately the flow of blood dried up, and she felt in her body that she was healed of her disease. Mark 5:27-29*

Oral Roberts used the same idea when he would talk about the "point of contact," which was an action you take to release your faith.

Activating Faith

Faith can be present both in a person as well as in the atmosphere in general (see the "Discerning Atmospheres" skill). When you recognize faith, try to activate it through one of two means as the Spirit leads. Activating faith can be one of the keys to moving up to more powerful healings:

Declaration

- Declare the healing. (This is different than commanding the healing)
- Immediately test the condition, if possible, to see if it has been healed.

Prophetic Act

- Ask God what prophetic act to have the person do, and then have them do that action.
- If it is possible, immediately test the condition afterwards.

school of
KINGDOM
MINISTRY

Ministry Practice Journal

Ministry Practice Journal

This last section of your student manual is meant to be a journal that you can use to track your ministry activities and reflect on them to learn where to continue to invest your energy in developing your abilities. Here is how it works:

- Each day you'll mark down the ministry you participated in that day. You'll simply check boxes as to whether or not you ministered in that way on that day. You'll check all that apply under three separate categories:

  Ministries—Check off the different types of ministry you may have participated in:

  Healing: ministering healing to some aspect of the person (not necessarily physical).

  Deliverance: Freeing a person from the holds of demons and addictions.

  Prophetic: ministering in revelatory gifts and prophetic words.

  Presence: Ministering the manifest presence of God directly someone.

  Contexts—Check off the different contexts you ministered in that day:

  Created spaces within church: Times and situations where ministry is the expected activity (services, small groups, etc.).
  Non-created spaces within church: Times and situations within church culture, but ministry is not the expected activity (meaning you create the opportunity)
  Public: Outside of the church context.

  Situational Gifts—Check off the situational gifts you ministered in that day.

- As you check off the ministries, contexts and gifts, we suggest that you check off any **attempted ministry**, regardless of the success. This is because we're trying to encourage a lifestyle of going for it, not an expectation of perfection.
- At the end of each week, total the number of days you ministered in the different ways.
- After a few weeks, examine what is normal for you. Where are you strong? What could you continue to grow in?

We've given you enough sheets to track your progress during the entire 28 weeks of the School of Kingdom Ministry classes. We stopped there just for length. We hope this is a helpful tool for you.

Week 1

Sunday

Ministries

- ☐ Healing
- ☐ Prophetic
- ☐ Deliverance
- ☐ Presence

Contexts

- ☐ Created spaces within church
- ☐ Non-created spaces within church
- ☐ Public

Situational Gifts

- ☐ Word of Knowledge
- ☐ Word of Wisdom
- ☐ Discerning of Spirits
- ☐ Prophecy
- ☐ Tongues
- ☐ Interpretation
- ☐ Gifts of Healing
- ☐ Working of Miracles
- ☐ Faith

Monday

Ministries

- ☐ Healing
- ☐ Prophetic
- ☐ Deliverance
- ☐ Presence

Contexts

- ☐ Created spaces within church
- ☐ Non-created spaces within church
- ☐ Public

Situational Gifts

- ☐ Word of Knowledge
- ☐ Word of Wisdom
- ☐ Discerning of Spirits
- ☐ Prophecy
- ☐ Tongues
- ☐ Interpretation
- ☐ Gifts of Healing
- ☐ Working of Miracles
- ☐ Faith

Tuesday

Ministries

- ☐ Healing
- ☐ Prophetic
- ☐ Deliverance
- ☐ Presence

Contexts

- ☐ Created spaces within church
- ☐ Non-created spaces within church
- ☐ Public

Situational Gifts

- ☐ Word of Knowledge
- ☐ Word of Wisdom
- ☐ Discerning of Spirits
- ☐ Prophecy
- ☐ Tongues
- ☐ Interpretation
- ☐ Gifts of Healing
- ☐ Working of Miracles
- ☐ Faith

Wednesday

Ministries

- ☐ Healing
- ☐ Prophetic
- ☐ Deliverance
- ☐ Presence

Contexts

- ☐ Created spaces within church
- ☐ Non-created spaces within church
- ☐ Public

Situational Gifts

- ☐ Word of Knowledge
- ☐ Word of Wisdom
- ☐ Discerning of Spirits
- ☐ Prophecy
- ☐ Tongues
- ☐ Interpretation
- ☐ Gifts of Healing
- ☐ Working of Miracles
- ☐ Faith

Thursday

Ministries

- ☐ Healing
- ☐ Prophetic
- ☐ Deliverance
- ☐ Presence

Contexts

- ☐ Created spaces within church
- ☐ Non-created spaces within church
- ☐ Public

Situational Gifts

- ☐ Word of Knowledge
- ☐ Word of Wisdom
- ☐ Discerning of Spirits
- ☐ Prophecy
- ☐ Tongues
- ☐ Interpretation
- ☐ Gifts of Healing
- ☐ Working of Miracles
- ☐ Faith

Friday

Ministries

- ☐ Healing
- ☐ Prophetic
- ☐ Deliverance
- ☐ Presence

Contexts

- ☐ Created spaces within church
- ☐ Non-created spaces within church
- ☐ Public

Situational Gifts

- ☐ Word of Knowledge
- ☐ Word of Wisdom
- ☐ Discerning of Spirits
- ☐ Prophecy
- ☐ Tongues
- ☐ Interpretation
- ☐ Gifts of Healing
- ☐ Working of Miracles
- ☐ Faith

Saturday

Ministries

- ☐ Healing
- ☐ Prophetic
- ☐ Deliverance
- ☐ Presence

Contexts

- ☐ Created spaces within church
- ☐ Non-created spaces within church
- ☐ Public

Situational Gifts

- ☐ Word of Knowledge
- ☐ Word of Wisdom
- ☐ Discerning of Spirits
- ☐ Prophecy
- ☐ Tongues
- ☐ Interpretation
- ☐ Gifts of Healing
- ☐ Working of Miracles
- ☐ Faith

Weekly Total:

Ministries

_____ Healing
_____ Prophetic
_____ Deliverance
_____ Presence

Contexts

_____ Created spaces within church
_____ Non-created spaces within church
_____ Public

Situational Gifts

_____ Word of Knowledge
_____ Word of Wisdom
_____ Discerning of Spirits
_____ Prophecy
_____ Tongues
_____ Interpretation
_____ Gifts of Healing
_____ Working of Miracles
_____ Faith

Week 2

Sunday

Ministries

- ☐ Healing
- ☐ Prophetic
- ☐ Deliverance
- ☐ Presence

Contexts

- ☐ Created spaces within church
- ☐ Non-created spaces within church
- ☐ Public

Situational Gifts

- ☐ Word of Knowledge
- ☐ Word of Wisdom
- ☐ Discerning of Spirits
- ☐ Prophecy
- ☐ Tongues
- ☐ Interpretation
- ☐ Gifts of Healing
- ☐ Working of Miracles
- ☐ Faith

Monday

Ministries

- ☐ Healing
- ☐ Prophetic
- ☐ Deliverance
- ☐ Presence

Contexts

- ☐ Created spaces within church
- ☐ Non-created spaces within church
- ☐ Public

Situational Gifts

- ☐ Word of Knowledge
- ☐ Word of Wisdom
- ☐ Discerning of Spirits
- ☐ Prophecy
- ☐ Tongues
- ☐ Interpretation
- ☐ Gifts of Healing
- ☐ Working of Miracles
- ☐ Faith

Tuesday

Ministries

- ☐ Healing
- ☐ Prophetic
- ☐ Deliverance
- ☐ Presence

Contexts

- ☐ Created spaces within church
- ☐ Non-created spaces within church
- ☐ Public

Situational Gifts

- ☐ Word of Knowledge
- ☐ Word of Wisdom
- ☐ Discerning of Spirits
- ☐ Prophecy
- ☐ Tongues
- ☐ Interpretation
- ☐ Gifts of Healing
- ☐ Working of Miracles
- ☐ Faith

Wednesday

Ministries

- ☐ Healing
- ☐ Prophetic
- ☐ Deliverance
- ☐ Presence

Contexts

- ☐ Created spaces within church
- ☐ Non-created spaces within church
- ☐ Public

Situational Gifts

- ☐ Word of Knowledge
- ☐ Word of Wisdom
- ☐ Discerning of Spirits
- ☐ Prophecy
- ☐ Tongues
- ☐ Interpretation
- ☐ Gifts of Healing
- ☐ Working of Miracles
- ☐ Faith

Thursday

Ministries
- ☐ Healing
- ☐ Prophetic
- ☐ Deliverance
- ☐ Presence

Contexts
- ☐ Created spaces within church
- ☐ Non-created spaces within church
- ☐ Public

Situational Gifts
- ☐ Word of Knowledge
- ☐ Word of Wisdom
- ☐ Discerning of Spirits
- ☐ Prophecy
- ☐ Tongues
- ☐ Interpretation
- ☐ Gifts of Healing
- ☐ Working of Miracles
- ☐ Faith

Friday

Ministries
- ☐ Healing
- ☐ Prophetic
- ☐ Deliverance
- ☐ Presence

Contexts
- ☐ Created spaces within church
- ☐ Non-created spaces within church
- ☐ Public

Situational Gifts
- ☐ Word of Knowledge
- ☐ Word of Wisdom
- ☐ Discerning of Spirits
- ☐ Prophecy
- ☐ Tongues
- ☐ Interpretation
- ☐ Gifts of Healing
- ☐ Working of Miracles
- ☐ Faith

Saturday

Ministries
- ☐ Healing
- ☐ Prophetic
- ☐ Deliverance
- ☐ Presence

Contexts
- ☐ Created spaces within church
- ☐ Non-created spaces within church
- ☐ Public

Situational Gifts
- ☐ Word of Knowledge
- ☐ Word of Wisdom
- ☐ Discerning of Spirits
- ☐ Prophecy
- ☐ Tongues
- ☐ Interpretation
- ☐ Gifts of Healing
- ☐ Working of Miracles
- ☐ Faith

Weekly Total:

Ministries

_____ Healing
_____ Prophetic
_____ Deliverance
_____ Presence

Contexts

_____ Created spaces within church
_____ Non-created spaces within church
_____ Public

Situational Gifts

_____ Word of Knowledge
_____ Word of Wisdom
_____ Discerning of Spirits
_____ Prophecy
_____ Tongues
_____ Interpretation
_____ Gifts of Healing
_____ Working of Miracles
_____ Faith

Week 3

Sunday

<u>Ministries</u>
- ☐ Healing
- ☐ Prophetic
- ☐ Deliverance
- ☐ Presence

<u>Contexts</u>
- ☐ Created spaces within church
- ☐ Non-created spaces within church
- ☐ Public

<u>Situational Gifts</u>
- ☐ Word of Knowledge
- ☐ Word of Wisdom
- ☐ Discerning of Spirits
- ☐ Prophecy
- ☐ Tongues
- ☐ Interpretation
- ☐ Gifts of Healing
- ☐ Working of Miracles
- ☐ Faith

Monday

<u>Ministries</u>
- ☐ Healing
- ☐ Prophetic
- ☐ Deliverance
- ☐ Presence

<u>Contexts</u>
- ☐ Created spaces within church
- ☐ Non-created spaces within church
- ☐ Public

<u>Situational Gifts</u>
- ☐ Word of Knowledge
- ☐ Word of Wisdom
- ☐ Discerning of Spirits
- ☐ Prophecy
- ☐ Tongues
- ☐ Interpretation
- ☐ Gifts of Healing
- ☐ Working of Miracles
- ☐ Faith

Tuesday

<u>Ministries</u>
- ☐ Healing
- ☐ Prophetic
- ☐ Deliverance
- ☐ Presence

<u>Contexts</u>
- ☐ Created spaces within church
- ☐ Non-created spaces within church
- ☐ Public

<u>Situational Gifts</u>
- ☐ Word of Knowledge
- ☐ Word of Wisdom
- ☐ Discerning of Spirits
- ☐ Prophecy
- ☐ Tongues
- ☐ Interpretation
- ☐ Gifts of Healing
- ☐ Working of Miracles
- ☐ Faith

Wednesday

<u>Ministries</u>
- ☐ Healing
- ☐ Prophetic
- ☐ Deliverance
- ☐ Presence

<u>Contexts</u>
- ☐ Created spaces within church
- ☐ Non-created spaces within church
- ☐ Public

<u>Situational Gifts</u>
- ☐ Word of Knowledge
- ☐ Word of Wisdom
- ☐ Discerning of Spirits
- ☐ Prophecy
- ☐ Tongues
- ☐ Interpretation
- ☐ Gifts of Healing
- ☐ Working of Miracles
- ☐ Faith

Thursday		
	Ministries ☐ Healing ☐ Prophetic ☐ Deliverance ☐ Presence **Contexts** ☐ Created spaces within church ☐ Non-created spaces within church ☐ Public	**Situational Gifts** ☐ Word of Knowledge ☐ Word of Wisdom ☐ Discerning of Spirits ☐ Prophecy ☐ Tongues ☐ Interpretation ☐ Gifts of Healing ☐ Working of Miracles ☐ Faith
Friday	**Ministries** ☐ Healing ☐ Prophetic ☐ Deliverance ☐ Presence **Contexts** ☐ Created spaces within church ☐ Non-created spaces within church ☐ Public	**Situational Gifts** ☐ Word of Knowledge ☐ Word of Wisdom ☐ Discerning of Spirits ☐ Prophecy ☐ Tongues ☐ Interpretation ☐ Gifts of Healing ☐ Working of Miracles ☐ Faith
Saturday	**Ministries** ☐ Healing ☐ Prophetic ☐ Deliverance ☐ Presence **Contexts** ☐ Created spaces within church ☐ Non-created spaces within church ☐ Public	**Situational Gifts** ☐ Word of Knowledge ☐ Word of Wisdom ☐ Discerning of Spirits ☐ Prophecy ☐ Tongues ☐ Interpretation ☐ Gifts of Healing ☐ Working of Miracles ☐ Faith

Weekly Total:

Ministries

_____ Healing
_____ Prophetic
_____ Deliverance
_____ Presence

Contexts

_____ Created spaces within church
_____ Non-created spaces within church
_____ Public

Situational Gifts

_____ Word of Knowledge
_____ Word of Wisdom
_____ Discerning of Spirits
_____ Prophecy
_____ Tongues
_____ Interpretation
_____ Gifts of Healing
_____ Working of Miracles
_____ Faith

Week 4

Sunday	**Ministries** ☐ Healing ☐ Prophetic ☐ Deliverance ☐ Presence **Contexts** ☐ Created spaces within church ☐ Non-created spaces within church ☐ Public	**Situational Gifts** ☐ Word of Knowledge ☐ Word of Wisdom ☐ Discerning of Spirits ☐ Prophecy ☐ Tongues ☐ Interpretation ☐ Gifts of Healing ☐ Working of Miracles ☐ Faith
Monday	**Ministries** ☐ Healing ☐ Prophetic ☐ Deliverance ☐ Presence **Contexts** ☐ Created spaces within church ☐ Non-created spaces within church ☐ Public	**Situational Gifts** ☐ Word of Knowledge ☐ Word of Wisdom ☐ Discerning of Spirits ☐ Prophecy ☐ Tongues ☐ Interpretation ☐ Gifts of Healing ☐ Working of Miracles ☐ Faith
Tuesday	**Ministries** ☐ Healing ☐ Prophetic ☐ Deliverance ☐ Presence **Contexts** ☐ Created spaces within church ☐ Non-created spaces within church ☐ Public	**Situational Gifts** ☐ Word of Knowledge ☐ Word of Wisdom ☐ Discerning of Spirits ☐ Prophecy ☐ Tongues ☐ Interpretation ☐ Gifts of Healing ☐ Working of Miracles ☐ Faith
Wednesday	**Ministries** ☐ Healing ☐ Prophetic ☐ Deliverance ☐ Presence **Contexts** ☐ Created spaces within church ☐ Non-created spaces within church ☐ Public	**Situational Gifts** ☐ Word of Knowledge ☐ Word of Wisdom ☐ Discerning of Spirits ☐ Prophecy ☐ Tongues ☐ Interpretation ☐ Gifts of Healing ☐ Working of Miracles ☐ Faith

Thursday

Ministries
- ☐ Healing
- ☐ Prophetic
- ☐ Deliverance
- ☐ Presence

Contexts
- ☐ Created spaces within church
- ☐ Non-created spaces within church
- ☐ Public

Situational Gifts
- ☐ Word of Knowledge
- ☐ Word of Wisdom
- ☐ Discerning of Spirits
- ☐ Prophecy
- ☐ Tongues
- ☐ Interpretation
- ☐ Gifts of Healing
- ☐ Working of Miracles
- ☐ Faith

Friday

Ministries
- ☐ Healing
- ☐ Prophetic
- ☐ Deliverance
- ☐ Presence

Contexts
- ☐ Created spaces within church
- ☐ Non-created spaces within church
- ☐ Public

Situational Gifts
- ☐ Word of Knowledge
- ☐ Word of Wisdom
- ☐ Discerning of Spirits
- ☐ Prophecy
- ☐ Tongues
- ☐ Interpretation
- ☐ Gifts of Healing
- ☐ Working of Miracles
- ☐ Faith

Saturday

Ministries
- ☐ Healing
- ☐ Prophetic
- ☐ Deliverance
- ☐ Presence

Contexts
- ☐ Created spaces within church
- ☐ Non-created spaces within church
- ☐ Public

Situational Gifts
- ☐ Word of Knowledge
- ☐ Word of Wisdom
- ☐ Discerning of Spirits
- ☐ Prophecy
- ☐ Tongues
- ☐ Interpretation
- ☐ Gifts of Healing
- ☐ Working of Miracles
- ☐ Faith

Weekly Total:

Ministries

_____ Healing
_____ Prophetic
_____ Deliverance
_____ Presence

Contexts

_____ Created spaces within church
_____ Non-created spaces within church
_____ Public

Situational Gifts

_____ Word of Knowledge
_____ Word of Wisdom
_____ Discerning of Spirits
_____ Prophecy
_____ Tongues
_____ Interpretation
_____ Gifts of Healing
_____ Working of Miracles
_____ Faith

Week 5

Sunday	**Ministries** ☐ Healing ☐ Prophetic ☐ Deliverance ☐ Presence **Contexts** ☐ Created spaces within church ☐ Non-created spaces within church ☐ Public	**Situational Gifts** ☐ Word of Knowledge ☐ Word of Wisdom ☐ Discerning of Spirits ☐ Prophecy ☐ Tongues ☐ Interpretation ☐ Gifts of Healing ☐ Working of Miracles ☐ Faith
Monday	**Ministries** ☐ Healing ☐ Prophetic ☐ Deliverance ☐ Presence **Contexts** ☐ Created spaces within church ☐ Non-created spaces within church ☐ Public	**Situational Gifts** ☐ Word of Knowledge ☐ Word of Wisdom ☐ Discerning of Spirits ☐ Prophecy ☐ Tongues ☐ Interpretation ☐ Gifts of Healing ☐ Working of Miracles ☐ Faith
Tuesday	**Ministries** ☐ Healing ☐ Prophetic ☐ Deliverance ☐ Presence **Contexts** ☐ Created spaces within church ☐ Non-created spaces within church ☐ Public	**Situational Gifts** ☐ Word of Knowledge ☐ Word of Wisdom ☐ Discerning of Spirits ☐ Prophecy ☐ Tongues ☐ Interpretation ☐ Gifts of Healing ☐ Working of Miracles ☐ Faith
Wednesday	**Ministries** ☐ Healing ☐ Prophetic ☐ Deliverance ☐ Presence **Contexts** ☐ Created spaces within church ☐ Non-created spaces within church ☐ Public	**Situational Gifts** ☐ Word of Knowledge ☐ Word of Wisdom ☐ Discerning of Spirits ☐ Prophecy ☐ Tongues ☐ Interpretation ☐ Gifts of Healing ☐ Working of Miracles ☐ Faith

Day	Ministries / Contexts	Situational Gifts
Thursday	**Ministries** ☐ Healing ☐ Prophetic ☐ Deliverance ☐ Presence **Contexts** ☐ Created spaces within church ☐ Non-created spaces within church ☐ Public	**Situational Gifts** ☐ Word of Knowledge ☐ Word of Wisdom ☐ Discerning of Spirits ☐ Prophecy ☐ Tongues ☐ Interpretation ☐ Gifts of Healing ☐ Working of Miracles ☐ Faith
Friday	**Ministries** ☐ Healing ☐ Prophetic ☐ Deliverance ☐ Presence **Contexts** ☐ Created spaces within church ☐ Non-created spaces within church ☐ Public	**Situational Gifts** ☐ Word of Knowledge ☐ Word of Wisdom ☐ Discerning of Spirits ☐ Prophecy ☐ Tongues ☐ Interpretation ☐ Gifts of Healing ☐ Working of Miracles ☐ Faith
Saturday	**Ministries** ☐ Healing ☐ Prophetic ☐ Deliverance ☐ Presence **Contexts** ☐ Created spaces within church ☐ Non-created spaces within church ☐ Public	**Situational Gifts** ☐ Word of Knowledge ☐ Word of Wisdom ☐ Discerning of Spirits ☐ Prophecy ☐ Tongues ☐ Interpretation ☐ Gifts of Healing ☐ Working of Miracles ☐ Faith

Weekly Total:

Ministries

_____ Healing
_____ Prophetic
_____ Deliverance
_____ Presence

Contexts

_____ Created spaces within church
_____ Non-created spaces within church
_____ Public

Situational Gifts

_____ Word of Knowledge
_____ Word of Wisdom
_____ Discerning of Spirits
_____ Prophecy
_____ Tongues
_____ Interpretation
_____ Gifts of Healing
_____ Working of Miracles
_____ Faith

Week 6

Sunday

Ministries
- ☐ Healing
- ☐ Prophetic
- ☐ Deliverance
- ☐ Presence

Contexts
- ☐ Created spaces within church
- ☐ Non-created spaces within church
- ☐ Public

Situational Gifts
- ☐ Word of Knowledge
- ☐ Word of Wisdom
- ☐ Discerning of Spirits
- ☐ Prophecy
- ☐ Tongues
- ☐ Interpretation
- ☐ Gifts of Healing
- ☐ Working of Miracles
- ☐ Faith

Monday

Ministries
- ☐ Healing
- ☐ Prophetic
- ☐ Deliverance
- ☐ Presence

Contexts
- ☐ Created spaces within church
- ☐ Non-created spaces within church
- ☐ Public

Situational Gifts
- ☐ Word of Knowledge
- ☐ Word of Wisdom
- ☐ Discerning of Spirits
- ☐ Prophecy
- ☐ Tongues
- ☐ Interpretation
- ☐ Gifts of Healing
- ☐ Working of Miracles
- ☐ Faith

Tuesday

Ministries
- ☐ Healing
- ☐ Prophetic
- ☐ Deliverance
- ☐ Presence

Contexts
- ☐ Created spaces within church
- ☐ Non-created spaces within church
- ☐ Public

Situational Gifts
- ☐ Word of Knowledge
- ☐ Word of Wisdom
- ☐ Discerning of Spirits
- ☐ Prophecy
- ☐ Tongues
- ☐ Interpretation
- ☐ Gifts of Healing
- ☐ Working of Miracles
- ☐ Faith

Wednesday

Ministries
- ☐ Healing
- ☐ Prophetic
- ☐ Deliverance
- ☐ Presence

Contexts
- ☐ Created spaces within church
- ☐ Non-created spaces within church
- ☐ Public

Situational Gifts
- ☐ Word of Knowledge
- ☐ Word of Wisdom
- ☐ Discerning of Spirits
- ☐ Prophecy
- ☐ Tongues
- ☐ Interpretation
- ☐ Gifts of Healing
- ☐ Working of Miracles
- ☐ Faith

Thursday

Ministries
- ☐ Healing
- ☐ Prophetic
- ☐ Deliverance
- ☐ Presence

Contexts
- ☐ Created spaces within church
- ☐ Non-created spaces within church
- ☐ Public

Situational Gifts
- ☐ Word of Knowledge
- ☐ Word of Wisdom
- ☐ Discerning of Spirits
- ☐ Prophecy
- ☐ Tongues
- ☐ Interpretation
- ☐ Gifts of Healing
- ☐ Working of Miracles
- ☐ Faith

Friday

Ministries
- ☐ Healing
- ☐ Prophetic
- ☐ Deliverance
- ☐ Presence

Contexts
- ☐ Created spaces within church
- ☐ Non-created spaces within church
- ☐ Public

Situational Gifts
- ☐ Word of Knowledge
- ☐ Word of Wisdom
- ☐ Discerning of Spirits
- ☐ Prophecy
- ☐ Tongues
- ☐ Interpretation
- ☐ Gifts of Healing
- ☐ Working of Miracles
- ☐ Faith

Saturday

Ministries
- ☐ Healing
- ☐ Prophetic
- ☐ Deliverance
- ☐ Presence

Contexts
- ☐ Created spaces within church
- ☐ Non-created spaces within church
- ☐ Public

Situational Gifts
- ☐ Word of Knowledge
- ☐ Word of Wisdom
- ☐ Discerning of Spirits
- ☐ Prophecy
- ☐ Tongues
- ☐ Interpretation
- ☐ Gifts of Healing
- ☐ Working of Miracles
- ☐ Faith

Weekly Total:

Ministries

_____ Healing
_____ Prophetic
_____ Deliverance
_____ Presence

Contexts

_____ Created spaces within church
_____ Non-created spaces within church
_____ Public

Situational Gifts

_____ Word of Knowledge
_____ Word of Wisdom
_____ Discerning of Spirits
_____ Prophecy
_____ Tongues
_____ Interpretation
_____ Gifts of Healing
_____ Working of Miracles
_____ Faith

Week 7

Day	Ministries / Contexts	Situational Gifts
Sunday	**Ministries** ☐ Healing ☐ Prophetic ☐ Deliverance ☐ Presence **Contexts** ☐ Created spaces within church ☐ Non-created spaces within church ☐ Public	**Situational Gifts** ☐ Word of Knowledge ☐ Word of Wisdom ☐ Discerning of Spirits ☐ Prophecy ☐ Tongues ☐ Interpretation ☐ Gifts of Healing ☐ Working of Miracles ☐ Faith
Monday	**Ministries** ☐ Healing ☐ Prophetic ☐ Deliverance ☐ Presence **Contexts** ☐ Created spaces within church ☐ Non-created spaces within church ☐ Public	**Situational Gifts** ☐ Word of Knowledge ☐ Word of Wisdom ☐ Discerning of Spirits ☐ Prophecy ☐ Tongues ☐ Interpretation ☐ Gifts of Healing ☐ Working of Miracles ☐ Faith
Tuesday	**Ministries** ☐ Healing ☐ Prophetic ☐ Deliverance ☐ Presence **Contexts** ☐ Created spaces within church ☐ Non-created spaces within church ☐ Public	**Situational Gifts** ☐ Word of Knowledge ☐ Word of Wisdom ☐ Discerning of Spirits ☐ Prophecy ☐ Tongues ☐ Interpretation ☐ Gifts of Healing ☐ Working of Miracles ☐ Faith
Wednesday	**Ministries** ☐ Healing ☐ Prophetic ☐ Deliverance ☐ Presence **Contexts** ☐ Created spaces within church ☐ Non-created spaces within church ☐ Public	**Situational Gifts** ☐ Word of Knowledge ☐ Word of Wisdom ☐ Discerning of Spirits ☐ Prophecy ☐ Tongues ☐ Interpretation ☐ Gifts of Healing ☐ Working of Miracles ☐ Faith

Day	Ministries / Contexts	Situational Gifts
Thursday	**Ministries** ☐ Healing ☐ Prophetic ☐ Deliverance ☐ Presence **Contexts** ☐ Created spaces within church ☐ Non-created spaces within church ☐ Public	**Situational Gifts** ☐ Word of Knowledge ☐ Word of Wisdom ☐ Discerning of Spirits ☐ Prophecy ☐ Tongues ☐ Interpretation ☐ Gifts of Healing ☐ Working of Miracles ☐ Faith
Friday	**Ministries** ☐ Healing ☐ Prophetic ☐ Deliverance ☐ Presence **Contexts** ☐ Created spaces within church ☐ Non-created spaces within church ☐ Public	**Situational Gifts** ☐ Word of Knowledge ☐ Word of Wisdom ☐ Discerning of Spirits ☐ Prophecy ☐ Tongues ☐ Interpretation ☐ Gifts of Healing ☐ Working of Miracles ☐ Faith
Saturday	**Ministries** ☐ Healing ☐ Prophetic ☐ Deliverance ☐ Presence **Contexts** ☐ Created spaces within church ☐ Non-created spaces within church ☐ Public	**Situational Gifts** ☐ Word of Knowledge ☐ Word of Wisdom ☐ Discerning of Spirits ☐ Prophecy ☐ Tongues ☐ Interpretation ☐ Gifts of Healing ☐ Working of Miracles ☐ Faith

Weekly Total:

Ministries

_____ Healing
_____ Prophetic
_____ Deliverance
_____ Presence

Contexts

_____ Created spaces within church
_____ Non-created spaces within church
_____ Public

Situational Gifts

_____ Word of Knowledge
_____ Word of Wisdom
_____ Discerning of Spirits
_____ Prophecy
_____ Tongues
_____ Interpretation
_____ Gifts of Healing
_____ Working of Miracles
_____ Faith

Week 8

Sunday

Ministries

- ☐ Healing
- ☐ Prophetic
- ☐ Deliverance
- ☐ Presence

Contexts

- ☐ Created spaces within church
- ☐ Non-created spaces within church
- ☐ Public

Situational Gifts

- ☐ Word of Knowledge
- ☐ Word of Wisdom
- ☐ Discerning of Spirits
- ☐ Prophecy
- ☐ Tongues
- ☐ Interpretation
- ☐ Gifts of Healing
- ☐ Working of Miracles
- ☐ Faith

Monday

Ministries

- ☐ Healing
- ☐ Prophetic
- ☐ Deliverance
- ☐ Presence

Contexts

- ☐ Created spaces within church
- ☐ Non-created spaces within church
- ☐ Public

Situational Gifts

- ☐ Word of Knowledge
- ☐ Word of Wisdom
- ☐ Discerning of Spirits
- ☐ Prophecy
- ☐ Tongues
- ☐ Interpretation
- ☐ Gifts of Healing
- ☐ Working of Miracles
- ☐ Faith

Tuesday

Ministries

- ☐ Healing
- ☐ Prophetic
- ☐ Deliverance
- ☐ Presence

Contexts

- ☐ Created spaces within church
- ☐ Non-created spaces within church
- ☐ Public

Situational Gifts

- ☐ Word of Knowledge
- ☐ Word of Wisdom
- ☐ Discerning of Spirits
- ☐ Prophecy
- ☐ Tongues
- ☐ Interpretation
- ☐ Gifts of Healing
- ☐ Working of Miracles
- ☐ Faith

Wednesday

Ministries

- ☐ Healing
- ☐ Prophetic
- ☐ Deliverance
- ☐ Presence

Contexts

- ☐ Created spaces within church
- ☐ Non-created spaces within church
- ☐ Public

Situational Gifts

- ☐ Word of Knowledge
- ☐ Word of Wisdom
- ☐ Discerning of Spirits
- ☐ Prophecy
- ☐ Tongues
- ☐ Interpretation
- ☐ Gifts of Healing
- ☐ Working of Miracles
- ☐ Faith

Day	Ministries / Contexts	Situational Gifts
Thursday	**Ministries** ☐ Healing ☐ Prophetic ☐ Deliverance ☐ Presence **Contexts** ☐ Created spaces within church ☐ Non-created spaces within church ☐ Public	**Situational Gifts** ☐ Word of Knowledge ☐ Word of Wisdom ☐ Discerning of Spirits ☐ Prophecy ☐ Tongues ☐ Interpretation ☐ Gifts of Healing ☐ Working of Miracles ☐ Faith
Friday	**Ministries** ☐ Healing ☐ Prophetic ☐ Deliverance ☐ Presence **Contexts** ☐ Created spaces within church ☐ Non-created spaces within church ☐ Public	**Situational Gifts** ☐ Word of Knowledge ☐ Word of Wisdom ☐ Discerning of Spirits ☐ Prophecy ☐ Tongues ☐ Interpretation ☐ Gifts of Healing ☐ Working of Miracles ☐ Faith
Saturday	**Ministries** ☐ Healing ☐ Prophetic ☐ Deliverance ☐ Presence **Contexts** ☐ Created spaces within church ☐ Non-created spaces within church ☐ Public	**Situational Gifts** ☐ Word of Knowledge ☐ Word of Wisdom ☐ Discerning of Spirits ☐ Prophecy ☐ Tongues ☐ Interpretation ☐ Gifts of Healing ☐ Working of Miracles ☐ Faith

Weekly Total:

Ministries

_____ Healing
_____ Prophetic
_____ Deliverance
_____ Presence

Contexts

_____ Created spaces within church
_____ Non-created spaces within church
_____ Public

Situational Gifts

_____ Word of Knowledge
_____ Word of Wisdom
_____ Discerning of Spirits
_____ Prophecy
_____ Tongues
_____ Interpretation
_____ Gifts of Healing
_____ Working of Miracles
_____ Faith

Week 9

Sunday

Ministries
- ☐ Healing
- ☐ Prophetic
- ☐ Deliverance
- ☐ Presence

Contexts
- ☐ Created spaces within church
- ☐ Non-created spaces within church
- ☐ Public

Situational Gifts
- ☐ Word of Knowledge
- ☐ Word of Wisdom
- ☐ Discerning of Spirits
- ☐ Prophecy
- ☐ Tongues
- ☐ Interpretation
- ☐ Gifts of Healing
- ☐ Working of Miracles
- ☐ Faith

Monday

Ministries
- ☐ Healing
- ☐ Prophetic
- ☐ Deliverance
- ☐ Presence

Contexts
- ☐ Created spaces within church
- ☐ Non-created spaces within church
- ☐ Public

Situational Gifts
- ☐ Word of Knowledge
- ☐ Word of Wisdom
- ☐ Discerning of Spirits
- ☐ Prophecy
- ☐ Tongues
- ☐ Interpretation
- ☐ Gifts of Healing
- ☐ Working of Miracles
- ☐ Faith

Tuesday

Ministries
- ☐ Healing
- ☐ Prophetic
- ☐ Deliverance
- ☐ Presence

Contexts
- ☐ Created spaces within church
- ☐ Non-created spaces within church
- ☐ Public

Situational Gifts
- ☐ Word of Knowledge
- ☐ Word of Wisdom
- ☐ Discerning of Spirits
- ☐ Prophecy
- ☐ Tongues
- ☐ Interpretation
- ☐ Gifts of Healing
- ☐ Working of Miracles
- ☐ Faith

Wednesday

Ministries
- ☐ Healing
- ☐ Prophetic
- ☐ Deliverance
- ☐ Presence

Contexts
- ☐ Created spaces within church
- ☐ Non-created spaces within church
- ☐ Public

Situational Gifts
- ☐ Word of Knowledge
- ☐ Word of Wisdom
- ☐ Discerning of Spirits
- ☐ Prophecy
- ☐ Tongues
- ☐ Interpretation
- ☐ Gifts of Healing
- ☐ Working of Miracles
- ☐ Faith

Day	Ministries / Contexts	Situational Gifts
Thursday	**Ministries** ☐ Healing ☐ Prophetic ☐ Deliverance ☐ Presence **Contexts** ☐ Created spaces within church ☐ Non-created spaces within church ☐ Public	**Situational Gifts** ☐ Word of Knowledge ☐ Word of Wisdom ☐ Discerning of Spirits ☐ Prophecy ☐ Tongues ☐ Interpretation ☐ Gifts of Healing ☐ Working of Miracles ☐ Faith
Friday	**Ministries** ☐ Healing ☐ Prophetic ☐ Deliverance ☐ Presence **Contexts** ☐ Created spaces within church ☐ Non-created spaces within church ☐ Public	**Situational Gifts** ☐ Word of Knowledge ☐ Word of Wisdom ☐ Discerning of Spirits ☐ Prophecy ☐ Tongues ☐ Interpretation ☐ Gifts of Healing ☐ Working of Miracles ☐ Faith
Saturday	**Ministries** ☐ Healing ☐ Prophetic ☐ Deliverance ☐ Presence **Contexts** ☐ Created spaces within church ☐ Non-created spaces within church ☐ Public	**Situational Gifts** ☐ Word of Knowledge ☐ Word of Wisdom ☐ Discerning of Spirits ☐ Prophecy ☐ Tongues ☐ Interpretation ☐ Gifts of Healing ☐ Working of Miracles ☐ Faith

Weekly Total:

Ministries

_____ Healing
_____ Prophetic
_____ Deliverance
_____ Presence

Contexts

_____ Created spaces within church
_____ Non-created spaces within church
_____ Public

Situational Gifts

_____ Word of Knowledge
_____ Word of Wisdom
_____ Discerning of Spirits
_____ Prophecy
_____ Tongues
_____ Interpretation
_____ Gifts of Healing
_____ Working of Miracles
_____ Faith

Week 10

Sunday

Ministries
- ☐ Healing
- ☐ Prophetic
- ☐ Deliverance
- ☐ Presence

Contexts
- ☐ Created spaces within church
- ☐ Non-created spaces within church
- ☐ Public

Situational Gifts
- ☐ Word of Knowledge
- ☐ Word of Wisdom
- ☐ Discerning of Spirits
- ☐ Prophecy
- ☐ Tongues
- ☐ Interpretation
- ☐ Gifts of Healing
- ☐ Working of Miracles
- ☐ Faith

Monday

Ministries
- ☐ Healing
- ☐ Prophetic
- ☐ Deliverance
- ☐ Presence

Contexts
- ☐ Created spaces within church
- ☐ Non-created spaces within church
- ☐ Public

Situational Gifts
- ☐ Word of Knowledge
- ☐ Word of Wisdom
- ☐ Discerning of Spirits
- ☐ Prophecy
- ☐ Tongues
- ☐ Interpretation
- ☐ Gifts of Healing
- ☐ Working of Miracles
- ☐ Faith

Tuesday

Ministries
- ☐ Healing
- ☐ Prophetic
- ☐ Deliverance
- ☐ Presence

Contexts
- ☐ Created spaces within church
- ☐ Non-created spaces within church
- ☐ Public

Situational Gifts
- ☐ Word of Knowledge
- ☐ Word of Wisdom
- ☐ Discerning of Spirits
- ☐ Prophecy
- ☐ Tongues
- ☐ Interpretation
- ☐ Gifts of Healing
- ☐ Working of Miracles
- ☐ Faith

Wednesday

Ministries
- ☐ Healing
- ☐ Prophetic
- ☐ Deliverance
- ☐ Presence

Contexts
- ☐ Created spaces within church
- ☐ Non-created spaces within church
- ☐ Public

Situational Gifts
- ☐ Word of Knowledge
- ☐ Word of Wisdom
- ☐ Discerning of Spirits
- ☐ Prophecy
- ☐ Tongues
- ☐ Interpretation
- ☐ Gifts of Healing
- ☐ Working of Miracles
- ☐ Faith

Day	Ministries	Contexts	Situational Gifts
Thursday	☐ Healing ☐ Prophetic ☐ Deliverance ☐ Presence	☐ Created spaces within church ☐ Non-created spaces within church ☐ Public	☐ Word of Knowledge ☐ Word of Wisdom ☐ Discerning of Spirits ☐ Prophecy ☐ Tongues ☐ Interpretation ☐ Gifts of Healing ☐ Working of Miracles ☐ Faith
Friday	☐ Healing ☐ Prophetic ☐ Deliverance ☐ Presence	☐ Created spaces within church ☐ Non-created spaces within church ☐ Public	☐ Word of Knowledge ☐ Word of Wisdom ☐ Discerning of Spirits ☐ Prophecy ☐ Tongues ☐ Interpretation ☐ Gifts of Healing ☐ Working of Miracles ☐ Faith
Saturday	☐ Healing ☐ Prophetic ☐ Deliverance ☐ Presence	☐ Created spaces within church ☐ Non-created spaces within church ☐ Public	☐ Word of Knowledge ☐ Word of Wisdom ☐ Discerning of Spirits ☐ Prophecy ☐ Tongues ☐ Interpretation ☐ Gifts of Healing ☐ Working of Miracles ☐ Faith

Weekly Total:

Ministries

_____ Healing
_____ Prophetic
_____ Deliverance
_____ Presence

Contexts

_____ Created spaces within church
_____ Non-created spaces within church
_____ Public

Situational Gifts

_____ Word of Knowledge
_____ Word of Wisdom
_____ Discerning of Spirits
_____ Prophecy
_____ Tongues
_____ Interpretation
_____ Gifts of Healing
_____ Working of Miracles
_____ Faith

Week 11

Sunday

Ministries
- ☐ Healing
- ☐ Prophetic
- ☐ Deliverance
- ☐ Presence

Contexts
- ☐ Created spaces within church
- ☐ Non-created spaces within church
- ☐ Public

Situational Gifts
- ☐ Word of Knowledge
- ☐ Word of Wisdom
- ☐ Discerning of Spirits
- ☐ Prophecy
- ☐ Tongues
- ☐ Interpretation
- ☐ Gifts of Healing
- ☐ Working of Miracles
- ☐ Faith

Monday

Ministries
- ☐ Healing
- ☐ Prophetic
- ☐ Deliverance
- ☐ Presence

Contexts
- ☐ Created spaces within church
- ☐ Non-created spaces within church
- ☐ Public

Situational Gifts
- ☐ Word of Knowledge
- ☐ Word of Wisdom
- ☐ Discerning of Spirits
- ☐ Prophecy
- ☐ Tongues
- ☐ Interpretation
- ☐ Gifts of Healing
- ☐ Working of Miracles
- ☐ Faith

Tuesday

Ministries
- ☐ Healing
- ☐ Prophetic
- ☐ Deliverance
- ☐ Presence

Contexts
- ☐ Created spaces within church
- ☐ Non-created spaces within church
- ☐ Public

Situational Gifts
- ☐ Word of Knowledge
- ☐ Word of Wisdom
- ☐ Discerning of Spirits
- ☐ Prophecy
- ☐ Tongues
- ☐ Interpretation
- ☐ Gifts of Healing
- ☐ Working of Miracles
- ☐ Faith

Wednesday

Ministries
- ☐ Healing
- ☐ Prophetic
- ☐ Deliverance
- ☐ Presence

Contexts
- ☐ Created spaces within church
- ☐ Non-created spaces within church
- ☐ Public

Situational Gifts
- ☐ Word of Knowledge
- ☐ Word of Wisdom
- ☐ Discerning of Spirits
- ☐ Prophecy
- ☐ Tongues
- ☐ Interpretation
- ☐ Gifts of Healing
- ☐ Working of Miracles
- ☐ Faith

Thursday

Ministries
- ☐ Healing
- ☐ Prophetic
- ☐ Deliverance
- ☐ Presence

Contexts
- ☐ Created spaces within church
- ☐ Non-created spaces within church
- ☐ Public

Situational Gifts
- ☐ Word of Knowledge
- ☐ Word of Wisdom
- ☐ Discerning of Spirits
- ☐ Prophecy
- ☐ Tongues
- ☐ Interpretation
- ☐ Gifts of Healing
- ☐ Working of Miracles
- ☐ Faith

Friday

Ministries
- ☐ Healing
- ☐ Prophetic
- ☐ Deliverance
- ☐ Presence

Contexts
- ☐ Created spaces within church
- ☐ Non-created spaces within church
- ☐ Public

Situational Gifts
- ☐ Word of Knowledge
- ☐ Word of Wisdom
- ☐ Discerning of Spirits
- ☐ Prophecy
- ☐ Tongues
- ☐ Interpretation
- ☐ Gifts of Healing
- ☐ Working of Miracles
- ☐ Faith

Saturday

Ministries
- ☐ Healing
- ☐ Prophetic
- ☐ Deliverance
- ☐ Presence

Contexts
- ☐ Created spaces within church
- ☐ Non-created spaces within church
- ☐ Public

Situational Gifts
- ☐ Word of Knowledge
- ☐ Word of Wisdom
- ☐ Discerning of Spirits
- ☐ Prophecy
- ☐ Tongues
- ☐ Interpretation
- ☐ Gifts of Healing
- ☐ Working of Miracles
- ☐ Faith

Weekly Total:

Ministries

_____ Healing
_____ Prophetic
_____ Deliverance
_____ Presence

Contexts

_____ Created spaces within church
_____ Non-created spaces within church
_____ Public

Situational Gifts

_____ Word of Knowledge
_____ Word of Wisdom
_____ Discerning of Spirits
_____ Prophecy
_____ Tongues
_____ Interpretation
_____ Gifts of Healing
_____ Working of Miracles
_____ Faith

Week 12

Sunday

<u>**Ministries**</u>
- ☐ Healing
- ☐ Prophetic
- ☐ Deliverance
- ☐ Presence

<u>**Contexts**</u>
- ☐ Created spaces within church
- ☐ Non-created spaces within church
- ☐ Public

<u>**Situational Gifts**</u>
- ☐ Word of Knowledge
- ☐ Word of Wisdom
- ☐ Discerning of Spirits
- ☐ Prophecy
- ☐ Tongues
- ☐ Interpretation
- ☐ Gifts of Healing
- ☐ Working of Miracles
- ☐ Faith

Monday

<u>**Ministries**</u>
- ☐ Healing
- ☐ Prophetic
- ☐ Deliverance
- ☐ Presence

<u>**Contexts**</u>
- ☐ Created spaces within church
- ☐ Non-created spaces within church
- ☐ Public

<u>**Situational Gifts**</u>
- ☐ Word of Knowledge
- ☐ Word of Wisdom
- ☐ Discerning of Spirits
- ☐ Prophecy
- ☐ Tongues
- ☐ Interpretation
- ☐ Gifts of Healing
- ☐ Working of Miracles
- ☐ Faith

Tuesday

<u>**Ministries**</u>
- ☐ Healing
- ☐ Prophetic
- ☐ Deliverance
- ☐ Presence

<u>**Contexts**</u>
- ☐ Created spaces within church
- ☐ Non-created spaces within church
- ☐ Public

<u>**Situational Gifts**</u>
- ☐ Word of Knowledge
- ☐ Word of Wisdom
- ☐ Discerning of Spirits
- ☐ Prophecy
- ☐ Tongues
- ☐ Interpretation
- ☐ Gifts of Healing
- ☐ Working of Miracles
- ☐ Faith

Wednesday

<u>**Ministries**</u>
- ☐ Healing
- ☐ Prophetic
- ☐ Deliverance
- ☐ Presence

<u>**Contexts**</u>
- ☐ Created spaces within church
- ☐ Non-created spaces within church
- ☐ Public

<u>**Situational Gifts**</u>
- ☐ Word of Knowledge
- ☐ Word of Wisdom
- ☐ Discerning of Spirits
- ☐ Prophecy
- ☐ Tongues
- ☐ Interpretation
- ☐ Gifts of Healing
- ☐ Working of Miracles
- ☐ Faith

	Ministries	Situational Gifts
Thursday	**Ministries** ☐ Healing ☐ Prophetic ☐ Deliverance ☐ Presence **Contexts** ☐ Created spaces within church ☐ Non-created spaces within church ☐ Public	**Situational Gifts** ☐ Word of Knowledge ☐ Word of Wisdom ☐ Discerning of Spirits ☐ Prophecy ☐ Tongues ☐ Interpretation ☐ Gifts of Healing ☐ Working of Miracles ☐ Faith
Friday	**Ministries** ☐ Healing ☐ Prophetic ☐ Deliverance ☐ Presence **Contexts** ☐ Created spaces within church ☐ Non-created spaces within church ☐ Public	**Situational Gifts** ☐ Word of Knowledge ☐ Word of Wisdom ☐ Discerning of Spirits ☐ Prophecy ☐ Tongues ☐ Interpretation ☐ Gifts of Healing ☐ Working of Miracles ☐ Faith
Saturday	**Ministries** ☐ Healing ☐ Prophetic ☐ Deliverance ☐ Presence **Contexts** ☐ Created spaces within church ☐ Non-created spaces within church ☐ Public	**Situational Gifts** ☐ Word of Knowledge ☐ Word of Wisdom ☐ Discerning of Spirits ☐ Prophecy ☐ Tongues ☐ Interpretation ☐ Gifts of Healing ☐ Working of Miracles ☐ Faith

Weekly Total:

Ministries

_____ Healing
_____ Prophetic
_____ Deliverance
_____ Presence

Contexts

_____ Created spaces within church
_____ Non-created spaces within church
_____ Public

Situational Gifts

_____ Word of Knowledge
_____ Word of Wisdom
_____ Discerning of Spirits
_____ Prophecy
_____ Tongues
_____ Interpretation
_____ Gifts of Healing
_____ Working of Miracles
_____ Faith

Week 13

Day	Ministries	Contexts	Situational Gifts
Sunday	☐ Healing ☐ Prophetic ☐ Deliverance ☐ Presence	☐ Created spaces within church ☐ Non-created spaces within church ☐ Public	☐ Word of Knowledge ☐ Word of Wisdom ☐ Discerning of Spirits ☐ Prophecy ☐ Tongues ☐ Interpretation ☐ Gifts of Healing ☐ Working of Miracles ☐ Faith
Monday	☐ Healing ☐ Prophetic ☐ Deliverance ☐ Presence	☐ Created spaces within church ☐ Non-created spaces within church ☐ Public	☐ Word of Knowledge ☐ Word of Wisdom ☐ Discerning of Spirits ☐ Prophecy ☐ Tongues ☐ Interpretation ☐ Gifts of Healing ☐ Working of Miracles ☐ Faith
Tuesday	☐ Healing ☐ Prophetic ☐ Deliverance ☐ Presence	☐ Created spaces within church ☐ Non-created spaces within church ☐ Public	☐ Word of Knowledge ☐ Word of Wisdom ☐ Discerning of Spirits ☐ Prophecy ☐ Tongues ☐ Interpretation ☐ Gifts of Healing ☐ Working of Miracles ☐ Faith
Wednesday	☐ Healing ☐ Prophetic ☐ Deliverance ☐ Presence	☐ Created spaces within church ☐ Non-created spaces within church ☐ Public	☐ Word of Knowledge ☐ Word of Wisdom ☐ Discerning of Spirits ☐ Prophecy ☐ Tongues ☐ Interpretation ☐ Gifts of Healing ☐ Working of Miracles ☐ Faith

Day	Ministries / Contexts	Situational Gifts
Thursday	**Ministries** ☐ Healing ☐ Prophetic ☐ Deliverance ☐ Presence **Contexts** ☐ Created spaces within church ☐ Non-created spaces within church ☐ Public	**Situational Gifts** ☐ Word of Knowledge ☐ Word of Wisdom ☐ Discerning of Spirits ☐ Prophecy ☐ Tongues ☐ Interpretation ☐ Gifts of Healing ☐ Working of Miracles ☐ Faith
Friday	**Ministries** ☐ Healing ☐ Prophetic ☐ Deliverance ☐ Presence **Contexts** ☐ Created spaces within church ☐ Non-created spaces within church ☐ Public	**Situational Gifts** ☐ Word of Knowledge ☐ Word of Wisdom ☐ Discerning of Spirits ☐ Prophecy ☐ Tongues ☐ Interpretation ☐ Gifts of Healing ☐ Working of Miracles ☐ Faith
Saturday	**Ministries** ☐ Healing ☐ Prophetic ☐ Deliverance ☐ Presence **Contexts** ☐ Created spaces within church ☐ Non-created spaces within church ☐ Public	**Situational Gifts** ☐ Word of Knowledge ☐ Word of Wisdom ☐ Discerning of Spirits ☐ Prophecy ☐ Tongues ☐ Interpretation ☐ Gifts of Healing ☐ Working of Miracles ☐ Faith

Weekly Total:

Ministries

_____ Healing
_____ Prophetic
_____ Deliverance
_____ Presence

Contexts

_____ Created spaces within church
_____ Non-created spaces within church
_____ Public

Situational Gifts

_____ Word of Knowledge
_____ Word of Wisdom
_____ Discerning of Spirits
_____ Prophecy
_____ Tongues
_____ Interpretation
_____ Gifts of Healing
_____ Working of Miracles
_____ Faith

Week 14

Day	Ministries / Contexts	Situational Gifts
Sunday	**Ministries** ☐ Healing ☐ Prophetic ☐ Deliverance ☐ Presence **Contexts** ☐ Created spaces within church ☐ Non-created spaces within church ☐ Public	**Situational Gifts** ☐ Word of Knowledge ☐ Word of Wisdom ☐ Discerning of Spirits ☐ Prophecy ☐ Tongues ☐ Interpretation ☐ Gifts of Healing ☐ Working of Miracles ☐ Faith
Monday	**Ministries** ☐ Healing ☐ Prophetic ☐ Deliverance ☐ Presence **Contexts** ☐ Created spaces within church ☐ Non-created spaces within church ☐ Public	**Situational Gifts** ☐ Word of Knowledge ☐ Word of Wisdom ☐ Discerning of Spirits ☐ Prophecy ☐ Tongues ☐ Interpretation ☐ Gifts of Healing ☐ Working of Miracles ☐ Faith
Tuesday	**Ministries** ☐ Healing ☐ Prophetic ☐ Deliverance ☐ Presence **Contexts** ☐ Created spaces within church ☐ Non-created spaces within church ☐ Public	**Situational Gifts** ☐ Word of Knowledge ☐ Word of Wisdom ☐ Discerning of Spirits ☐ Prophecy ☐ Tongues ☐ Interpretation ☐ Gifts of Healing ☐ Working of Miracles ☐ Faith
Wednesday	**Ministries** ☐ Healing ☐ Prophetic ☐ Deliverance ☐ Presence **Contexts** ☐ Created spaces within church ☐ Non-created spaces within church ☐ Public	**Situational Gifts** ☐ Word of Knowledge ☐ Word of Wisdom ☐ Discerning of Spirits ☐ Prophecy ☐ Tongues ☐ Interpretation ☐ Gifts of Healing ☐ Working of Miracles ☐ Faith

Thursday

Ministries
- ☐ Healing
- ☐ Prophetic
- ☐ Deliverance
- ☐ Presence

Contexts
- ☐ Created spaces within church
- ☐ Non-created spaces within church
- ☐ Public

Situational Gifts
- ☐ Word of Knowledge
- ☐ Word of Wisdom
- ☐ Discerning of Spirits
- ☐ Prophecy
- ☐ Tongues
- ☐ Interpretation
- ☐ Gifts of Healing
- ☐ Working of Miracles
- ☐ Faith

Friday

Ministries
- ☐ Healing
- ☐ Prophetic
- ☐ Deliverance
- ☐ Presence

Contexts
- ☐ Created spaces within church
- ☐ Non-created spaces within church
- ☐ Public

Situational Gifts
- ☐ Word of Knowledge
- ☐ Word of Wisdom
- ☐ Discerning of Spirits
- ☐ Prophecy
- ☐ Tongues
- ☐ Interpretation
- ☐ Gifts of Healing
- ☐ Working of Miracles
- ☐ Faith

Saturday

Ministries
- ☐ Healing
- ☐ Prophetic
- ☐ Deliverance
- ☐ Presence

Contexts
- ☐ Created spaces within church
- ☐ Non-created spaces within church
- ☐ Public

Situational Gifts
- ☐ Word of Knowledge
- ☐ Word of Wisdom
- ☐ Discerning of Spirits
- ☐ Prophecy
- ☐ Tongues
- ☐ Interpretation
- ☐ Gifts of Healing
- ☐ Working of Miracles
- ☐ Faith

Weekly Total:

Ministries

_____ Healing
_____ Prophetic
_____ Deliverance
_____ Presence

Contexts

_____ Created spaces within church
_____ Non-created spaces within church
_____ Public

Situational Gifts

_____ Word of Knowledge
_____ Word of Wisdom
_____ Discerning of Spirits
_____ Prophecy
_____ Tongues
_____ Interpretation
_____ Gifts of Healing
_____ Working of Miracles
_____ Faith

Week 15

Sunday

Ministries
- ☐ Healing
- ☐ Prophetic
- ☐ Deliverance
- ☐ Presence

Contexts
- ☐ Created spaces within church
- ☐ Non-created spaces within church
- ☐ Public

Situational Gifts
- ☐ Word of Knowledge
- ☐ Word of Wisdom
- ☐ Discerning of Spirits
- ☐ Prophecy
- ☐ Tongues
- ☐ Interpretation
- ☐ Gifts of Healing
- ☐ Working of Miracles
- ☐ Faith

Monday

Ministries
- ☐ Healing
- ☐ Prophetic
- ☐ Deliverance
- ☐ Presence

Contexts
- ☐ Created spaces within church
- ☐ Non-created spaces within church
- ☐ Public

Situational Gifts
- ☐ Word of Knowledge
- ☐ Word of Wisdom
- ☐ Discerning of Spirits
- ☐ Prophecy
- ☐ Tongues
- ☐ Interpretation
- ☐ Gifts of Healing
- ☐ Working of Miracles
- ☐ Faith

Tuesday

Ministries
- ☐ Healing
- ☐ Prophetic
- ☐ Deliverance
- ☐ Presence

Contexts
- ☐ Created spaces within church
- ☐ Non-created spaces within church
- ☐ Public

Situational Gifts
- ☐ Word of Knowledge
- ☐ Word of Wisdom
- ☐ Discerning of Spirits
- ☐ Prophecy
- ☐ Tongues
- ☐ Interpretation
- ☐ Gifts of Healing
- ☐ Working of Miracles
- ☐ Faith

Wednesday

Ministries
- ☐ Healing
- ☐ Prophetic
- ☐ Deliverance
- ☐ Presence

Contexts
- ☐ Created spaces within church
- ☐ Non-created spaces within church
- ☐ Public

Situational Gifts
- ☐ Word of Knowledge
- ☐ Word of Wisdom
- ☐ Discerning of Spirits
- ☐ Prophecy
- ☐ Tongues
- ☐ Interpretation
- ☐ Gifts of Healing
- ☐ Working of Miracles
- ☐ Faith

Day	Ministries / Contexts	Situational Gifts
Thursday	**Ministries** ☐ Healing ☐ Prophetic ☐ Deliverance ☐ Presence **Contexts** ☐ Created spaces within church ☐ Non-created spaces within church ☐ Public	**Situational Gifts** ☐ Word of Knowledge ☐ Word of Wisdom ☐ Discerning of Spirits ☐ Prophecy ☐ Tongues ☐ Interpretation ☐ Gifts of Healing ☐ Working of Miracles ☐ Faith
Friday	**Ministries** ☐ Healing ☐ Prophetic ☐ Deliverance ☐ Presence **Contexts** ☐ Created spaces within church ☐ Non-created spaces within church ☐ Public	**Situational Gifts** ☐ Word of Knowledge ☐ Word of Wisdom ☐ Discerning of Spirits ☐ Prophecy ☐ Tongues ☐ Interpretation ☐ Gifts of Healing ☐ Working of Miracles ☐ Faith
Saturday	**Ministries** ☐ Healing ☐ Prophetic ☐ Deliverance ☐ Presence **Contexts** ☐ Created spaces within church ☐ Non-created spaces within church ☐ Public	**Situational Gifts** ☐ Word of Knowledge ☐ Word of Wisdom ☐ Discerning of Spirits ☐ Prophecy ☐ Tongues ☐ Interpretation ☐ Gifts of Healing ☐ Working of Miracles ☐ Faith

Weekly Total:

Ministries

_____ Healing
_____ Prophetic
_____ Deliverance
_____ Presence

Contexts

_____ Created spaces within church
_____ Non-created spaces within church
_____ Public

Situational Gifts

_____ Word of Knowledge
_____ Word of Wisdom
_____ Discerning of Spirits
_____ Prophecy
_____ Tongues
_____ Interpretation
_____ Gifts of Healing
_____ Working of Miracles
_____ Faith

Week 16

Sunday

Ministries
- ☐ Healing
- ☐ Prophetic
- ☐ Deliverance
- ☐ Presence

Contexts
- ☐ Created spaces within church
- ☐ Non-created spaces within church
- ☐ Public

Situational Gifts
- ☐ Word of Knowledge
- ☐ Word of Wisdom
- ☐ Discerning of Spirits
- ☐ Prophecy
- ☐ Tongues
- ☐ Interpretation
- ☐ Gifts of Healing
- ☐ Working of Miracles
- ☐ Faith

Monday

Ministries
- ☐ Healing
- ☐ Prophetic
- ☐ Deliverance
- ☐ Presence

Contexts
- ☐ Created spaces within church
- ☐ Non-created spaces within church
- ☐ Public

Situational Gifts
- ☐ Word of Knowledge
- ☐ Word of Wisdom
- ☐ Discerning of Spirits
- ☐ Prophecy
- ☐ Tongues
- ☐ Interpretation
- ☐ Gifts of Healing
- ☐ Working of Miracles
- ☐ Faith

Tuesday

Ministries
- ☐ Healing
- ☐ Prophetic
- ☐ Deliverance
- ☐ Presence

Contexts
- ☐ Created spaces within church
- ☐ Non-created spaces within church
- ☐ Public

Situational Gifts
- ☐ Word of Knowledge
- ☐ Word of Wisdom
- ☐ Discerning of Spirits
- ☐ Prophecy
- ☐ Tongues
- ☐ Interpretation
- ☐ Gifts of Healing
- ☐ Working of Miracles
- ☐ Faith

Wednesday

Ministries
- ☐ Healing
- ☐ Prophetic
- ☐ Deliverance
- ☐ Presence

Contexts
- ☐ Created spaces within church
- ☐ Non-created spaces within church
- ☐ Public

Situational Gifts
- ☐ Word of Knowledge
- ☐ Word of Wisdom
- ☐ Discerning of Spirits
- ☐ Prophecy
- ☐ Tongues
- ☐ Interpretation
- ☐ Gifts of Healing
- ☐ Working of Miracles
- ☐ Faith

Thursday

Ministries
- ☐ Healing
- ☐ Prophetic
- ☐ Deliverance
- ☐ Presence

Contexts
- ☐ Created spaces within church
- ☐ Non-created spaces within church
- ☐ Public

Situational Gifts
- ☐ Word of Knowledge
- ☐ Word of Wisdom
- ☐ Discerning of Spirits
- ☐ Prophecy
- ☐ Tongues
- ☐ Interpretation
- ☐ Gifts of Healing
- ☐ Working of Miracles
- ☐ Faith

Friday

Ministries
- ☐ Healing
- ☐ Prophetic
- ☐ Deliverance
- ☐ Presence

Contexts
- ☐ Created spaces within church
- ☐ Non-created spaces within church
- ☐ Public

Situational Gifts
- ☐ Word of Knowledge
- ☐ Word of Wisdom
- ☐ Discerning of Spirits
- ☐ Prophecy
- ☐ Tongues
- ☐ Interpretation
- ☐ Gifts of Healing
- ☐ Working of Miracles
- ☐ Faith

Saturday

Ministries
- ☐ Healing
- ☐ Prophetic
- ☐ Deliverance
- ☐ Presence

Contexts
- ☐ Created spaces within church
- ☐ Non-created spaces within church
- ☐ Public

Situational Gifts
- ☐ Word of Knowledge
- ☐ Word of Wisdom
- ☐ Discerning of Spirits
- ☐ Prophecy
- ☐ Tongues
- ☐ Interpretation
- ☐ Gifts of Healing
- ☐ Working of Miracles
- ☐ Faith

Weekly Total:

Ministries

_____ Healing
_____ Prophetic
_____ Deliverance
_____ Presence

Contexts

_____ Created spaces within church
_____ Non-created spaces within church
_____ Public

Situational Gifts

_____ Word of Knowledge
_____ Word of Wisdom
_____ Discerning of Spirits
_____ Prophecy
_____ Tongues
_____ Interpretation
_____ Gifts of Healing
_____ Working of Miracles
_____ Faith

Week 17

Sunday

Ministries
- ☐ Healing
- ☐ Prophetic
- ☐ Deliverance
- ☐ Presence

Contexts
- ☐ Created spaces within church
- ☐ Non-created spaces within church
- ☐ Public

Situational Gifts
- ☐ Word of Knowledge
- ☐ Word of Wisdom
- ☐ Discerning of Spirits
- ☐ Prophecy
- ☐ Tongues
- ☐ Interpretation
- ☐ Gifts of Healing
- ☐ Working of Miracles
- ☐ Faith

Monday

Ministries
- ☐ Healing
- ☐ Prophetic
- ☐ Deliverance
- ☐ Presence

Contexts
- ☐ Created spaces within church
- ☐ Non-created spaces within church
- ☐ Public

Situational Gifts
- ☐ Word of Knowledge
- ☐ Word of Wisdom
- ☐ Discerning of Spirits
- ☐ Prophecy
- ☐ Tongues
- ☐ Interpretation
- ☐ Gifts of Healing
- ☐ Working of Miracles
- ☐ Faith

Tuesday

Ministries
- ☐ Healing
- ☐ Prophetic
- ☐ Deliverance
- ☐ Presence

Contexts
- ☐ Created spaces within church
- ☐ Non-created spaces within church
- ☐ Public

Situational Gifts
- ☐ Word of Knowledge
- ☐ Word of Wisdom
- ☐ Discerning of Spirits
- ☐ Prophecy
- ☐ Tongues
- ☐ Interpretation
- ☐ Gifts of Healing
- ☐ Working of Miracles
- ☐ Faith

Wednesday

Ministries
- ☐ Healing
- ☐ Prophetic
- ☐ Deliverance
- ☐ Presence

Contexts
- ☐ Created spaces within church
- ☐ Non-created spaces within church
- ☐ Public

Situational Gifts
- ☐ Word of Knowledge
- ☐ Word of Wisdom
- ☐ Discerning of Spirits
- ☐ Prophecy
- ☐ Tongues
- ☐ Interpretation
- ☐ Gifts of Healing
- ☐ Working of Miracles
- ☐ Faith

Thursday

Ministries	Situational Gifts
☐ Healing	☐ Word of Knowledge
☐ Prophetic	☐ Word of Wisdom
☐ Deliverance	☐ Discerning of Spirits
☐ Presence	☐ Prophecy
	☐ Tongues
Contexts	☐ Interpretation
☐ Created spaces within church	☐ Gifts of Healing
☐ Non-created spaces within church	☐ Working of Miracles
☐ Public	☐ Faith

Friday

Ministries	Situational Gifts
☐ Healing	☐ Word of Knowledge
☐ Prophetic	☐ Word of Wisdom
☐ Deliverance	☐ Discerning of Spirits
☐ Presence	☐ Prophecy
	☐ Tongues
Contexts	☐ Interpretation
☐ Created spaces within church	☐ Gifts of Healing
☐ Non-created spaces within church	☐ Working of Miracles
☐ Public	☐ Faith

Saturday

Ministries	Situational Gifts
☐ Healing	☐ Word of Knowledge
☐ Prophetic	☐ Word of Wisdom
☐ Deliverance	☐ Discerning of Spirits
☐ Presence	☐ Prophecy
	☐ Tongues
Contexts	☐ Interpretation
☐ Created spaces within church	☐ Gifts of Healing
☐ Non-created spaces within church	☐ Working of Miracles
☐ Public	☐ Faith

Weekly Total:

Ministries

_____ Healing
_____ Prophetic
_____ Deliverance
_____ Presence

Contexts

_____ Created spaces within church
_____ Non-created spaces within church
_____ Public

Situational Gifts

_____ Word of Knowledge
_____ Word of Wisdom
_____ Discerning of Spirits
_____ Prophecy
_____ Tongues
_____ Interpretation
_____ Gifts of Healing
_____ Working of Miracles
_____ Faith

Week 18

Sunday

Ministries
- ☐ Healing
- ☐ Prophetic
- ☐ Deliverance
- ☐ Presence

Contexts
- ☐ Created spaces within church
- ☐ Non-created spaces within church
- ☐ Public

Situational Gifts
- ☐ Word of Knowledge
- ☐ Word of Wisdom
- ☐ Discerning of Spirits
- ☐ Prophecy
- ☐ Tongues
- ☐ Interpretation
- ☐ Gifts of Healing
- ☐ Working of Miracles
- ☐ Faith

Monday

Ministries
- ☐ Healing
- ☐ Prophetic
- ☐ Deliverance
- ☐ Presence

Contexts
- ☐ Created spaces within church
- ☐ Non-created spaces within church
- ☐ Public

Situational Gifts
- ☐ Word of Knowledge
- ☐ Word of Wisdom
- ☐ Discerning of Spirits
- ☐ Prophecy
- ☐ Tongues
- ☐ Interpretation
- ☐ Gifts of Healing
- ☐ Working of Miracles
- ☐ Faith

Tuesday

Ministries
- ☐ Healing
- ☐ Prophetic
- ☐ Deliverance
- ☐ Presence

Contexts
- ☐ Created spaces within church
- ☐ Non-created spaces within church
- ☐ Public

Situational Gifts
- ☐ Word of Knowledge
- ☐ Word of Wisdom
- ☐ Discerning of Spirits
- ☐ Prophecy
- ☐ Tongues
- ☐ Interpretation
- ☐ Gifts of Healing
- ☐ Working of Miracles
- ☐ Faith

Wednesday

Ministries
- ☐ Healing
- ☐ Prophetic
- ☐ Deliverance
- ☐ Presence

Contexts
- ☐ Created spaces within church
- ☐ Non-created spaces within church
- ☐ Public

Situational Gifts
- ☐ Word of Knowledge
- ☐ Word of Wisdom
- ☐ Discerning of Spirits
- ☐ Prophecy
- ☐ Tongues
- ☐ Interpretation
- ☐ Gifts of Healing
- ☐ Working of Miracles
- ☐ Faith

	Ministries	Situational Gifts
Thursday	**Ministries** ☐ Healing ☐ Prophetic ☐ Deliverance ☐ Presence **Contexts** ☐ Created spaces within church ☐ Non-created spaces within church ☐ Public	**Situational Gifts** ☐ Word of Knowledge ☐ Word of Wisdom ☐ Discerning of Spirits ☐ Prophecy ☐ Tongues ☐ Interpretation ☐ Gifts of Healing ☐ Working of Miracles ☐ Faith
Friday	**Ministries** ☐ Healing ☐ Prophetic ☐ Deliverance ☐ Presence **Contexts** ☐ Created spaces within church ☐ Non-created spaces within church ☐ Public	**Situational Gifts** ☐ Word of Knowledge ☐ Word of Wisdom ☐ Discerning of Spirits ☐ Prophecy ☐ Tongues ☐ Interpretation ☐ Gifts of Healing ☐ Working of Miracles ☐ Faith
Saturday	**Ministries** ☐ Healing ☐ Prophetic ☐ Deliverance ☐ Presence **Contexts** ☐ Created spaces within church ☐ Non-created spaces within church ☐ Public	**Situational Gifts** ☐ Word of Knowledge ☐ Word of Wisdom ☐ Discerning of Spirits ☐ Prophecy ☐ Tongues ☐ Interpretation ☐ Gifts of Healing ☐ Working of Miracles ☐ Faith

Weekly Total:

Ministries

_____ Healing
_____ Prophetic
_____ Deliverance
_____ Presence

Contexts

_____ Created spaces within church
_____ Non-created spaces within church
_____ Public

Situational Gifts

_____ Word of Knowledge
_____ Word of Wisdom
_____ Discerning of Spirits
_____ Prophecy
_____ Tongues
_____ Interpretation
_____ Gifts of Healing
_____ Working of Miracles
_____ Faith

Week 19

Sunday

Ministries

- ☐ Healing
- ☐ Prophetic
- ☐ Deliverance
- ☐ Presence

Contexts

- ☐ Created spaces within church
- ☐ Non-created spaces within church
- ☐ Public

Situational Gifts

- ☐ Word of Knowledge
- ☐ Word of Wisdom
- ☐ Discerning of Spirits
- ☐ Prophecy
- ☐ Tongues
- ☐ Interpretation
- ☐ Gifts of Healing
- ☐ Working of Miracles
- ☐ Faith

Monday

Ministries

- ☐ Healing
- ☐ Prophetic
- ☐ Deliverance
- ☐ Presence

Contexts

- ☐ Created spaces within church
- ☐ Non-created spaces within church
- ☐ Public

Situational Gifts

- ☐ Word of Knowledge
- ☐ Word of Wisdom
- ☐ Discerning of Spirits
- ☐ Prophecy
- ☐ Tongues
- ☐ Interpretation
- ☐ Gifts of Healing
- ☐ Working of Miracles
- ☐ Faith

Tuesday

Ministries

- ☐ Healing
- ☐ Prophetic
- ☐ Deliverance
- ☐ Presence

Contexts

- ☐ Created spaces within church
- ☐ Non-created spaces within church
- ☐ Public

Situational Gifts

- ☐ Word of Knowledge
- ☐ Word of Wisdom
- ☐ Discerning of Spirits
- ☐ Prophecy
- ☐ Tongues
- ☐ Interpretation
- ☐ Gifts of Healing
- ☐ Working of Miracles
- ☐ Faith

Wednesday

Ministries

- ☐ Healing
- ☐ Prophetic
- ☐ Deliverance
- ☐ Presence

Contexts

- ☐ Created spaces within church
- ☐ Non-created spaces within church
- ☐ Public

Situational Gifts

- ☐ Word of Knowledge
- ☐ Word of Wisdom
- ☐ Discerning of Spirits
- ☐ Prophecy
- ☐ Tongues
- ☐ Interpretation
- ☐ Gifts of Healing
- ☐ Working of Miracles
- ☐ Faith

Thursday		
	Ministries ☐ Healing ☐ Prophetic ☐ Deliverance ☐ Presence **Contexts** ☐ Created spaces within church ☐ Non-created spaces within church ☐ Public	**Situational Gifts** ☐ Word of Knowledge ☐ Word of Wisdom ☐ Discerning of Spirits ☐ Prophecy ☐ Tongues ☐ Interpretation ☐ Gifts of Healing ☐ Working of Miracles ☐ Faith
Friday	**Ministries** ☐ Healing ☐ Prophetic ☐ Deliverance ☐ Presence **Contexts** ☐ Created spaces within church ☐ Non-created spaces within church ☐ Public	**Situational Gifts** ☐ Word of Knowledge ☐ Word of Wisdom ☐ Discerning of Spirits ☐ Prophecy ☐ Tongues ☐ Interpretation ☐ Gifts of Healing ☐ Working of Miracles ☐ Faith
Saturday	**Ministries** ☐ Healing ☐ Prophetic ☐ Deliverance ☐ Presence **Contexts** ☐ Created spaces within church ☐ Non-created spaces within church ☐ Public	**Situational Gifts** ☐ Word of Knowledge ☐ Word of Wisdom ☐ Discerning of Spirits ☐ Prophecy ☐ Tongues ☐ Interpretation ☐ Gifts of Healing ☐ Working of Miracles ☐ Faith

Weekly Total:

Ministries

_____ Healing
_____ Prophetic
_____ Deliverance
_____ Presence

Contexts

_____ Created spaces within church
_____ Non-created spaces within church
_____ Public

Situational Gifts

_____ Word of Knowledge
_____ Word of Wisdom
_____ Discerning of Spirits
_____ Prophecy
_____ Tongues
_____ Interpretation
_____ Gifts of Healing
_____ Working of Miracles
_____ Faith

Week 20

Sunday

Ministries
- ☐ Healing
- ☐ Prophetic
- ☐ Deliverance
- ☐ Presence

Contexts
- ☐ Created spaces within church
- ☐ Non-created spaces within church
- ☐ Public

Situational Gifts
- ☐ Word of Knowledge
- ☐ Word of Wisdom
- ☐ Discerning of Spirits
- ☐ Prophecy
- ☐ Tongues
- ☐ Interpretation
- ☐ Gifts of Healing
- ☐ Working of Miracles
- ☐ Faith

Monday

Ministries
- ☐ Healing
- ☐ Prophetic
- ☐ Deliverance
- ☐ Presence

Contexts
- ☐ Created spaces within church
- ☐ Non-created spaces within church
- ☐ Public

Situational Gifts
- ☐ Word of Knowledge
- ☐ Word of Wisdom
- ☐ Discerning of Spirits
- ☐ Prophecy
- ☐ Tongues
- ☐ Interpretation
- ☐ Gifts of Healing
- ☐ Working of Miracles
- ☐ Faith

Tuesday

Ministries
- ☐ Healing
- ☐ Prophetic
- ☐ Deliverance
- ☐ Presence

Contexts
- ☐ Created spaces within church
- ☐ Non-created spaces within church
- ☐ Public

Situational Gifts
- ☐ Word of Knowledge
- ☐ Word of Wisdom
- ☐ Discerning of Spirits
- ☐ Prophecy
- ☐ Tongues
- ☐ Interpretation
- ☐ Gifts of Healing
- ☐ Working of Miracles
- ☐ Faith

Wednesday

Ministries
- ☐ Healing
- ☐ Prophetic
- ☐ Deliverance
- ☐ Presence

Contexts
- ☐ Created spaces within church
- ☐ Non-created spaces within church
- ☐ Public

Situational Gifts
- ☐ Word of Knowledge
- ☐ Word of Wisdom
- ☐ Discerning of Spirits
- ☐ Prophecy
- ☐ Tongues
- ☐ Interpretation
- ☐ Gifts of Healing
- ☐ Working of Miracles
- ☐ Faith

Thursday

Ministries	Situational Gifts
☐ Healing	☐ Word of Knowledge
☐ Prophetic	☐ Word of Wisdom
☐ Deliverance	☐ Discerning of Spirits
☐ Presence	☐ Prophecy
	☐ Tongues
Contexts	☐ Interpretation
☐ Created spaces within church	☐ Gifts of Healing
☐ Non-created spaces within church	☐ Working of Miracles
☐ Public	☐ Faith

Friday

Ministries	Situational Gifts
☐ Healing	☐ Word of Knowledge
☐ Prophetic	☐ Word of Wisdom
☐ Deliverance	☐ Discerning of Spirits
☐ Presence	☐ Prophecy
	☐ Tongues
Contexts	☐ Interpretation
☐ Created spaces within church	☐ Gifts of Healing
☐ Non-created spaces within church	☐ Working of Miracles
☐ Public	☐ Faith

Saturday

Ministries	Situational Gifts
☐ Healing	☐ Word of Knowledge
☐ Prophetic	☐ Word of Wisdom
☐ Deliverance	☐ Discerning of Spirits
☐ Presence	☐ Prophecy
	☐ Tongues
Contexts	☐ Interpretation
☐ Created spaces within church	☐ Gifts of Healing
☐ Non-created spaces within church	☐ Working of Miracles
☐ Public	☐ Faith

Weekly Total:

Ministries

_____ Healing
_____ Prophetic
_____ Deliverance
_____ Presence

Contexts

_____ Created spaces within church
_____ Non-created spaces within church
_____ Public

Situational Gifts

_____ Word of Knowledge
_____ Word of Wisdom
_____ Discerning of Spirits
_____ Prophecy
_____ Tongues
_____ Interpretation
_____ Gifts of Healing
_____ Working of Miracles
_____ Faith

Week 21

Sunday

Ministries

- ☐ Healing
- ☐ Prophetic
- ☐ Deliverance
- ☐ Presence

Contexts

- ☐ Created spaces within church
- ☐ Non-created spaces within church
- ☐ Public

Situational Gifts

- ☐ Word of Knowledge
- ☐ Word of Wisdom
- ☐ Discerning of Spirits
- ☐ Prophecy
- ☐ Tongues
- ☐ Interpretation
- ☐ Gifts of Healing
- ☐ Working of Miracles
- ☐ Faith

Monday

Ministries

- ☐ Healing
- ☐ Prophetic
- ☐ Deliverance
- ☐ Presence

Contexts

- ☐ Created spaces within church
- ☐ Non-created spaces within church
- ☐ Public

Situational Gifts

- ☐ Word of Knowledge
- ☐ Word of Wisdom
- ☐ Discerning of Spirits
- ☐ Prophecy
- ☐ Tongues
- ☐ Interpretation
- ☐ Gifts of Healing
- ☐ Working of Miracles
- ☐ Faith

Tuesday

Ministries

- ☐ Healing
- ☐ Prophetic
- ☐ Deliverance
- ☐ Presence

Contexts

- ☐ Created spaces within church
- ☐ Non-created spaces within church
- ☐ Public

Situational Gifts

- ☐ Word of Knowledge
- ☐ Word of Wisdom
- ☐ Discerning of Spirits
- ☐ Prophecy
- ☐ Tongues
- ☐ Interpretation
- ☐ Gifts of Healing
- ☐ Working of Miracles
- ☐ Faith

Wednesday

Ministries

- ☐ Healing
- ☐ Prophetic
- ☐ Deliverance
- ☐ Presence

Contexts

- ☐ Created spaces within church
- ☐ Non-created spaces within church
- ☐ Public

Situational Gifts

- ☐ Word of Knowledge
- ☐ Word of Wisdom
- ☐ Discerning of Spirits
- ☐ Prophecy
- ☐ Tongues
- ☐ Interpretation
- ☐ Gifts of Healing
- ☐ Working of Miracles
- ☐ Faith

Thursday	**Ministries** ☐ Healing ☐ Prophetic ☐ Deliverance ☐ Presence **Contexts** ☐ Created spaces within church ☐ Non-created spaces within church ☐ Public	**Situational Gifts** ☐ Word of Knowledge ☐ Word of Wisdom ☐ Discerning of Spirits ☐ Prophecy ☐ Tongues ☐ Interpretation ☐ Gifts of Healing ☐ Working of Miracles ☐ Faith
Friday	**Ministries** ☐ Healing ☐ Prophetic ☐ Deliverance ☐ Presence **Contexts** ☐ Created spaces within church ☐ Non-created spaces within church ☐ Public	**Situational Gifts** ☐ Word of Knowledge ☐ Word of Wisdom ☐ Discerning of Spirits ☐ Prophecy ☐ Tongues ☐ Interpretation ☐ Gifts of Healing ☐ Working of Miracles ☐ Faith
Saturday	**Ministries** ☐ Healing ☐ Prophetic ☐ Deliverance ☐ Presence **Contexts** ☐ Created spaces within church ☐ Non-created spaces within church ☐ Public	**Situational Gifts** ☐ Word of Knowledge ☐ Word of Wisdom ☐ Discerning of Spirits ☐ Prophecy ☐ Tongues ☐ Interpretation ☐ Gifts of Healing ☐ Working of Miracles ☐ Faith

Weekly Total:

Ministries

_____ Healing
_____ Prophetic
_____ Deliverance
_____ Presence

Contexts

_____ Created spaces within church
_____ Non-created spaces within church
_____ Public

Situational Gifts

_____ Word of Knowledge
_____ Word of Wisdom
_____ Discerning of Spirits
_____ Prophecy
_____ Tongues
_____ Interpretation
_____ Gifts of Healing
_____ Working of Miracles
_____ Faith

Week 22

<table>
<tr><td>Sunday</td><td>

Ministries
- ☐ Healing
- ☐ Prophetic
- ☐ Deliverance
- ☐ Presence

Contexts
- ☐ Created spaces within church
- ☐ Non-created spaces within church
- ☐ Public

</td><td>

Situational Gifts
- ☐ Word of Knowledge
- ☐ Word of Wisdom
- ☐ Discerning of Spirits
- ☐ Prophecy
- ☐ Tongues
- ☐ Interpretation
- ☐ Gifts of Healing
- ☐ Working of Miracles
- ☐ Faith

</td></tr>
<tr><td>Monday</td><td>

Ministries
- ☐ Healing
- ☐ Prophetic
- ☐ Deliverance
- ☐ Presence

Contexts
- ☐ Created spaces within church
- ☐ Non-created spaces within church
- ☐ Public

</td><td>

Situational Gifts
- ☐ Word of Knowledge
- ☐ Word of Wisdom
- ☐ Discerning of Spirits
- ☐ Prophecy
- ☐ Tongues
- ☐ Interpretation
- ☐ Gifts of Healing
- ☐ Working of Miracles
- ☐ Faith

</td></tr>
<tr><td>Tuesday</td><td>

Ministries
- ☐ Healing
- ☐ Prophetic
- ☐ Deliverance
- ☐ Presence

Contexts
- ☐ Created spaces within church
- ☐ Non-created spaces within church
- ☐ Public

</td><td>

Situational Gifts
- ☐ Word of Knowledge
- ☐ Word of Wisdom
- ☐ Discerning of Spirits
- ☐ Prophecy
- ☐ Tongues
- ☐ Interpretation
- ☐ Gifts of Healing
- ☐ Working of Miracles
- ☐ Faith

</td></tr>
<tr><td>Wednesday</td><td>

Ministries
- ☐ Healing
- ☐ Prophetic
- ☐ Deliverance
- ☐ Presence

Contexts
- ☐ Created spaces within church
- ☐ Non-created spaces within church
- ☐ Public

</td><td>

Situational Gifts
- ☐ Word of Knowledge
- ☐ Word of Wisdom
- ☐ Discerning of Spirits
- ☐ Prophecy
- ☐ Tongues
- ☐ Interpretation
- ☐ Gifts of Healing
- ☐ Working of Miracles
- ☐ Faith

</td></tr>
</table>

Thursday

Ministries
- ☐ Healing
- ☐ Prophetic
- ☐ Deliverance
- ☐ Presence

Contexts
- ☐ Created spaces within church
- ☐ Non-created spaces within church
- ☐ Public

Situational Gifts
- ☐ Word of Knowledge
- ☐ Word of Wisdom
- ☐ Discerning of Spirits
- ☐ Prophecy
- ☐ Tongues
- ☐ Interpretation
- ☐ Gifts of Healing
- ☐ Working of Miracles
- ☐ Faith

Friday

Ministries
- ☐ Healing
- ☐ Prophetic
- ☐ Deliverance
- ☐ Presence

Contexts
- ☐ Created spaces within church
- ☐ Non-created spaces within church
- ☐ Public

Situational Gifts
- ☐ Word of Knowledge
- ☐ Word of Wisdom
- ☐ Discerning of Spirits
- ☐ Prophecy
- ☐ Tongues
- ☐ Interpretation
- ☐ Gifts of Healing
- ☐ Working of Miracles
- ☐ Faith

Saturday

Ministries
- ☐ Healing
- ☐ Prophetic
- ☐ Deliverance
- ☐ Presence

Contexts
- ☐ Created spaces within church
- ☐ Non-created spaces within church
- ☐ Public

Situational Gifts
- ☐ Word of Knowledge
- ☐ Word of Wisdom
- ☐ Discerning of Spirits
- ☐ Prophecy
- ☐ Tongues
- ☐ Interpretation
- ☐ Gifts of Healing
- ☐ Working of Miracles
- ☐ Faith

Weekly Total:

Ministries

_____ Healing
_____ Prophetic
_____ Deliverance
_____ Presence

Contexts

_____ Created spaces within church
_____ Non-created spaces within church
_____ Public

Situational Gifts

_____ Word of Knowledge
_____ Word of Wisdom
_____ Discerning of Spirits
_____ Prophecy
_____ Tongues
_____ Interpretation
_____ Gifts of Healing
_____ Working of Miracles
_____ Faith

Week 23

Sunday	**Ministries** ☐ Healing ☐ Prophetic ☐ Deliverance ☐ Presence **Contexts** ☐ Created spaces within church ☐ Non-created spaces within church ☐ Public	**Situational Gifts** ☐ Word of Knowledge ☐ Word of Wisdom ☐ Discerning of Spirits ☐ Prophecy ☐ Tongues ☐ Interpretation ☐ Gifts of Healing ☐ Working of Miracles ☐ Faith
Monday	**Ministries** ☐ Healing ☐ Prophetic ☐ Deliverance ☐ Presence **Contexts** ☐ Created spaces within church ☐ Non-created spaces within church ☐ Public	**Situational Gifts** ☐ Word of Knowledge ☐ Word of Wisdom ☐ Discerning of Spirits ☐ Prophecy ☐ Tongues ☐ Interpretation ☐ Gifts of Healing ☐ Working of Miracles ☐ Faith
Tuesday	**Ministries** ☐ Healing ☐ Prophetic ☐ Deliverance ☐ Presence **Contexts** ☐ Created spaces within church ☐ Non-created spaces within church ☐ Public	**Situational Gifts** ☐ Word of Knowledge ☐ Word of Wisdom ☐ Discerning of Spirits ☐ Prophecy ☐ Tongues ☐ Interpretation ☐ Gifts of Healing ☐ Working of Miracles ☐ Faith
Wednesday	**Ministries** ☐ Healing ☐ Prophetic ☐ Deliverance ☐ Presence **Contexts** ☐ Created spaces within church ☐ Non-created spaces within church ☐ Public	**Situational Gifts** ☐ Word of Knowledge ☐ Word of Wisdom ☐ Discerning of Spirits ☐ Prophecy ☐ Tongues ☐ Interpretation ☐ Gifts of Healing ☐ Working of Miracles ☐ Faith

	Ministries	Situational Gifts
Thursday	**Ministries** ☐ Healing ☐ Prophetic ☐ Deliverance ☐ Presence **Contexts** ☐ Created spaces within church ☐ Non-created spaces within church ☐ Public	**Situational Gifts** ☐ Word of Knowledge ☐ Word of Wisdom ☐ Discerning of Spirits ☐ Prophecy ☐ Tongues ☐ Interpretation ☐ Gifts of Healing ☐ Working of Miracles ☐ Faith
Friday	**Ministries** ☐ Healing ☐ Prophetic ☐ Deliverance ☐ Presence **Contexts** ☐ Created spaces within church ☐ Non-created spaces within church ☐ Public	**Situational Gifts** ☐ Word of Knowledge ☐ Word of Wisdom ☐ Discerning of Spirits ☐ Prophecy ☐ Tongues ☐ Interpretation ☐ Gifts of Healing ☐ Working of Miracles ☐ Faith
Saturday	**Ministries** ☐ Healing ☐ Prophetic ☐ Deliverance ☐ Presence **Contexts** ☐ Created spaces within church ☐ Non-created spaces within church ☐ Public	**Situational Gifts** ☐ Word of Knowledge ☐ Word of Wisdom ☐ Discerning of Spirits ☐ Prophecy ☐ Tongues ☐ Interpretation ☐ Gifts of Healing ☐ Working of Miracles ☐ Faith

Weekly Total:

Ministries

_____ Healing
_____ Prophetic
_____ Deliverance
_____ Presence

Contexts

_____ Created spaces within church
_____ Non-created spaces within church
_____ Public

Situational Gifts

_____ Word of Knowledge
_____ Word of Wisdom
_____ Discerning of Spirits
_____ Prophecy
_____ Tongues
_____ Interpretation
_____ Gifts of Healing
_____ Working of Miracles
_____ Faith

Week 24

Sunday

Ministries
- ☐ Healing
- ☐ Prophetic
- ☐ Deliverance
- ☐ Presence

Contexts
- ☐ Created spaces within church
- ☐ Non-created spaces within church
- ☐ Public

Situational Gifts
- ☐ Word of Knowledge
- ☐ Word of Wisdom
- ☐ Discerning of Spirits
- ☐ Prophecy
- ☐ Tongues
- ☐ Interpretation
- ☐ Gifts of Healing
- ☐ Working of Miracles
- ☐ Faith

Monday

Ministries
- ☐ Healing
- ☐ Prophetic
- ☐ Deliverance
- ☐ Presence

Contexts
- ☐ Created spaces within church
- ☐ Non-created spaces within church
- ☐ Public

Situational Gifts
- ☐ Word of Knowledge
- ☐ Word of Wisdom
- ☐ Discerning of Spirits
- ☐ Prophecy
- ☐ Tongues
- ☐ Interpretation
- ☐ Gifts of Healing
- ☐ Working of Miracles
- ☐ Faith

Tuesday

Ministries
- ☐ Healing
- ☐ Prophetic
- ☐ Deliverance
- ☐ Presence

Contexts
- ☐ Created spaces within church
- ☐ Non-created spaces within church
- ☐ Public

Situational Gifts
- ☐ Word of Knowledge
- ☐ Word of Wisdom
- ☐ Discerning of Spirits
- ☐ Prophecy
- ☐ Tongues
- ☐ Interpretation
- ☐ Gifts of Healing
- ☐ Working of Miracles
- ☐ Faith

Wednesday

Ministries
- ☐ Healing
- ☐ Prophetic
- ☐ Deliverance
- ☐ Presence

Contexts
- ☐ Created spaces within church
- ☐ Non-created spaces within church
- ☐ Public

Situational Gifts
- ☐ Word of Knowledge
- ☐ Word of Wisdom
- ☐ Discerning of Spirits
- ☐ Prophecy
- ☐ Tongues
- ☐ Interpretation
- ☐ Gifts of Healing
- ☐ Working of Miracles
- ☐ Faith

Thursday

Ministries
- ☐ Healing
- ☐ Prophetic
- ☐ Deliverance
- ☐ Presence

Contexts
- ☐ Created spaces within church
- ☐ Non-created spaces within church
- ☐ Public

Situational Gifts
- ☐ Word of Knowledge
- ☐ Word of Wisdom
- ☐ Discerning of Spirits
- ☐ Prophecy
- ☐ Tongues
- ☐ Interpretation
- ☐ Gifts of Healing
- ☐ Working of Miracles
- ☐ Faith

Friday

Ministries
- ☐ Healing
- ☐ Prophetic
- ☐ Deliverance
- ☐ Presence

Contexts
- ☐ Created spaces within church
- ☐ Non-created spaces within church
- ☐ Public

Situational Gifts
- ☐ Word of Knowledge
- ☐ Word of Wisdom
- ☐ Discerning of Spirits
- ☐ Prophecy
- ☐ Tongues
- ☐ Interpretation
- ☐ Gifts of Healing
- ☐ Working of Miracles
- ☐ Faith

Saturday

Ministries
- ☐ Healing
- ☐ Prophetic
- ☐ Deliverance
- ☐ Presence

Contexts
- ☐ Created spaces within church
- ☐ Non-created spaces within church
- ☐ Public

Situational Gifts
- ☐ Word of Knowledge
- ☐ Word of Wisdom
- ☐ Discerning of Spirits
- ☐ Prophecy
- ☐ Tongues
- ☐ Interpretation
- ☐ Gifts of Healing
- ☐ Working of Miracles
- ☐ Faith

Weekly Total:

Ministries

_____ Healing
_____ Prophetic
_____ Deliverance
_____ Presence

Contexts

_____ Created spaces within church
_____ Non-created spaces within church
_____ Public

Situational Gifts

_____ Word of Knowledge
_____ Word of Wisdom
_____ Discerning of Spirits
_____ Prophecy
_____ Tongues
_____ Interpretation
_____ Gifts of Healing
_____ Working of Miracles
_____ Faith

Week 25

	Ministries / Contexts	Situational Gifts
Sunday	**Ministries** ☐ Healing ☐ Prophetic ☐ Deliverance ☐ Presence **Contexts** ☐ Created spaces within church ☐ Non-created spaces within church ☐ Public	**Situational Gifts** ☐ Word of Knowledge ☐ Word of Wisdom ☐ Discerning of Spirits ☐ Prophecy ☐ Tongues ☐ Interpretation ☐ Gifts of Healing ☐ Working of Miracles ☐ Faith
Monday	**Ministries** ☐ Healing ☐ Prophetic ☐ Deliverance ☐ Presence **Contexts** ☐ Created spaces within church ☐ Non-created spaces within church ☐ Public	**Situational Gifts** ☐ Word of Knowledge ☐ Word of Wisdom ☐ Discerning of Spirits ☐ Prophecy ☐ Tongues ☐ Interpretation ☐ Gifts of Healing ☐ Working of Miracles ☐ Faith
Tuesday	**Ministries** ☐ Healing ☐ Prophetic ☐ Deliverance ☐ Presence **Contexts** ☐ Created spaces within church ☐ Non-created spaces within church ☐ Public	**Situational Gifts** ☐ Word of Knowledge ☐ Word of Wisdom ☐ Discerning of Spirits ☐ Prophecy ☐ Tongues ☐ Interpretation ☐ Gifts of Healing ☐ Working of Miracles ☐ Faith
Wednesday	**Ministries** ☐ Healing ☐ Prophetic ☐ Deliverance ☐ Presence **Contexts** ☐ Created spaces within church ☐ Non-created spaces within church ☐ Public	**Situational Gifts** ☐ Word of Knowledge ☐ Word of Wisdom ☐ Discerning of Spirits ☐ Prophecy ☐ Tongues ☐ Interpretation ☐ Gifts of Healing ☐ Working of Miracles ☐ Faith

Thursday

Ministries
- ☐ Healing
- ☐ Prophetic
- ☐ Deliverance
- ☐ Presence

Contexts
- ☐ Created spaces within church
- ☐ Non-created spaces within church
- ☐ Public

Situational Gifts
- ☐ Word of Knowledge
- ☐ Word of Wisdom
- ☐ Discerning of Spirits
- ☐ Prophecy
- ☐ Tongues
- ☐ Interpretation
- ☐ Gifts of Healing
- ☐ Working of Miracles
- ☐ Faith

Friday

Ministries
- ☐ Healing
- ☐ Prophetic
- ☐ Deliverance
- ☐ Presence

Contexts
- ☐ Created spaces within church
- ☐ Non-created spaces within church
- ☐ Public

Situational Gifts
- ☐ Word of Knowledge
- ☐ Word of Wisdom
- ☐ Discerning of Spirits
- ☐ Prophecy
- ☐ Tongues
- ☐ Interpretation
- ☐ Gifts of Healing
- ☐ Working of Miracles
- ☐ Faith

Saturday

Ministries
- ☐ Healing
- ☐ Prophetic
- ☐ Deliverance
- ☐ Presence

Contexts
- ☐ Created spaces within church
- ☐ Non-created spaces within church
- ☐ Public

Situational Gifts
- ☐ Word of Knowledge
- ☐ Word of Wisdom
- ☐ Discerning of Spirits
- ☐ Prophecy
- ☐ Tongues
- ☐ Interpretation
- ☐ Gifts of Healing
- ☐ Working of Miracles
- ☐ Faith

Weekly Total:

Ministries

_____ Healing
_____ Prophetic
_____ Deliverance
_____ Presence

Contexts

_____ Created spaces within church
_____ Non-created spaces within church
_____ Public

Situational Gifts

_____ Word of Knowledge
_____ Word of Wisdom
_____ Discerning of Spirits
_____ Prophecy
_____ Tongues
_____ Interpretation
_____ Gifts of Healing
_____ Working of Miracles
_____ Faith

Week 26

Sunday

Ministries
- ☐ Healing
- ☐ Prophetic
- ☐ Deliverance
- ☐ Presence

Contexts
- ☐ Created spaces within church
- ☐ Non-created spaces within church
- ☐ Public

Situational Gifts
- ☐ Word of Knowledge
- ☐ Word of Wisdom
- ☐ Discerning of Spirits
- ☐ Prophecy
- ☐ Tongues
- ☐ Interpretation
- ☐ Gifts of Healing
- ☐ Working of Miracles
- ☐ Faith

Monday

Ministries
- ☐ Healing
- ☐ Prophetic
- ☐ Deliverance
- ☐ Presence

Contexts
- ☐ Created spaces within church
- ☐ Non-created spaces within church
- ☐ Public

Situational Gifts
- ☐ Word of Knowledge
- ☐ Word of Wisdom
- ☐ Discerning of Spirits
- ☐ Prophecy
- ☐ Tongues
- ☐ Interpretation
- ☐ Gifts of Healing
- ☐ Working of Miracles
- ☐ Faith

Tuesday

Ministries
- ☐ Healing
- ☐ Prophetic
- ☐ Deliverance
- ☐ Presence

Contexts
- ☐ Created spaces within church
- ☐ Non-created spaces within church
- ☐ Public

Situational Gifts
- ☐ Word of Knowledge
- ☐ Word of Wisdom
- ☐ Discerning of Spirits
- ☐ Prophecy
- ☐ Tongues
- ☐ Interpretation
- ☐ Gifts of Healing
- ☐ Working of Miracles
- ☐ Faith

Wednesday

Ministries
- ☐ Healing
- ☐ Prophetic
- ☐ Deliverance
- ☐ Presence

Contexts
- ☐ Created spaces within church
- ☐ Non-created spaces within church
- ☐ Public

Situational Gifts
- ☐ Word of Knowledge
- ☐ Word of Wisdom
- ☐ Discerning of Spirits
- ☐ Prophecy
- ☐ Tongues
- ☐ Interpretation
- ☐ Gifts of Healing
- ☐ Working of Miracles
- ☐ Faith

Day	Ministries	Contexts	Situational Gifts
Thursday	☐ Healing ☐ Prophetic ☐ Deliverance ☐ Presence	☐ Created spaces within church ☐ Non-created spaces within church ☐ Public	☐ Word of Knowledge ☐ Word of Wisdom ☐ Discerning of Spirits ☐ Prophecy ☐ Tongues ☐ Interpretation ☐ Gifts of Healing ☐ Working of Miracles ☐ Faith
Friday	☐ Healing ☐ Prophetic ☐ Deliverance ☐ Presence	☐ Created spaces within church ☐ Non-created spaces within church ☐ Public	☐ Word of Knowledge ☐ Word of Wisdom ☐ Discerning of Spirits ☐ Prophecy ☐ Tongues ☐ Interpretation ☐ Gifts of Healing ☐ Working of Miracles ☐ Faith
Saturday	☐ Healing ☐ Prophetic ☐ Deliverance ☐ Presence	☐ Created spaces within church ☐ Non-created spaces within church ☐ Public	☐ Word of Knowledge ☐ Word of Wisdom ☐ Discerning of Spirits ☐ Prophecy ☐ Tongues ☐ Interpretation ☐ Gifts of Healing ☐ Working of Miracles ☐ Faith

Weekly Total:

Ministries

_____ Healing
_____ Prophetic
_____ Deliverance
_____ Presence

Contexts

_____ Created spaces within church
_____ Non-created spaces within church
_____ Public

Situational Gifts

_____ Word of Knowledge
_____ Word of Wisdom
_____ Discerning of Spirits
_____ Prophecy
_____ Tongues
_____ Interpretation
_____ Gifts of Healing
_____ Working of Miracles
_____ Faith

Week 27

Sunday

Ministries
- ☐ Healing
- ☐ Prophetic
- ☐ Deliverance
- ☐ Presence

Contexts
- ☐ Created spaces within church
- ☐ Non-created spaces within church
- ☐ Public

Situational Gifts
- ☐ Word of Knowledge
- ☐ Word of Wisdom
- ☐ Discerning of Spirits
- ☐ Prophecy
- ☐ Tongues
- ☐ Interpretation
- ☐ Gifts of Healing
- ☐ Working of Miracles
- ☐ Faith

Monday

Ministries
- ☐ Healing
- ☐ Prophetic
- ☐ Deliverance
- ☐ Presence

Contexts
- ☐ Created spaces within church
- ☐ Non-created spaces within church
- ☐ Public

Situational Gifts
- ☐ Word of Knowledge
- ☐ Word of Wisdom
- ☐ Discerning of Spirits
- ☐ Prophecy
- ☐ Tongues
- ☐ Interpretation
- ☐ Gifts of Healing
- ☐ Working of Miracles
- ☐ Faith

Tuesday

Ministries
- ☐ Healing
- ☐ Prophetic
- ☐ Deliverance
- ☐ Presence

Contexts
- ☐ Created spaces within church
- ☐ Non-created spaces within church
- ☐ Public

Situational Gifts
- ☐ Word of Knowledge
- ☐ Word of Wisdom
- ☐ Discerning of Spirits
- ☐ Prophecy
- ☐ Tongues
- ☐ Interpretation
- ☐ Gifts of Healing
- ☐ Working of Miracles
- ☐ Faith

Wednesday

Ministries
- ☐ Healing
- ☐ Prophetic
- ☐ Deliverance
- ☐ Presence

Contexts
- ☐ Created spaces within church
- ☐ Non-created spaces within church
- ☐ Public

Situational Gifts
- ☐ Word of Knowledge
- ☐ Word of Wisdom
- ☐ Discerning of Spirits
- ☐ Prophecy
- ☐ Tongues
- ☐ Interpretation
- ☐ Gifts of Healing
- ☐ Working of Miracles
- ☐ Faith

Thursday

<u>Ministries</u>
- ☐ Healing
- ☐ Prophetic
- ☐ Deliverance
- ☐ Presence

<u>Contexts</u>
- ☐ Created spaces within church
- ☐ Non-created spaces within church
- ☐ Public

<u>Situational Gifts</u>
- ☐ Word of Knowledge
- ☐ Word of Wisdom
- ☐ Discerning of Spirits
- ☐ Prophecy
- ☐ Tongues
- ☐ Interpretation
- ☐ Gifts of Healing
- ☐ Working of Miracles
- ☐ Faith

Friday

<u>Ministries</u>
- ☐ Healing
- ☐ Prophetic
- ☐ Deliverance
- ☐ Presence

<u>Contexts</u>
- ☐ Created spaces within church
- ☐ Non-created spaces within church
- ☐ Public

<u>Situational Gifts</u>
- ☐ Word of Knowledge
- ☐ Word of Wisdom
- ☐ Discerning of Spirits
- ☐ Prophecy
- ☐ Tongues
- ☐ Interpretation
- ☐ Gifts of Healing
- ☐ Working of Miracles
- ☐ Faith

Saturday

<u>Ministries</u>
- ☐ Healing
- ☐ Prophetic
- ☐ Deliverance
- ☐ Presence

<u>Contexts</u>
- ☐ Created spaces within church
- ☐ Non-created spaces within church
- ☐ Public

<u>Situational Gifts</u>
- ☐ Word of Knowledge
- ☐ Word of Wisdom
- ☐ Discerning of Spirits
- ☐ Prophecy
- ☐ Tongues
- ☐ Interpretation
- ☐ Gifts of Healing
- ☐ Working of Miracles
- ☐ Faith

Weekly Total:

<u>Ministries</u>

_____ Healing
_____ Prophetic
_____ Deliverance
_____ Presence

<u>Contexts</u>

_____ Created spaces within church
_____ Non-created spaces within church
_____ Public

<u>Situational Gifts</u>

_____ Word of Knowledge
_____ Word of Wisdom
_____ Discerning of Spirits
_____ Prophecy
_____ Tongues
_____ Interpretation
_____ Gifts of Healing
_____ Working of Miracles
_____ Faith

Week 28

Sunday

Ministries
- ☐ Healing
- ☐ Prophetic
- ☐ Deliverance
- ☐ Presence

Contexts
- ☐ Created spaces within church
- ☐ Non-created spaces within church
- ☐ Public

Situational Gifts
- ☐ Word of Knowledge
- ☐ Word of Wisdom
- ☐ Discerning of Spirits
- ☐ Prophecy
- ☐ Tongues
- ☐ Interpretation
- ☐ Gifts of Healing
- ☐ Working of Miracles
- ☐ Faith

Monday

Ministries
- ☐ Healing
- ☐ Prophetic
- ☐ Deliverance
- ☐ Presence

Contexts
- ☐ Created spaces within church
- ☐ Non-created spaces within church
- ☐ Public

Situational Gifts
- ☐ Word of Knowledge
- ☐ Word of Wisdom
- ☐ Discerning of Spirits
- ☐ Prophecy
- ☐ Tongues
- ☐ Interpretation
- ☐ Gifts of Healing
- ☐ Working of Miracles
- ☐ Faith

Tuesday

Ministries
- ☐ Healing
- ☐ Prophetic
- ☐ Deliverance
- ☐ Presence

Contexts
- ☐ Created spaces within church
- ☐ Non-created spaces within church
- ☐ Public

Situational Gifts
- ☐ Word of Knowledge
- ☐ Word of Wisdom
- ☐ Discerning of Spirits
- ☐ Prophecy
- ☐ Tongues
- ☐ Interpretation
- ☐ Gifts of Healing
- ☐ Working of Miracles
- ☐ Faith

Wednesday

Ministries
- ☐ Healing
- ☐ Prophetic
- ☐ Deliverance
- ☐ Presence

Contexts
- ☐ Created spaces within church
- ☐ Non-created spaces within church
- ☐ Public

Situational Gifts
- ☐ Word of Knowledge
- ☐ Word of Wisdom
- ☐ Discerning of Spirits
- ☐ Prophecy
- ☐ Tongues
- ☐ Interpretation
- ☐ Gifts of Healing
- ☐ Working of Miracles
- ☐ Faith

Thursday

Ministries	Situational Gifts
☐ Healing	☐ Word of Knowledge
☐ Prophetic	☐ Word of Wisdom
☐ Deliverance	☐ Discerning of Spirits
☐ Presence	☐ Prophecy
	☐ Tongues
Contexts	☐ Interpretation
☐ Created spaces within church	☐ Gifts of Healing
☐ Non-created spaces within church	☐ Working of Miracles
☐ Public	☐ Faith

Friday

Ministries	Situational Gifts
☐ Healing	☐ Word of Knowledge
☐ Prophetic	☐ Word of Wisdom
☐ Deliverance	☐ Discerning of Spirits
☐ Presence	☐ Prophecy
	☐ Tongues
Contexts	☐ Interpretation
☐ Created spaces within church	☐ Gifts of Healing
☐ Non-created spaces within church	☐ Working of Miracles
☐ Public	☐ Faith

Saturday

Ministries	Situational Gifts
☐ Healing	☐ Word of Knowledge
☐ Prophetic	☐ Word of Wisdom
☐ Deliverance	☐ Discerning of Spirits
☐ Presence	☐ Prophecy
	☐ Tongues
Contexts	☐ Interpretation
☐ Created spaces within church	☐ Gifts of Healing
☐ Non-created spaces within church	☐ Working of Miracles
☐ Public	☐ Faith

Weekly Total:

Ministries

_____ Healing
_____ Prophetic
_____ Deliverance
_____ Presence

Contexts

_____ Created spaces within church
_____ Non-created spaces within church
_____ Public

Situational Gifts

_____ Word of Knowledge
_____ Word of Wisdom
_____ Discerning of Spirits
_____ Prophecy
_____ Tongues
_____ Interpretation
_____ Gifts of Healing
_____ Working of Miracles
_____ Faith

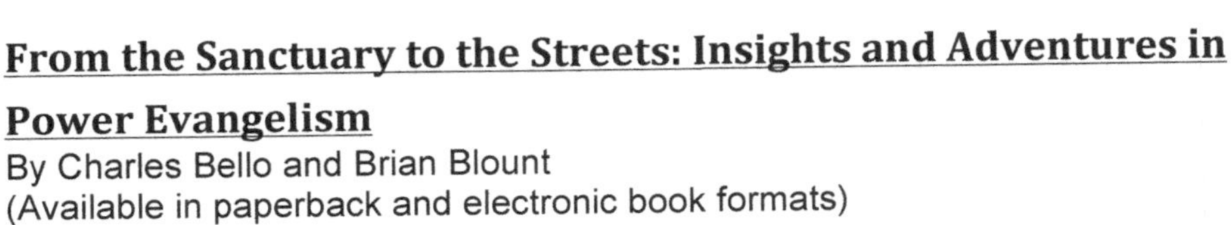

From the Sanctuary to the Streets: Insights and Adventures in Power Evangelism

By Charles Bello and Brian Blount
(Available in paperback and electronic book formats)

From the Sanctuary to the Streets is a practical guide written to propel the reader into a lifestyle marked by intimacy with God and power evangelism. Through teaching and personal stories, the authors share with humor and honesty their own efforts to embrace the empowering activity of the Holy Spirit. As the authors state, "We are not called to be spiritual recluses or trail blazing burnouts. Rather, we are called to be friends of God who live a life of intimacy and impact as we simply do life with God in a naturally supernatural way."

Kingdom Encounters

DVD featuring Brian Blount

In Matthew 10:7-8, Jesus commissioned his disciples into a supernatural ministry. He instructed them to proclaim the message of God's kingdom, heal the sick, cast out demons, and raise the dead. He told them to do these things "as you go."

Brian Blount has taken this commission seriously and set out on a mission to live a naturally supernatural life as he goes about his day. Included in this DVD are over 30 video testimonies of people who have been radically touched by God as Brian prayed for them on the streets. Some of these kingdom encounters occurred during planned outreaches with teams. Most of these encounters, however, occurred in Brian's everyday life as he simply went about his day. From Walmart to fast food drive thru windows to Starbucks, Brian demonstrates that the kingdom of God is truly at hand everywhere you go. Join Brian on this journey to take love and power to the streets by putting Jesus on display. Brian's desire is that these testimonies will give you the encouragement to take a risk and follow Jesus' commission of Matthew 10:7-8 "as you go."

Live It! with Love and Power

5-DVD set from the Live It! Conference
Speakers: Robby Dawkins, Brian Blount, Charles Bello, A.T. Hargrave, and Shane Jason Mock

The Live It! With Love and Power conference is designed to equip you in empowered evangelism, healing the sick, prophetic ministry, living from the inner life outward, and knowing our gospel identity. We believe that Jesus called the church to continue in his ministry, which was not only proclaiming the gospel of the kingdom but also demonstrating the reality of his kingdom by healing the sick, hearing God's heart for others, setting people free from darkness, and bringing them into the love of the Father (Matthew 10:7-8).

This 5-DVD set will equip you to continue the ministry of Jesus through its valuable teaching, practical tools, models, and values for living out a naturally supernatural lifestyle. You will be encouraged to look, listen, and respond to Jesus' commission and his activity around you. This DVD set, consisting of over 17 hours of video, includes all eight conference sessions with teaching and ministry, personal interviews with all the conference speakers, and 25 video testimonies from people being encountered and healed on the streets by the love and power of Jesus. Whether you are at Walmart, the mall, school, work, church, or home, may you live it with love and power, not only proclaiming the good news, but also demonstrating it.

Prayer as a Place: Spirituality that Transforms

By Charles Bello
(Available in electronic book formats)

Prayer as a Place is an invitation to partner with Christ as he leads the believer into the dark places of his or her own heart. The purpose of this journey is to bring holiness and wholeness to the child of God. With candor and brutal honesty, Pastor Charles Bello shares his own reluctance and then resolve to follow Christ on this inward journey. In sharing his story, readers gain insight into what their own personal journeys may look like. *Prayer as a Place* reads like a road map as it explores the contemporary use of contemplative prayer as a means of following Christ inward.

Learning to Suffer Well

By Peter Fitch, DMin
(Available in paperback and electronic book formats)

Learning to Suffer Well is an interactive devotional study designed to help you think through some of the Bible's teaching about how to face suffering in different situations. It is meant to force you to interact with ideas from the Scriptures in such a way that you will be challenged to grow as a Christian in terms of understanding, honesty, behavior, attitude, and level of spiritual maturity.

Recycled Spirituality: Ancient Ways Made New

By Charles Bello
(Available in electronic book formats)

Recycled Spirituality is like browsing through a mysterious, ancient resale shop filled with treasures from the rich heritage of historical Christianity. Many of the ancient spiritual disciplines have continued to be in use for thousands of years—others are being newly rediscovered. These classical disciplines are drawn from our shared Catholic, Orthodox, Protestant, Evangelical and Pentecostal traditions. The purpose of these disciplines is always transformation, renewal and missional living. As Charles writes, "The gift of tradition is meant to be received. The essence of tradition is meant to be rediscovered. And if the practice of a tradition helps form you into the image of Christ, it is meant to be recycled."

The Re-Imaging of God

By Dr. Richard Clinton
(Available in paperback and electronic book formats)

In *The Re-Imaging of God*, Richard Clinton takes us on a journey to explore the ways we perceive God. Our image of God affects every aspect of our lives and our leadership. It is paramount that we begin the adventure to understand our images of God and re-image God based on Biblical images of God. Filled with personal examples, thorough study and reflection questions, Clinton guides us in our endeavor to re-image God.

The Christian Leader's Wish List

A Quick Read Book
By Bill Faris, MPC
(Available in paperback and electronic book formats)

The Christian Leaders' Wish List speaks straight to the hearts of men and women who are fulfilling their call to a lifestyle of Christian leadership. While every minister faces unique challenges, many stresses are widely experienced, and this book addresses six of the most common wishes leaders express. This concise, useful, and uplifting volume offers timely encouragement and practical tools in a format that can be read in about an hour and referred to again and again as a personal resource. The topics covered in this book include: I wish I could find stress relief, I wish for some close relationships, I wish I could prioritize my personal development, I wish I could thrive through transition, I wish my marriage and family could be renewed, and I wish I could run long and finish well.

You can order these books and additional copies of *The School of Kingdom Ministry Manual* by visiting coachingsaints.com.

CPSIA information can be obtained at www.ICGtesting.com
Printed in the USA
LVOW02s1953230814

400561LV00003B/4/P

9 780989 832113